The years 1955–59 were a vital transitional
period for the Anglo-American relationship in the
Middle East. British and American leaders sought
to protect cold war and oil interests in the region
against the background of a renaissance of Arab
nationalism personified by the Egyptian leader
Nasser. With the aid of extensive declassified
official documentation, this study traces the
British and American responses to the Turco-Iraqi
Pact of 1955, the Suez crisis, the Syrian crisis of
1957, the outbreak of civil strife in Lebanon, and
the Iraqi Revolution of 1958. It shows how the
differing priorities of the two powers in the region
promoted a patchwork of confrontation and
cooperation over Middle Eastern questions. For
Britain, this study reveals that it was the Iraqi
Revolution rather than Suez which led to a
redefinition of strategy in the region, and a
concentration on the defence of her oil interests in
the Gulf.

For a note on the author, please see the back flap

EISENHOWER, MACMILLAN AND THE PROBLEM OF NASSER

STUDIES IN MILITARY AND STRATEGIC HISTORY

General Editor: Michael Dockrill, Reader in War Studies, King's College London

Published titles include:

G. H. Bennett
BRITISH FOREIGN POLICY DURING THE CURZON PERIOD, 1919–24

David A. Charters
THE BRITISH ARMY AND JEWISH INSURGENCY IN PALESTINE, 1945–47

Paul Cornish
BRITISH MILITARY PLANNING FOR THE DEFENCE OF GERMANY, 1945–50

Robert Frazier
ANGLO-AMERICAN RELATIONS WITH GREECE: The Coming of the Cold War, 1942–47

Brian Holden Reid
J. F. C. FULLER: Military Thinker

Stewart Lone
JAPAN'S FIRST MODERN WAR: Army and Society in the Conflict with China, 1894–95

Thomas R. Mockaitis
BRITISH COUNTERINSURGENCY, 1919–60

Roger Woodhouse
BRITISH FOREIGN POLICY TOWARDS FRANCE, 1945–51

Eisenhower, Macmillan and the Problem of Nasser

Anglo-American Relations and Arab Nationalism, 1955–59

Nigel John Ashton
Lecturer
Department of History
University of Liverpool

 in association with
KING'S COLLEGE LONDON

First published in Great Britain 1996 by
MACMILLAN PRESS LTD
Houndmills, Basingstoke, Hampshire RG21 6XS
and London
Companies and representatives
throughout the world

A catalogue record for this book is available
from the British Library.

ISBN 0–333–64455–7

First published in the United States of America 1996 by
ST. MARTIN'S PRESS, INC.,
Scholarly and Reference Division,
175 Fifth Avenue,
New York, N.Y. 10010

ISBN 0–312–16108–5

Library of Congress Cataloging-in-Publication Data
Ashton, Nigel John.
Eisenhower, Macmillan and the problem of Nasser : Anglo-American
relations and Arab nationalism, 1955–59 / Nigel John Ashton.
p.   cm. — (Studies in military and strategic history)
Includes bibliographical references (p.   ) and index.
ISBN 0–312–16108–5
1. Arab countries—Foreign relations—United States.   2. United
States—Foreign relations—Arab countries.   3. United States–
–Foreign relations—1953–1961.   4. Arab countries—Foreign
relations—Great Britain.   5. Great Britain—Foreign relations—Arab
countries.   6. United States—Foreign relations—Great Britain.
7. Great Britain—Foreign relations—United States.   I. Title.
II. Series.
DS63.2.U5A865   1996
327.730174927—dc20   96–10395
                                                                 CIP

10   9   8   7   6   5   4   3   2   1
05   04   03   02   01   00   99   98   97   96

Printed and bound in Great Britain by
Ipswich Book Co Ltd, Ipswich, Suffolk

For my parents
and Danielle

Contents

Preface

This book is the product of my own work. It is not the result of any collaborative efforts with others. In writing it I have incurred a number of debts.

The first and by far the most important of these debts is to my former doctoral supervisor, Dr David Reynolds. His guidance, insight and encouragement assisted me at every stage of my original research work. In addition I would like to thank Dr Ian Clark, who not only offered valuable advice, but also, by coincidence, shared my time at the Eisenhower Library, Abilene, Kansas. Thanks go also to Richard Langhorne, former Director of the Centre of International Studies in Cambridge. Dr David Dutton of the Department of History at the University of Liverpool generously read through my work and offered valuable suggestions as to how it might be improved. Others who cannot go without mention include HRH Prince Zeid bin Raad al-Hussein whose knowledge of the complexities of Middle Eastern history, politics and culture has helped to remedy my own deficiencies in these areas. His unfailing sense of humour also enlivened the task of graduate research.

I have worked in a number of archives during the course of my research, and must single out in particular the staff of the Eisenhower Library, Abilene, Kansas, for their efficiency, helpfulness and knowledge of their material. In addition, however, I would also like to thank the staff of the Public Records Office, Kew, London, the United States National Archives, Washington, DC, the Library of Congress, Washington, DC, the Seeley G. Mudd Manuscript Library, Princeton, New Jersey, and the John Fitzgerald Kennedy Library, Boston, Massachusetts.

Financial assistance for my research has been provided at various stages by the British Academy, Christ's College, Cambridge, the Eisenhower Foundation, the Kennedy Foundation, and the University of Liverpool. Without this generous support I would have been unable to conduct my archival visits.

Finally, my thanks go to my parents, without whose sacrifices in funding my earlier education this book could certainly not have been produced, and to Danielle.

1 Introduction

'We fully agree that [the] UK is and should be [a] world power, and the more powerful and the more worldly the better', commented Philip Jessup, a member of the American team which negotiated the Tripartite Declaration on the Middle East with Britain and France in 1950.[1] However, one could be forgiven for thinking, in view of the divergence in approach of the two powers to certain regional problems during the post-war years, that the Middle East was in fact one area to which this dictum did not apply. The paradox in Anglo-American relations in the Middle East is that while there were major disagreements over, for instance, the Palestine Mandate, Mossadegh's Iran, and the Suez Crisis, the two countries were capable, when it suited their respective interests, of cooperating remarkably closely in the region. The key to this paradox lies, as might be expected, in the question of interests, which, despite the nobler historical and ideological sentiments often attributed to it, lay at the heart of the Anglo-American relationship. The Middle East was no exception in this respect. The reason why it proved to be such fertile ground for conflict between the two powers was simply that their interests here often failed to coincide.

Discussions of Anglo-American relations in the Middle East during the later 1950s have, of course, been dominated by the Suez Crisis. Described variously as the 'lion's last roar',[2] the end of empire, and Great Britain's 'last battle' in the Middle East,[3] Suez has exerted a strong teleological pull over the historiography of the British role in the region. Despite recent revisionist attempts to play down the significance of the crisis,[4] due both to the fascination of the Suez drama itself, and the constraints of the 'thirty year rule', no detailed attempt has yet been made to set the crisis in context by exploring the subsequent course of Anglo-American relations in the Middle East. This account sets out, among other objectives, to achieve this goal.

Suez from the British perspective has often been regarded

as something of an aberration, even as a temporary loss of sanity on behalf of the British Cabinet and the Prime Minister in particular. Indeed, there is no better illustration of this sentiment than the amount of discussion which has been devoted to the state of the Anthony Eden's health during the crisis, and the likely impact on his judgement caused by the cocktail of drugs prescribed to him by his doctors.[5] Although to someone of the present generation the sort of assumptions about Britain's place in the world, and the means by which it should be maintained, epitomized by Suez, appear extraordinary, to those in power in the later 1950s they were the foundations of foreign policy. Britain was a great power and should use all necessary means to secure her economic and political position should it appear to be challenged.

Donald Cameron Watt, in his enlightening discussion of Anglo-American relations throughout the twentieth century, has stressed the importance of historical generations in shaping the outlook of statesmen.[6] All of the important members of Eden's cabinet had served their political apprenticeships during the inter-war years when, with both the United States and Soviet Union preoccupied with internal problems, Britain's role as a leading world power was unquestioned. The most significant political lesson which they had learned from this period was the danger of appeasing dictators, a lesson which they were to apply out of context during the Suez Crisis.

It follows then, that the attitudes which shaped the response of the government to the Suez Crisis did not disappear overnight. Rather, as this study will show, there was a surprising degree of continuity in British strategy both before and after Suez. Suez will emerge as an aberration only to the extent that Eden acted without ensuring at least American acquiescence. His successor, Harold Macmillan, while intent on pursuing the same strategy of defeating the Egyptian leader, Colonel Gamal Abdel Nasser, used different means and tried, admittedly with limited success, to carry the Americans with him. Continuity will emerge not just in British strategy, but also in Anglo-American relations in the Middle East during the period under review. What we will find in this respect is essentially a patchwork of conflict and cooperation governed by the overriding importance of interests. Where interests coincided, both before and after Suez, cooperation could be very close. Where they diverged, conflict could be correspondingly bitter.

The importance of regionality in modifying analyses of the Anglo-American relationship should already be clear in other theatres from such examples as the conflict over policy towards Communist China, and towards South East Asia after Dien Bien Phu. While the two powers might have clear ideas of what interests they sought to protect in a particular region, events often overtook them. As will be seen, when added to the question of how best to secure oil supplies against the perceived Soviet threat, the rise of radical Arab nationalism personified by Nasser was to place great strains on the Anglo-American relationship in the Middle East in the 1950s.

Foreign policy in any part of the world cannot, of course, be divorced from the personalities of the men who shape and implement it. In this respect, there are clearly five characters who head the Anglo-American list of dramatis personae; Dwight D. Eisenhower, John Foster Dulles, Harold Macmillan, Anthony Eden, and Selwyn Lloyd. In fact, in view of the ground covered by this study, this list might be reduced even further to four and a half characters. Without seeking to belittle the role of Anthony Eden, much of the new ground covered here on the British side is in relation to the policies pursued under Harold Macmillan.

On the American side, the relationship between Dwight D. Eisenhower and John Foster Dulles, President and Secretary of State from January 1953 until Dulles's resignation and death split their partnership in 1959, has received a great deal of attention from historians. Contemporaries, including, it should be noted, informed representatives of the British Government, tended to take the view that the President was somewhat detached from the day-to-day conduct of foreign policy, leaving many important decisions to his Secretary of State.[7] More recently, however, a great deal of literature has been devoted to rehabilitating the President as a shrewd political operator, who cultivated the impression of detachment while at the same time retaining a firm grip on the reins of power. The concept of a 'hidden-hand Presidency' has gained a great deal of currency.[8]

Eisenhower will emerge in this study as a man of strong

convictions, many of them bred by his time in the military, first as commander of the allied forces which liberated Western Europe in the Second World War, and latterly as Supreme Commander of NATO. Foremost among these convictions was the belief that communism should be opposed and if possible defeated. To achieve this, the 'free world', especially the countries of Western Europe, should be supported and a strong alliance of the democracies maintained. The United Nations should be promoted as the guardian of the international order, and encouragement should be given to the nations emerging from colonial rule to adopt democratic institutions and look to the United States for protection against the intrigues of 'international communism'. Whether one shared his ethical code or not, the strength of his own conviction could not be denied. What certainly can be said of the President is that when he felt any of these principal concerns to be involved, then he was very closely engaged with the formulation of policy. To this extent, the revisionists are right to stress his role behind the scenes directing the actions of the Secretary of State. However, it is important to note that Dulles, because of the closeness of the relationship he achieved with the President, was entrusted with a great deal of latitude in the interpretation and implementation of broad lines of policy agreed with Eisenhower.[9]

The only respect in which I would beg to diverge from what may be termed the revisionist synthesis on Eisenhower is in dissenting from Stephen Ambrose's view of the emphasis placed by the President on institutions of government as opposed to personalities.[10] I have found that Eisenhower laid great stress on the qualities of individual leaders. So, he referred to his disappointment at having 'continually to downgrade' his estimate of Eden,[11] while in a meeting three days later he noted that 'he had always thought most highly of Macmillan'.[12] Perhaps the best example of this sentiment, however, was Eisenhower's extraordinary belief that King Saud of Saudi Arabia could be the man to divert the course of the whole Arab nationalist movement, and rival the leadership of Nasser. Again, here, his first question about Saud was 'what kind of a man is he?'[13] This stress on the qualities of leadership may again perhaps be attributed to Eisenhower's military background.

If Eisenhower emerges as a relatively straightforward character, deceiving contemporaries only as to the degree of his involvement in policy making, the opposite can be said of John Foster Dulles. An owlish and meticulous man with a penchant for sharpening his own pencils and measuring distances on the globe with his handkerchief, Dulles had served his apprenticeship as an international lawyer. Latterly, he had been foreign policy adviser to Thomas Dewey, the defeated Republican candidate in the 1948 election. This, and his subsequent experience of the Truman Administration's policy of the 'containment' of Communism, had convinced him that a radical and more aggressive approach was needed to prevent the resources of the US being dissipated in a protracted global war of attrition with Communism. The US should be prepared to place a much greater reliance on the deterrent effect of its superior nuclear, as opposed to conventional, forces.

Dulles's puritanical character and his rhetorical contributions to the so-called 'New Look' foreign policy adopted by Eisenhower made him a controversial figure and the butt of many contemporary jokes. His boast that he had been three times to the brink of nuclear war coined not only the term 'brinkmanship' to describe his brand of nuclear diplomacy, but also the jibe at his character, 'three brinks, and he's brunk'. His call for an 'agonizing reappraisal' of US foreign policy inspired a cartoon in the *Saturday Review of Literature* depicting a jeweller's store window. In the bottom corner appeared the caption 'appraisals $2; agonizing reappraisals $5'.[14] Finally, a night club singer, Carol Burnett, provoked fifty calls of complaint to the NBC television station, when she appeared on the network singing her satirical composition, 'I made a fool of myself over John Foster Dulles'.[15] This jibe at Dulles' priggishness evidently did not strike a cord with all Americans.

On the other side of the Atlantic, Dulles's blend of self-righteousness and personal and political puritanism provoked a decidedly mixed response. His relationship with Eden was at best strained. Churchill could not abide him and famously dismissed him in three words, 'dull, duller, Dulles'. As Winthrop Aldrich, US Ambassador to Britain at the time of the Suez crisis later recollected, 'you have no idea, you couldn't have any idea, how much he was mistrusted by Winston Churchill, and Winston Churchill's mistrust of Dulles permeated the whole Cabinet.'[16]

What, then, were the principal foreign policy goals of this controversial Secretary of State? In fact, although one may lay out a similar list of concerns in his conduct of policy to those entertained by Eisenhower, with Dulles the defeat of Communism assumed such a primacy that it blinkered his outlook in many other respects. His view of Communism, founded on his reading of Stalin's 'Problems of Leninism', emphasized the twin threats which he believed it posed to the West. The Soviet Union was intent not only on direct national expansion into the states on its borders, but also on fostering social revolution throughout the world. US foreign policy must aim to thwart both designs.[17] The US was in a unique position to take on this role, given something of the character of a moral crusade by Dulles, because of its economic and military strength. Not only this, however, but to Dulles's mind the US operated on a different moral plane in the conduct of its foreign policy. As he told foreign service personnel in April 1956, 'the United States is, I suppose, the only country in the world which has foreign policies which are not primarily designed for its own aggrandizement.'[18]

One source of confusion about Dulles's role as Secretary of State stemmed from the contemporary misinterpretation of his relationship with Eisenhower, which, as has been suggested, seems to have been shared to some extent by the British Government. So, during the Suez Crisis, for instance, it seems fair to conclude that Eden underestimated both the strength of Eisenhower's convictions and the degree of control he exerted over Dulles's manoeuvrings. Dulles's much publicised comment that the Egyptian leader, Nasser, should be made to 'disgorge' the Canal may well explain Eden's annotation of the words 'Foster advocated going in' on one of the President's many warnings about the inadvisability of using force to settle the dispute.[19]

What Dulles's statements appear to have illustrated is a method of action which seems to have recurred again and again in his conduct of foreign policy. Because of what may be termed his lawyer's instincts, the Secretary was often prepared to say one thing in public on one occasion and another in private at a later date if this served to 'win the case' for him at that particular time. A good example of this was his anti-colonialist statements during the Senate hearings on the Eisenhower Doctrine early in 1957. At the same time as he and the President were manoeuvring to restore some form of cooperation, or at least consultation, with the British over Middle Eastern problems, Dulles was telling the senators: 'if I were an American boy going to fight in the Middle East I would rather not have a British and a Frenchman, one on my right hand, one on my left . . .'[20]

In addition to these well-known examples, however, this study will present several new instances of Dulles acting in haste and repenting at leisure in circumstances which seem explicable only by reference both to his isolation from advisers in Washington, and to his own personal prejudices. A good example of the former circumstances at work will be provided by Dulles's initial reaction to the formation of the United Arab Republic of Egypt and Syria, news of which broke while he was attending a Baghdad Pact Council meeting in Ankara at the end of January 1958. Having first encouraged the Iraqi Government to take the initiative in devising some counterstroke to Nasser's coup, Dulles back-pedalled somewhat when, on his return to Washington, he was advised that the formation of the union had served to block Communist intrigues in Syria.

An example of the latter circumstances in action is provided by Dulles's statements in private during 1958 to the British about Nasser. Dulles had viewed the Egyptian leader with some distaste since well before the Suez crisis but, because of the primacy of the communist threat, had always been prepared to countenance the possibility of working with him if he could be shown to be opposing the designs of the Soviet Union. Still, the British consistently found it difficult to interpret his policy when on the one hand the US Administration pursued a pragmatic approach in public towards the Egyptian leader, while on the other Dulles compared him in private to Hitler.[21] With Dulles, it seems appropriate to predict his actions by reference to what we may term a hierarchy of threats. Top of the list, and far outweighing any other threat, was that of Communism. Next came that of radical, neutralist, or anti-Western nationalism. Finally came imperialism and colonialism. While it is often

difficult to isolate these factors from one another we can norm-
ally safely predict his response by following his view of the likely
gains for Communism in any situation.

On the British side, this study has little that is new to add
to the many assessments already made of Anthony Eden's
character and qualities as Prime Minister. Eden had been
heir apparent to the premiership, occupying the position of
Foreign Secretary throughout Churchill's long Indian summer as Prime Minister from 1951 until April 1955. The years
in waiting undoubtedly embittered him to some extent, and
perhaps inclined him all the more towards an autocratic
form of premiership, and an impatience with those who
failed to see his point of view. Perhaps, too, those years, which
had witnessed conspicuous diplomatic successes for the Foreign Secretary, most notably in Indo-China and over German
incorporation into NATO, had dimmed somewhat his sense of
Britain's position in the world between the superpowers. This
was all the more surprising since in 1952 Eden himself had
been the author of a paper advising the shedding of overseas
commitments, and the recognition of the strict limitations on
British power.[22] Whatever the explanation, Eden appears here
as a man preoccupied with the importance of the Middle East
to Britain, and increasingly incensed by the behaviour of the
challenger to British power there, Nasser. As was suggested earlier, his experience in government in the inter-war years had
ingrained what he believed to be the lessons of appeasement on
his outlook. The false parallel between the actions of Hitler and
Mussolini and those of Nasser was one which came to dominate his perceptions.

Harold Macmillan, too, was preoccupied with these lessons.
The beginning of the period covered by this study saw his star
in the ascendant. Having completed a successful term as Housing Minister in October 1954, Macmillan moved on briefly to
Defence. On Eden's assumption of the premiership in April
1955 Macmillan was promoted again, this time to Eden's old job
at the Foreign Office. Formative political appointments in his
earlier career had included a spell as British Minister with the
allied forces in North Africa during the war, where he had built
up a close association with one General Dwight D. Eisenhower,
soon to be a close colleague again.

Macmillan emerges here as every bit as complex a character as Eden himself. On the one hand, renowned as a great political showman, Macmillan was in fact an intensely private and insecure man prone to bouts of melancholy. These could strike in the midst of crises and leave him incapable of taking action. In terms of political instincts it seems fair to say that he was far more of a pragmatist than an idealist. Indeed, some have gone so far as to portray him as an unprincipled opportunist intent only on seeking and retaining power for himself.[23] His biographer, on the other hand, inclines to put a more charitable light on his career.[24] However, it must be admitted that this study unearths some startling examples of Macmillan's political recklessness. His pursuit of the defeat of Nasser in the Middle East was every bit as hot as that of his predecessor. The only difference between the two men in this respect was to prove to be that Macmillan saw the need at least to keep the Americans informed of British intentions. It was this which saved him from a situation which in some respects had the makings of another Suez when, in response to the revolution in Iraq in July 1958, he recklessly sent British paratroops into a precarious position in Jordan. More than this, the Iraqi crisis also reveals Macmillan taking the need to practise 'economy with the truth' to a new extreme which can only be termed 'austerity with the truth' in his explanations to Parliament of the circumstances surrounding the intervention.

Nevertheless, in spite of these serious strictures, Macmillan at least avoided overturning the Anglo-American boat in the Middle East as Eden had done. He also avoided humiliations of the scale of Suez and has been judged comparatively favourably because of the fortuitous success of such actions as that undertaken in Jordan. Although intent on exercising power, he did at least prove to be more prepared than his predecessor to entertain the opinions of others.

Macmillan's principal source of advice and information on foreign affairs was of course his Foreign Secretary, Selwyn Lloyd. Lloyd is in one sense an interesting political figure in that he held on to his post after the Suez crisis and thus spanned the premierships of both Eden and Macmillan. On the other hand, he can certainly not be described as a charismatic politician, or one who left a particular imprint on the office of Foreign

Secretary. It could perhaps be said not unfairly of him, in the words of T. S. Eliot, that he was 'not Prince Hamlet', but 'an attendant lord', 'deferential, glad to be of use, politic, cautious and meticulous'. His prominent characteristics were loyalty, industry and diligence, which overlaid a sense of personal insecurity. There was also an element of naivety in his nature typified by his first reaction when the Profumo affair broke: 'but he couldn't have had the time'.[25] Both Eden and Macmillan, who were previous holders of the office of Foreign Secretary, found it useful to have a steady rather than a flamboyant man at the Foreign Office. This is not to say that Lloyd was a mere cypher. On occasion he proposed important initiatives himself, including his suggestion to Macmillan in May 1959 that Britain should begin the process of restoring diplomatic relations with Nasser's Egypt.[26] However, unlike Macmillan under Eden, Lloyd was unlikely to attempt to plough his own furrow in foreign affairs behind the back of the Prime Minister. It seems fair to say that even as Foreign Secretary in the Macmillan years, he never quite lived down Nye Bevan's reference to him during the Suez crisis as the monkey to Eden's organ-grinder.

These then, were the characters, who were to direct the course of Anglo-American relations in the Middle East during the period under review. It is fair to say that their efforts to maintain Western influence in the region were to be dominated by relations with one indigenous personality, the Egyptian leader, Colonel Gamal Abdel Nasser. However, before outlining his role, it is important to examine the legacy which British and American leaders inherited in the Middle East at the start of 1955, a legacy which had in fact done much to shape Nasser's own outlook.

It is clear that British interests in the Middle East in the years after the Second World War were dominated by the need to secure access to oil supplies. An important element in the economic vulnerability of the country in the post-war period was the American insistence on making progress towards the convertibility of sterling a condition of loans to bail out the British economy. These requirements had been made clear by the Bretton Woods agreement of 1944, which, despite British acquiescence, effectively represented the imposition of the

American vision for the future of the Western economy. However, the effect on Britain, when combined with the swift termination of Lend-Lease at the end of the war, was devastating. The defence of sterling as a major international reserve currency, an assumption unquestioned by British post-war planners, put a premium on the maintenance of sizeable dollar reserves. However, although a large loan was negotiated with the Truman Administration in 1946, the extent of Britain's overseas commitments, including the British zone in Germany, meant that it was spent at what could only be viewed as an alarming rate over the next two years. The abandonment of the British commitments to defend Greece and Turkey followed by the American espousal of the Truman Doctrine illustrated all too readily the impact of economic stringency on Britain's ability to maintain her role as a world power.

Of course, a way out of the dilemma would have been to abandon this attempt. However, one result of the wartime coalition government had been the development of a bipartisan consensus as to the need to maintain Britain's place at the high table of world politics. Ernest Bevin, the Foreign Secretary of the Labour Government during the years 1945–51, therefore set about finding ways of renewing the British Empire as an economic and political unit. On the one hand, he was helped by American recognition, embodied in the Marshall Plan, that the United States would have to help the Western European economies back on to their feet, even if only out of her own economic self-interest. On the other, he developed his own schemes for renewing the empire, at the heart of which were his plans to exploit the oil resources of the Middle East and develop the British colonies in Africa. 'In peace and in war', he stated, in a memorandum circulated to his cabinet colleagues, 'the Middle East is an area of cardinal importance to the UK, second only to the UK itself.'[27]

The particular importance of the Persian Gulf to Britain in these years was that it was a source of extensive oil reserves comparatively close to Western Europe, which could be bought from British companies and paid for in sterling.. In addition, oil sold on world markets was a significant source of revenue for Britain. Unlike the US which could still at this stage fulfil its own needs from indigenous resources, by the early 1950s

Britain had no real alternative to oil supplies drawn from the Persian Gulf area.[28] Whereas in 1938 only 19 per cent of Western Europe's oil supplies had come from the Middle East, by 1955, British Government figures showed that 90 per cent of supplies came from the area. This was an extraordinary expansion by any standards.[29] Thus from the point of view of the economic recovery of Britain and Western Europe, it seemed important to maintain the security of the Persian Gulf region, and access to its oil supplies.

In fact, as with many imperial commitments, Britain's involvement in the Gulf had originally grown up in a piecemeal fashion. The principal concern of the British in the early nineteenth century had been with the protection of the trade routes to India. Consequently, the earliest agreements with local rulers had concentrated first on securing the rights of the East India Company over its colonial rivals, and then on the suppression of piracy. Exclusive British political influence or 'protection' was not formalized until the end of the century. Contemporaneously, the notion of the Persian Gulf as a distinct political entity grew up as Curzon, the viceroy of India, identified the area as one which was vital to the interests of India and the British Empire.[30] During the inter-war years, the focus of British interests had begun to shift away from the protection of the trade routes to India, towards a competition with the United States to secure concessions for the exploitation of the oil reserves then being discovered in the region. This had started when the British Government had become a partner in the Anglo-Persian Oil Company as early as 1914, but was given added impetus by the First World War.

However, although the realization of the importance of oil to the military machine had begun to dawn in Washington, the natural reluctance of the US Government to become involved in what it regarded as primarily commercial squabbles, and the discovery of new reserves at home, meant that the issue diminished in importance during the 1920s. The Depression, and the glut in oil supplies which accompanied it, served only to further this trend. Thus, although Benjamin Shwadran argues that from the end of the First World War until the outbreak of the second 'a continuous struggle . . . [was] waged between the United States and Great Britain for the exploitation of the oil resources of the Middle East',[31] this struggle tended to take place more between companies than governments. Its net result was a series of victories for the American companies, which gained a quarter share in the Iraqi Petroleum Company, the entire concessions of Saudi Arabia and Bahrain, and one half of the Kuwait concession.

It was the Second World War that gave the greatest impetus to the American drive to secure a share in the oil resources of the Gulf region. The intention was to guard against the day when domestic supplies would no longer suffice. From Pearl Harbor until the defeat of Japan, nearly seven billion barrels of petroleum were produced for Allied use. Six billion came from the United States.[32] As will be seen, this was to have a profound impact on US relations with oil-producing countries in the region, foremost among which was to be Saudi Arabia.

Returning to British interests in the region, however, it is important to note that conceptions of the defence of the area's oil supplies in the post-Second World War years did not concentrate specifically on the defence of the Gulf. Just as, in the previous century, the maintenance of British leverage over the Ottoman Empire had been conceived of in terms of the protection of the trade routes to India, so British policy in the Middle East in the post-war years was to be dictated by the need to secure oil transit as well as supply. The attempt to renegotiate the basis of the British presence in Egypt undertaken by Ernest Bevin during these years was a clear example of this strategy. The Suez Canal, on which Britain had built up a vast military base during the war years, was viewed as a vital imperial artery. As its importance as a route east to India waned, so its value as a route west for Gulf oil supplies rose. However, the resentment generated by six decades of British occupation of the country proved to be an insurmountable barrier to Bevin's attempts to negotiate some new treaty relationship guaranteeing British access to the base. Hatred of the British was such that, as Sidqi Pasha was to discover to his cost, any Egyptian leader who dealt with them was likely to see his position at home undermined. British conceptions of the defence of the region, and of the secure passage of oil supplies, therefore, were dominated by the need for Egypt in these years.[33]

By contrast, the British were slow to recognize the strategic importance of Iraq, one of the three areas mandated to them by the League of Nations under the post-First World War imperialist carve-up of the region organized at the San Remo Conference of 1920. British moves to grant independence to the country under the treaty of 1930 seem to have been dictated at least in part by a sense of bad conscience about the failure to honour wartime promises to her Arab allies. Certainly, they seem to have been made without any real sense of the importance of Iraq, both as a future oil-producing state, reserves having first been discovered in 1927, and as a possible protector of, or danger to, the Gulf.[34] Although Bevin attempted to renegotiate Britain's treaty relationship with the country after the war, with the intention of securing continued access to the Habbinaya airbase, his efforts foundered as a result of the resentment generated by the Palestine War. The true importance of Iraq as a pivot of the British position in the Middle East was, as will be seen, only to emerge in 1955. Then, in a remarkable strategic shift, occasioned by Britain's failure to achieve agreement with Egypt, and the contemporaneous signing of the Baghdad Pact, Britain was to make Iraq the focus of her efforts to protect the oil supplies of the region.

Of the other mandates granted to Britain at the San Remo Conference, no study of British strategy in the Middle East in the 1950s could begin without some reference to the ramifications of the collapse of British policy in Palestine. In one of his moments of despair during the winter of 1955, Evelyn Shuckburgh, Under Secretary at the Foreign Office with responsibility for Middle Eastern affairs, was driven to comment, 'how the Arabs hate us really... they will never forgive us Israel.'[35] While this placed the difficulty confronting Britain in maintaining influence over the Arab world from 1948 onwards at its starkest, no amount of special pleading by the British, even if justified, could mitigate the sense of bitterness and betrayal felt towards them by the great majority of the Arabs. The British Government was 'caught on the horns of an insoluble dilemma' in Palestine after the Second World War.[36] On the one hand it was unable to create the state sought by Zionists for fear of undermining its position in the Arab world. On the other, it could not close the door to the hundreds of thousands of Jewish refugees seeking to flee Europe.

While the events in the mandate leading up to the war of 1948–9 are not directly relevant to this study, the collapse of the British attempt to maintain a middle way between the demands of the Zionists for a Jewish state, and the equally fervent opposition of the Arabs to what they regarded as an alien occupation of their lands, offered a portent of what was to come in several respects. Firstly, it underlined Britain's inability to operate in defiance of the wishes of the two emerging superpowers, America and the Soviet Union, who were somewhat incongruously allied, for widely diverging reasons, in opposition to the British policy in the mandate. Secondly, it introduced a permanent element of instability into the region, and created what the Arabs regarded as an internal threat which always overrode in importance the external danger from the Soviet Union, to which Britain tried to point in her subsequent attempts to organize the defence of the area. Put simply, Arab nationalists opposed to Britain could in future frustrate her policies, and vilify her allies in the eyes of the broad mass of Arabs, by pointing to the example of Palestine. The British betrayal here, they argued, was evidence that all British schemes were really intended to distract the Arabs' attention from their true enemy. Palestine eroded what trust there might have been left for Britain in the Arab world.

The Palestine War had also undermined somewhat Britain's position in Jordan, the third of her former mandates in the region. Although the British-officered Arab Legion had performed creditably, particularly in the first phase of the conflict, accusations were levelled that Britain had failed to supply it with sufficient quantities of arms and ammunition to enable it to conduct the war against the Jewish forces effectively. While the British treaty relationship with Jordan for defence purposes endured, and British officers maintained a high profile in the Arab Legion, British prestige here too had taken a serious blow during 1948–9.

The American role in the region up to the beginning of the Second World War had been very limited compared to that of Britain. Barring the competition between American and British oil companies for concessions between the wars, and the passing interest of the American Government in the wake of the First World War, the area had been one which had largely been left to the British. Again though, as has been suggested, the demands for oil engendered by war drew the attention of the American Government to the region. The principal country in which this interest was manifested was Saudi Arabia, where the Arabian American Oil Company [ARAMCO] had earlier won the concession for the exploitation of the country's oil reserves. Governmental disinterest had been such before the war that it was only under intense pressure from the oil companies that the State Department had relented and allocated a permanent diplomatic representative to the court of King Ibn Saud in June 1939.[37]

It was in the later years of the war, however, that American economic and military involvement in Saudi Arabia gathered pace. Firstly, in February 1943, Roosevelt informed Lend-Lease administrator Edward Stettinius that 'the defence of Saudi Arabia is vital to the defence of the United States' and ordered the extension of Lend-Lease aid to that country.[38] Then, in June 1943, the American Minister in Jeddah was instructed to inform his British counterpart that the Saudis would from now on be dealing directly with the US over arms sales, rather than going through the British as had formerly been the case. From this point onwards 'the idea of playing a role independent of the British had begun to gather momentum' in American minds.[39] Wartime rivalry between the two allies over Saudi Arabia reached a peak when, in October 1944, the American Minister learned that the British had been involved in the Saudi refusal to allow the US to build a military airfield at Dharan. In the face of vigorous American protests, the British retreated, and in the late months of the war, the airstrip which was to become the nucleus of the Dharan base was constructed. This gave the US, in addition to its substantial oil interests in the country, a strategic interest which, as will be seen, helped to influence its relations with Britain over policy in the region in the 1950s.

In addition to commercial and military links, a certain ideological bond was to develop between the United States and Saudi Arabia in the post-war years against the background of the outbreak of the cold war with the Soviet Union. While the Saudis were principally concerned with regional problems such as their rivalry with the Hashemites of Iraq and Jordan, there was a certain community of interest between them and the Americans in respect of resisting Communist penetration of the Arab world. The classical Islamic view of international relations envisioned a bipolar world, made up of Dar al-Islam (territory under the Islamic, or God's law) and the Dar al-Harb (territory of war). Within the Dar al-Islam could be numbered not only Muslims, but all monotheists. These people, known as Ahl al-Kitab, the 'People of the Book' could include Christians and Jews. Although there were obvious limitations on this philosophy, especially in relation to the state of Israel, it could nevertheless be easily adapted to the world order during the period of cold war. It was not difficult to classify the areas under Communist control as Dar al-Harb, and thus to justify an alliance with the leader of the 'Free World', America, as an alliance of monotheists against unbelievers.[40]

The other aspect of the US–Saudi relationship which was to have an impact on Anglo-American relations during the 1950s was the American support for Saudi territorial claims within the Arabian peninsula. During the 1950s, this support was principally to be concerned with the dispute over the Buraimi Oasis on the Saudi-Abu Dhabi-Omani borders. Although this issue will be discussed in more detail in Chapter 4, it should be noted here that the Saudis were prompted to press their claim in 1949 as a result of ARAMCO oil exploration in the vicinity of the oasis. Then, when, in April 1953, it was agreed to take the matter to international arbitration, the Saudis were aided in the preparation of their detailed case, known as the Saudi memorial, by ARAMCO officials. The suspicion of the British Government that ARAMCO was the unofficial arm of US policy in the region seemed to be confirmed by Eisenhower's comment during a discussion of Buraimi with Eden in January 1956, that 'we had to take account of world opinion. People in general were very ignorant about Muscat and Buraimi and tended to think that the whole Arabian peninsula belonged – or ought to belong – to King Saud.' Eden's record of the conversation contains the annotated comment 'what people'.[41]

The other specific interest of the US Government in the Middle East which also caused tension with the British in the post-war years lay in the creation and continued existence of the state of Israel. Anglo-American cooperation over Palestine had of course proven to be 'the single most frustrating and elusive goal of the Labour Government in imperial and colonial affairs'.[42] One important reason for this was the attitude of President Truman. Although the British were initially understanding about US election difficulties, this understanding was tempered by the belief that the President would eventually act on what they believed to be the obvious merits of the case, and bring British and American policies into line. The hoped-for convergence in approach never materialized, however, and Bevin in particular was left embittered at what he regarded as the sacrifice of vital Western security interests on the altar of US domestic politics.[43] In fact, it seems that Truman's view was conditioned not just by electoral considerations, but by a genuine belief that during the Palestine War the Jewish people were creating a state 'in a way perhaps comparable to the winning of the American West'.[44] It was not until January 1949 that anything like a breaking point appeared in Truman's tolerance for the expansion of Israel, brought on by Israeli strikes across the Egyptian frontier.

The British view of the likely future course of developments at the end of the Palestine War was decidedly pessimistic. Bevin described Israel as 'another China', and pointed towards the aid received from the Eastern bloc as evidence that the country might become a Soviet satellite state in the heart of the Middle East. The American view was much more positive, and saw the Israelis as potential regional allies, although they initially aimed at a neutral course between the two superpowers.[45] Nevertheless, both the British and the Americans, together with the French, were able to agree on the need to stabilize the Middle East in the short term after the negotiation of the armistices. The result was the Tripartite Declaration of 1950 which aimed to preserve the status quo in the region by the imposition of controls on arms supplies. However, the Declaration was little more than a stopgap measure, and failed to address the fundamental problem of why countries in the Middle East wanted to arm themselves.

A significant change in the American outlook on the region was, however, brought about by the election of Eisenhower to the presidency in January 1953. At much the same time as the Israelis were inclining towards a closer relationship with the

West, in the wake of the damage done to relations with the
Soviet Union by the so-called 'Doctors Plot', Dulles was announcing that the US would pursue a policy of 'friendly impar-
tiality' between Israel and the Arab states.[46] It would certainly
be true to say that the new incumbent of the White House was
far less pro-Zionist than his predecessor, an attitude mirrored by
his Secretary of State.[47] Eisenhower, although not anti-Semitic,
was 'uncomfortable with Jews'.[48] In addition, with the new
Administration making the waging of the cold war in the region
a priority, Arab sensitivities occupied a much higher place in
their list of priorities than had previously been the case.[49]

'Eisenhower . . . believed that the United States possessed a
moral obligation to employ its power in order to contain international Communism . . .'[50] Although the Middle East was not,
at the beginning of Eisenhower's first term as President, a
region in which the Soviet Union was manifesting much of
an interest, the philosophy of the Soviet threat embraced
by Eisenhower maintained that the Soviets would be bound,
sooner or later, to become involved in the area. It was of vital
importance to the economies of Western Europe, the undermining of which was presumed to be a principal goal of Soviet
strategy.

On the one hand, therefore, Eisenhower was prepared to
bury the differences of the previous Administration with the
British in order to seek a more effective community of effort
to defend the region against the Soviets. This approach manifested itself particularly in Iran, where Eisenhower backed a
CIA scheme, carried out in conjunction with the British, to overthrow the nationalist government of Mohammad Mossadegh,
which had earlier challenged British control over Iranian oil
production. Eisenhower's decision to act here was dominated
by the belief that Mossadegh was backed by the Communists.[51]
On the other hand, however, the activities of the CIA in Egypt,
which received strong backing from the new Administration,
were not so welcome to the British. The agency's operations
were dominated by the support given to Colonel Gamal Abdel
Nasser, both before and after the coup which brought him
and the junta of 'Free Officers' led initially by Mohammad
Neguib to power. The basis of the US Administration's action was the perceived need for the US to develop what Miles

Copeland has called an 'independent ally' in the region.[52] The idea behind the encouragement of Nasser was 'to have in power in one "key" Arab country a leader who would be strong enough to make unpopular decisions – like making peace with Israel'.[53] Since the thrust of Eisenhower's policy was concerned with the creation of stability, on the assumption that instability anywhere would provide fertile ground for the expansion of Communism, Nasser was to be the person backed by his Administration to bring such stability to the Middle East.

The initial problem for the British in all this was that they were engaged in a parallel attempt to try to wring concessions out of Nasser over the future status of the Canal Zone. More than this, however, they regarded Nasser as still too unpredictable a figure at this stage on whom to found a regional strategy, even though they welcomed the ending of the Farouk regime.[54] Indeed, Nasser's early experiences in life had been shaped by the fight against imperialism. In his youth he had joined in demonstrations against the British in Alexandria and had even suffered imprisonment.[55] From this point onwards, the search for 'dignity' for the Egyptian nation, which involved the casting off of the imperialist yoke, was to dominate his outlook. It was King Farouk's public humiliation by the British in 1942 that determined Nasser that if Egypt was to achieve such dignity it could only be under new rulers.

Although a natural demagogue from the outset, until the 1947 UN Resolution for the partition of Palestine Nasser could still more properly be termed an Egyptian nationalist. While the Palestine War broadened his consciousness of the role of Egypt in Arab affairs, even after the 1952 revolution he remained more preoccupied with internal Egyptian problems. It was the Baghdad Pact, and the perceived challenge which it laid down from Iraq to Egyptian leadership of the Arab world that was to change his outlook.[56]

Nasser's personal charisma was undeniable. Mahmoud Fawzi recalls that Nasser had 'a cultivated talent, if not a natural gift, of rapport with others when he put his mind to it'.[57] Even Julian Amery, a leading figure in the British Suez Group which opposed agreement with Nasser, 'found his frankness endearing' when they met.[58] Although prone to bursts of high-pitched laughter in conversation, Nasser was never lacking in self-confidence. His physical presence was imposing, and his ability to command an audience impressive. Speeches delivered in colloquial Arabic endeared him to the masses who saw him as a leader in touch with their lives. Although in private Nasser could be witty and urbane, with a dryness of humour which cut through formality, in his public political life he was a ruthless and effective operator. Julian Amery also recalled raising the issue of why Nasser opposed the Iraqi Prime Minister Nuri es-Said so strongly. 'Nuri is a dictator. He censors the press; he imprisons his political opponents . . .', Nasser argued. 'More than you do?', enquired Amery. 'No, not more, but less efficiently', Nasser replied.[59]

During the early stage of his career, however, it was Nasser's very demagogic appeal that made him seem such a great potential ally to the Americans. The vision of Nasser as a possible anti-Communist warrior which developed soon after the revolution, was one which was to prove surprisingly tenacious in Washington in the coming years. Although Nasser did not in any sense invent Arab nationalism, he was to prove remarkably successful in tapping the waves of resentment felt by the Arab peoples against their colonial oppressors. One could not talk of Arab nationalism in the 1950s without thinking of Nasser. He came to embody the movement. This despite the fact that his strategy remained rooted in 'long-standing Egyptian national interests'.[60]

The American support for Nasser in the early years was, however, not all that surprising in view of the well-established sympathy of the US for peoples it believed to be struggling to free themselves from colonial oppression. This point brings us naturally to the last background thread that must be picked up before we can plunge into the dramatic events of 1955 – that of the broader foundations of the Anglo-American relationship. It should be recognized from the start that, despite assumptions which may be current in the present day, the close association of the two powers was comparatively recent in the making. It had been bred in the special circumstances which existed in the early years of the Second World War when, after the fall of France, Britain was left to stand alone as America's perceived buffer against the triumph of fascism.[61] In the inter-war years, despite the ties of culture and language that should have bound the two countries, they had in fact known surprisingly

little about each other.[62] Indeed, in some areas, especially that
of their respective navies, the two had even found themselves
in competition.[63]

The example of the US role in Saudi Arabia which produced tension between the allies during the war years themselves illustrates the extent to which interests, despite all the
fair words spoken about ideological and cultural bonds, were
to be at the heart of the new relationship. Nor was it the natural state of affairs for America to engage herself in long-term
foreign alliances, especially with European powers. Immediately after the Second World War, as after the First, America initially sought to disengage herself from these bonds. The easy
credit arrangements provided by Lend-Lease, which had sus-
tained Britain during the war years, were cancelled within eight
days of the end of the war with Japan. Although a new loan
was negotiated to keep the British economy afloat, it was clear
that the US now expected Britain to fend for herself again,
both economically and politically.

It was the development of the cold war with the Soviet Union
during the years 1946–9, however, which changed all of this,
and renewed the US alliance with Britain, producing in successive years the Truman Doctrine for Greece and Turkey, the
Marshall Plan, and the North Atlantic Treaty Organization for
Western Europe. Once Soviet actions in constructing a sphere
of influence in Eastern Europe were rationalized as Communist expansionism, Western Europe came to be viewed as a
vital political and economic bastion for the United States. It
was here that the foundations of post-war Anglo-American
cooperation were laid. In addition, however, it should be noted
that the significance of the American concern over Communist expansionism manifested by these developments was not
lost on British policy-makers. If a particular problem faced
by the British in any area of the world could successfully be
presented to the Americans in terms of the Communist threat,
then US aid was much more likely to be forthcoming. In
fact one important aspect of the new US commitment to Europe, evidenced by the Marshall Plan and the creation of NATO,
from the point of view of British policy-makers, was that it
freed Britain's resources to enable her to maintain her role as
a world power. While there was agreement between Britain and

America on the overriding need to defend Western Europe, in the other theatres in which Britain manifested an interest, of which the Middle East was a prime example, the different interests of the two powers were to breed repeated disagreements.

Although British governments of whatever complexion in the post-war years believed it to be a good thing for Britain to be closely allied with US power, there were undercurrents of tension in the relationship which went beyond conflicts over specific interests. Bevin, for one, resented the American pressure for Britain to move into a closer political relationship with Western Europe which accompanied the Marshall Plan. 'Although the British saw nothing improper in a "special relationship" with their transatlantic relatives, they were appalled at the prospect of sharing close and continuous quarters with the Italians, the French, and the Germans.'[64] This was at least in part the result of a sentiment engendered in the war years, when, with Western Europe fallen to Hitler, it was the Anglo-American relationship which saved Britain. More than this, however, successive British governments still aspired to be treated on near equal terms by the Americans, as a great power, and not as a dependent ally tied to American coat-tails. This was made all the more difficult by the obvious dependence of the country on American financial largesse. Nevertheless, Anthony Eden like Bevin before him was determined that Britain should continue to be able to pursue independent initiatives on the international stage. These attitudes were to be of vital importance in shaping the outlook of British policy-makers towards the Middle East during the later 1950s.

Similarly, from the American side, suspicions were entertained in several respects about her ally's intentions. Washington officials were constantly beset by the fear that the goal of British policy was to use American money to gain British ends. In other words, for the Americans to pull British chestnuts out of the fire. Even more, they were suspicious and disapproving about the British Empire, both from the economic and from the moral point of view. The empire acted to some degree in the post-war years as a trading bloc based on the sterling area, in collision with the US aspiration for 'open door' economic policies. Furthermore, colonialism was viewed by many, including the new president Eisenhower, as morally unacceptable, an anachronism to be speeded on its way into the history books. The differing degrees of Anglophobia and Anglophilia between various branches of the US Administration, and between the individuals who went to make up these branches illustrates the particular care which must be taken when speaking of an opinion as current in 'Washington'. 'London' and 'Washington' 'are shorthand terms for vast machines of government' which should not be personified.[65] One very good example of the sorts of difference in opinion which might emerge between the various departments of the US Government will be outlined here. The Defense Department, backed by the Chiefs of Staff, repeatedly pushed for US adherence to the Baghdad Pact on military grounds. It was rebuffed on political grounds by the Near Eastern section of the State Department, which received the casting vote of the President as backing for its stance.

On the British side, career civil servants, of whom Evelyn Shuckburgh, Under Secretary at the Foreign Office, is a good example, had some latitude in the formation of policy. 'Project Alpha', which will be referred to in later chapters, was an Anglo-American attempt to solve the Arab–Israeli dispute in which the role of Shuckburgh, in formulating specific plans to give substance to the general sentiments of his political masters, was of great significance. Even more strikingly, Sir Ivone Kirkpatrick, Permanent Under Secretary at the Foreign Office, was responsible for drafting much of Eden's correspondence with Eisenhower during the Suez Crisis, with its loaded references to Nasser as Mussolini and the Soviet Union as Hitler.[66] It is also clear that the views of British ambassadors on the ground in the Middle East were given rather more weight in London than reports received in Washington from their American counterparts. The dismissive attitude adopted by Dulles to the warnings issued by Ambassador McClintock, the US representative in Beirut, at the time of the Lebanese crisis of May–July 1958 is a good illustration of this tendency.

Indeed, the very differences in systems of government between the two countries were often the source of misunderstanding. As will be seen, when Macmillan pressed Eisenhower to commit himself to some sweeping operation in the Middle East in the wake of the Iraqi Revolution of 14 July 1958, Eisenhower told Dulles that of course he could not and would not write a 'blank check' for the British. 'They just didn't understand our parliamentary system', he complained to the Secretary of State.[67] Disappointed expectations of the kind engendered in situations like these could and did lead to paranoid reactions on the part of the two governments.[68]

Suspicions and misconceptions were thus never far below the surface in Anglo-American relations even at the best of times. In dealings over the Middle East, where interests often collided, they found fertile ground in which to germinate. It was only the even greater fear of the advance of Communism in the region which held them in check. However, despite the breakdowns and conflicts which this study will detail, it should be noted that there was another side to the coin in Anglo-American relations. The coincidence of interests over, for example, Syria could and did produce instances of cooperation closer than anything which might have been achieved between other countries. Similarly, the new US Administration of President Kennedy was quick to offer diplomatic and logistical support for the British intervention in Kuwait in July 1961. It is certainly not my intention to carry revisionism to the point where such examples become inexplicable. Whatever their differences during these years, the two countries remained well aware of the need to pool their assets in the region, such as they were, in the fight against Communism. What follows, then, will be a chronicle of specialness in both conflict and cooperation.

2 The Middle East in 1955

The Middle East at the beginning of 1955 was entering a revolutionary era. The overthrow of the Farouk regime in Egypt in July 1952, and its replacement by a cadre of army officers, was the harbinger of far-reaching political changes which were to sweep the Arab world during the coming decade. In many respects, it seems fair to describe the period 1955–9 as a pivotal one in the post-war history of the region. Arab nationalist sentiment underwent a major renaissance at the same time as ruling elites were threatened or displaced by new social and political forces. The Western powers more often than not were to find themselves reacting to, rather than shaping events, while the influence of the Soviet Union with the Arab states seemed to be advancing on all fronts. Perhaps it is appropriate, therefore, to set the scene for these changes by sketching in brief details of the political situation in the major states of the region on which this study will touch at the beginning of 1955.

In Egypt, the so-called 'Free Officers' regime which had seized control in the July 1952 coup had consolidated its hold on power. The struggle for leadership between Colonel Gamal Abdel Nasser and General Mohammad Neguib during the course of 1954 had concluded with Nasser victorious. As will be seen, the country over which Nasser now ruled was struggling to emerge from the effects of a British imperial occupation dating back to the nineteenth century. The question of Egypt's relationship with Britain had been one of the dominant strands of the country's politics in the inter-war and immediate post-war years. The rise of the nationalist Wafd Party and periodic bouts of anti-British rioting had turned the maintenance of British control into a major political and military undertaking for the imperial power. It was not until the conclusion of the Anglo-Egyptian Treaty in 1936 that any meaningful accommodation was reached between the British Government and the Wafd. However, the Second World War was to prove to be a further unhappy chapter in Anglo-Egyptian relations. In the face of the threat from Rommel's Afrika Corps,

26

Britain moved to secure political stability in Egypt by forcing King Farouk to dismiss the government of Ali Maher Pasha, and appoint his personal enemy, Nahas Pasha, leader of the Wafd, as premier. Although the British move shrewdly secured the compliance of the Wafd in British policies for the duration of the war, it stored up political problems for the future. A change of government imposed by British armour surrounding Cairo's Royal Abdin Palace was the clearest indication possible of Britain's tutelage over Egypt.

After the war, new momentum was given to the nationalist struggle by Egypt's abject failure in the conflict of 1948–9, by Britain's continuing intransigence over reducing her military presence in the huge base which sat astride the Suez Canal, and by the evident corruption of the country's rulers. King Farouk according to one account 'withdrew into a world of constant excess in the late 1940s'.[1] Ralph Stevenson, the British Ambassador in Cairo, described the tension between the king's sense of duty to his people and his personal appetites. 'I would feel happier about it', Stevenson wrote in May 1951, 'had I not a sneaking suspicion that where his own amusement and distraction are concerned the king in him is fighting a losing battle against the man.'[2] The campaign to rid Egypt of the British reached its apogee with Prime Minister Mustafa Nahas Pasha's abrogation of the 1936 Anglo-Egyptian Treaty in October 1951. The riots which followed set the scene for the revolution of July 1952. Paradoxically, however, the advent of the new nationalist regime of the 'Free Officers', together with broader changes in Britain's strategic position, were ultimately to break the deadlock in Anglo-Egyptian relations. The Anglo-Egyptian Treaty of July 1954 might have heralded a new era in relations between the two countries. The reasons why the treaty proved in fact to be a false dawn will be central to this study.

In more general terms, it is arguable that at the beginning of 1955 Egypt could be regarded as the most politically significant of the Arab states. Her statesmen had played a leading part, for instance, in the formation of the Arab League, whose pact was signed in Egypt in 1945. In this context it seemed appropriate that the first Secretary General of the League should be an Egyptian, Abdur Rahman Azzam Pasha. The Arab

League undertaking was indicative of Egypt's aspirations to be seen as the political leader of the Arab world. Economically, although the country was the wealthiest of the Arab states, agriculture was still the most important single source of wealth and employment in the early 1950s. In 1952 agriculture produced about 40 per cent of GDP, employed about 65 per cent of the labour force and provided 90 per cent of exports. Cotton was the dominant crop. Industry, on the other hand, accounted for only 15 per cent of GDP and 10 per cent of the labour force.[3] Again, the pattern of the country's economy cannot be divorced from the British occupation. It had suited Britain's purposes to maintain Egypt as a market for British manufactured goods, and as a cotton plantation to supply the Lancashire mills.[4] Socially, Egypt was something of a polarized society. One of the goals of the 1952 Revolution was to narrow the wide gap between a small wealthy upper class and the mass of the peasantry. Much of the country's land was concentrated in the hands of a few absentee landlords. It is not surprising, therefore, that one of the main features of domestic policy set in train by the revolution was a programme of land reform intended to redistribute these large holdings among the peasantry. Thus, at the beginning of the period covered by this study, Egypt was a traditional society emerging from a prolonged period of imperial domination. Far-reaching domestic, social and economic changes were to be paralleled by new trends in foreign policy which will loom large in this study.

Iraq too had experienced a period of British domination. Indeed, it could be argued that at the beginning of 1955 Iraq had not yet emerged from the shadow of her imperial protector, much as the young King Feisal II still deferred to the regent Abdul Ilah in the conduct of government. The Hashemite Kingdom of Iraq had been forged under his grandfather, Feisal I, who had been installed by the British in the wake of the post-First World War carve-up of the Ottoman Empire. Although Iraq had gained independence from British-mandated rule through the Treaty of 1930, and had been admitted to the League of Nations in 1932, British influence remained strong in the country. The 1930 treaty maintained a defence relationship between the two countries, and allowed Britain access to air bases in the vicinity of Basra and west of the Euphrates.

During the early years of independence, continuing British interference in the country's affairs led to a decline in relations between the two, with the low point being reached in 1941. British reverses in the first phase of the war led former Prime Minister Rashid Ali el-Gailani to attempt a pro-Axis coup. This was put down by the British with the aid of forces sent by King Abdullah of Transjordan.

However, anti-British sentiment remained not far below the surface of Iraqi politics. It re-emerged during the Palestine War of 1948, when Britain's ill-timed attempt to secure a renewal of her treaty relationship with Iraq was scuppered by anti-British riots in Baghdad. Although conservative political elements in the country, led by the regent Abdul Ilah and the veteran politician Nuri es-Said, were able to restore calm for much of the early 1950s, social and political resentments lurked below the surface in the country. Nuri and his circle governed with the support of landowning elements, while the disenfranchised nationalist and socialist opposition built up support in the expanding cities. The population of Greater Baghdad had risen from 500 000 in 1947 to 800 000 by 1957, with many of the new immigrants finding only very poorly paid service jobs.[5] They thus provided a growing pool of support for those discontented with Hashemite rule. To this extent, the Hashemite dynasty of Iraq was a precarious edifice with little foundation in popular support.

One way in which the monarchy attempted to shore-up its position was through the use of revenues from Iraq's expanding oil industry for development programmes. Indeed, compared to the profligacy of Iraq's post-revolutionary regimes, it is arguable that economic policies under the monarchy were prudent and far-sighted. Oil revenues, which increased from 10 per cent of GNP in 1948 to 28 per cent in 1958, were invested in long-term agricultural development based on large-scale irrigation projects.[6] However, these well-intended schemes won the Government little in the way of popular support. In fact, the development programme was handicapped by the regime's refusal to address the question of land reform for fear of offending the landowners on whom it depended for political support.[7] In addition to the conservative upper classes, the Government also relied on the army to hold together the fissiparous elements of Iraqi society, among whom could be numbered the substantial Kurdish minority. Just as the military had been drawn into politics in Egypt, so in Iraq their political role was to prove to be significant. As will be seen, it was an army coup which was to sweep away the Hashemite monarchy in 1958.

If the roots of the Hashemite monarchy in Iraq could be described as shallow at the beginning of 1955, this surely could be said even more of the branch of the House of Hashem which ruled in Jordan. US Administration assessments of the political position in Jordan throughout the late 1950s are littered with references to the unviable nature of the regime of King Hussein.[8] Even British government officials, who were anxious on the whole to see the regime survive, sometimes admitted privately that its long-term prospects were bleak.[9] The fact that the king did survive, and moreover remains in power to this very day, is a remarkable testimony to the astuteness of his political instincts. Looking back to the beginning of 1955, the young Hussein had few political assets with which to work.

The Kingdom of Transjordan had been forged under his grandfather, Abdullah. It had been created as part of the Anglo-French division of the Ottoman Empire after the end of the First World War. Indeed, of all the artificial states formed at the San Remo Conference of April 1920, 'Transjordan was perhaps the most artificial of them all.'[10] It owed its birth both to Abdullah's determination that he should not be left without a kingdom, and to British indecision as to what to do with an area of land which did not seem to fall naturally under the jurisdiction of Syria, Iraq or Palestine. The country was only sparsely settled: by 1944, its population numbered a mere 340 000, and it had few natural resources.[11] Although the first two decades of the new country's history were relatively uneventful, the role of the Arab Legion, Abdullah's British-officered army, was crucial in securing the subservience to central authority of the heterogeneous population. It is not going too far indeed to argue that 'the army created the state'.[12] After the Second World War, in March 1946, the British mandate over Transjordan was formally ended, and an Anglo-Jordanian Treaty was signed. This was modelled on the Anglo-Iraqi Treaty of 1930, which afforded the country independence while reserving military rights for Britain. Although these rights were diminished through a revision of the treaty in 1948, Britain retained an important role in Jordan, not least through her continued funding and officering of the Jordanian Arab Legion.

It would be fair to say that Abdullah's influence in postwar regional politics was far greater than that warranted by the economic and political significance of his kingdom. As recent scholarship has shown, Abdullah was flexible in his dealings with the leaders of the Zionist movement in Palestine, entertaining notions of compromise which made him a controversial figure in the Arab world.[13] Although *realpolitik* may have been the dominant sentiment behind these moves, with Abdullah aiming to acquire a slice of Palestine through any partition of the mandate, it seems churlish to deny him an interest in the peaceful resolution of the Arab–Zionist dispute. During the 1948–9 War Abdullah's British-officered forces occupied and held an area of the mandate on the West Bank of the River Jordan, scoring the only Arab success in the conflict. Unfortunately, Abdullah paid dearly for the independent course he charted in Arab politics, being assassinated in Jerusalem in 1951.

After the brief rule of his son, Talal, was terminated by ill health, Abdullah was succeeded by the young Hussein in August 1952. From the attainment of his majority in May 1953, Hussein ruled over a kingdom beset by profound social and political problems. The acquisition of the West Bank had brought with it a substantial Palestinian problem. Politically, the new Palestinian citizens of Jordan were discontented, blaming Britain, the US and the Jordanian Government itself for the creation of Israel. Also, they resented the continuing leading role of East Bankers in the administration of the country. The large numbers of destitute refugees who had fled to the West Bank posed huge economic as well as political problems for the Jordanian Government. The only assets Hussein had in maintaining the integrity and order of his country were the army, and the circle of advisers bequeathed to him by his grandfather. These advisers included statesmen such as Samir Rifai, whose role was to loom large in Jordanian politics in the later 1950s. At the beginning of 1955, however, Jordan appeared to be a likely point of instability in the constellation of Middle Eastern states.

This was also undoubtedly true of Syria. The political history of the country since the formal attainment of independence from France in 1943 had been one of coup and counter-coup. The period 1955–9 was to be no different. The roots of the chronic instability of the Syrian state appear to have lain in a combination of domestic and foreign tensions. Domestically, post-war Syrian politics functioned as a competition for power between and within three broad groups: the traditional notables; the army; and the new ideological political parties. In the first instance, it was the notables, large landowners whose influence dated back to the Ottoman period, who inherited power from the French. They numbered perhaps as few as 50 influential families. Foremost among them was Shukri Quwatli who was installed as first President of the republic. However, the notables proved strangely inept at handling the business of government, and this, together with their split into factions based on the rival centres of Damascus and Aleppo, brought the military into politics. The year 1949 witnessed no less than three military coups in Syria. These were led respectively by Husni Zaim, Sami Hinnawi and, most significantly, Adib Shishakli. Shishakli's domination of Syrian politics was to last from 1949 to 1954, and was arguably the most stable and efficient period of government Syria witnessed before the consolidation of power in the hands of Hafez al-Asad after 1970. Although it was the notables who were to displace Shishakli in the coup of 1954, the elections of that year also witnessed the emergence of the third force in Syrian politics, ideological political parties. Foremost among these were the Communist and Baath parties. Of these two, the Baath Party, committed to pan-Arab unity and revolutionary socialism, was to prove the more significant in subsequent Syrian history.

Externally, influence in Syria was perceived as the prize in a struggle for leadership in the Arab world during the 1950s, involving Egypt, Iraq and Saudi Arabia. Instability in Syria was also to make it into a theatre of great power intervention and confrontation. Much as with Iraq and Egypt, Syria was a traditional society, with a predominantly agricultural economy, struggling to forge a new identity in the wake of imperialist occupation. The dynamic forces of economic and social change, including urbanization and population growth, drove on the process of political ferment.

The political balance in Lebanon, which had been carved from greater Syria during the period of the French mandate, was, if anything, the most complicated of all the states of the region. The state was founded on a confederation of 16 different communities or sects each of which could command the ultimate loyalty of their members. The political system which recognized the primacy of these religious communities came to be known as confessionalism. The most important of the sects were the Maronite Christians, the Sunni Muslims, the Shia Muslims and the Druze. The Maronites had prospered, politically and economically, under French rule and were Western-oriented in their outlook. The Sunnis were the traditional leaders of the Muslim communities of Lebanon, while the Shia tended to be the more economically and politically dispossessed. The Druze sect, although an offshoot of the Shia branch of Islam, was fiercely protective of its independent rights.

Lebanon achieved formal independence from France alongside Syria in 1943, and from this point onwards the country was governed according to the terms of the 'National Pact'. This divided out the principal political offices among the different religious groups and assigned seats in the legislature on the basis of the 1932 census of the population. Although the terms of the Pact were never formally spelt out, its principles were established when, in 1943, the Maronite Christian President Khoury called on the Sunni Muslim Riyadh al-Solh to be his Prime Minister. At the same time it was agreed that the Speaker of the Parliament should be a Shia Muslim, his deputy a Greek Orthodox Christian, the Commander of the army a Maronite, and his Chief of Staff a Druze. Since the 1932 census showed a six to five majority of Christians as against Muslims, seats in parliament were assigned on this basis, with the total number of members having to be a multiple of eleven.

The National Pact had four obvious weaknesses as a constitution for a state. Firstly, it was founded on the shifting sands of demography. The balance of the population was certain to change over time, and the Pact made no provision for redistributing representation to reflect this. Sure enough, the Christian majority was gradually eroded in the post-war years, but the Christian sects remained opposed to the taking of another census which might reveal this shift, never mind to any alterations in the National Pact. Secondly, because the terms of the Pact were never formally spelt out it was ambiguous and therefore provided no definite point of reference in times of political tension.[14] Thirdly, the Pact put a premium on attachment to religious communities as the basis for politics. It therefore reinforced the differences between the various sects. Finally, the Pact entrenched the power of the conservative leaders of the various sects who were able to exert their influence to secure the nominations for the parliamentary seats reserved for their community.

The Pact could be seen as a way of fudging the issue of Lebanon's national identity.[15] It expressed both the differences and the unity of the sects, for all could speak of a Lebanese nation but mean different things.[16] For some, therefore, Lebanon was still essentially a Western-oriented Maronite homeland, while for others it was 'a temporary expedient until a broad, secular Arab state should be ready to absorb it'. Although it gave the appearance of stability, 'the system was built for a liberal, mercantile epoch, not for an ideological or revolutionary one.'[17] The tensions in the system were to become all too apparent during the later 1950s.

Saudi Arabia too was not immune to the political currents of the Arab world in this era. The constitution of 1926 had vested all power in the hands of King Ibn Saud, who was bound only by the laws of the Sharia. Government other than that supplied by the king was minimal until the 1950s. Its expansion came about only with the dramatic increases in oil revenues which began after the Second World War. Revenue from this source rose from $13 million in 1946 to $172 million by 1952. The 1950s, therefore, witnessed the beginnings of the economic development of the country. These changes, together with the impact of pan-Arabism, were reflected in a struggle for political power after the death of King Ibn Saud between his sons Saud and Feisal. Saud stood for the maintenance of the traditional system of royal government, and a pro-Western tilt in foreign policy. Feisal wanted to develop more elaborate forms of government, and was sympathetic, at least during the 1950s, to the goals of Nasser and the pan-Arab movement.

Finally, it is important to devote some attention to the one non-Arab state in the region on which this study will touch: Israel. Forged in the war of 1948, the new state in the early 1950s was still only beginning to chart its course in domestic and foreign affairs. Not only was there the matter of feeding, housing and employing the hundreds of thousands of Jewish immigrants who flooded into the country during these years, there was the question of securing the borders of the new state. Many of the areas closest to the armistice lines were sparsely populated. This was due to the pre-existing distribution of population, the effects of the 1948 war, and continuing infiltration and raiding from neighbouring Arab states. Both in securing its borders, and in its more general position with regard to a peace settlement, Israel adopted a tough, uncompromising stand. The border areas of the state were treated as free-fire zones, with any Arabs crossing the armistice lines for whatever purposes liable to be shot on sight.[18] As regards a peace settlement, the Israeli Government led by David Ben Gurion refused to accept either that it should trade territory for peace, or that it should accept back large numbers of the Arab refugees who had fled Palestine during the 1948 conflict. The official Israeli line was that the refugees had left to facilitate an attack on Jewish forces by the neighbouring Arab states. The realities behind the exodus, as recent scholarship has shown, were far more complicated.[19] Although the attitude of the government was perhaps understandable in the context of the Holocaust syndrome or Masada complex, which saw threats to the security of the Jewish state around every corner, it helped to stymie any opportunities which may have existed to achieve a broader Arab–Israeli peace.[20]

In foreign affairs, although the Israeli state charted a neutralist course during the first five years of its existence, the government thereafter tilted towards the West. However, despite its pro-Western tendencies, Israel was to prove unable to secure either membership of NATO, or the signing of any bilateral pact with one or other of the major Western powers. This, together with the difficulties of securing a reliable Western arms supplier until 1955, did little to alleviate the Israeli sense of insecurity. Alongside the increasing assertiveness of Arab nationalism, and the growing instability of the armistice lines, this sense of insecurity made another round of fighting between Israel and her neighbours appear an ever great probability as the 1950s progressed.

This brief survey of the political state of affairs in some of the major countries of the region underlines the instability of the Middle East at the beginning of 1955. In protecting their considerable interests in the area, therefore, both Britain and America seemed likely to be faced with one of the most significant foreign policy challenges of the era.

3 The Background to the Formation of the Baghdad Pact

Viewed from one perspective, there was a broad unity of purpose between British and American aims in the Middle East at the start of 1955. Both countries wanted to protect access to the vast oil reserves of the region, and both thought that the principal threat to such access came ultimately from the Soviet Union. The importance of Middle Eastern oil to the economies of Western Europe was illustrated by British Government figures produced in early 1956. These showed that in 1955 the six main refining countries (the United Kingdom, France, Italy, the Netherlands, West Germany and Belgium) imported about 93 million tons of crude oil, of which 90 per cent came from the Middle East. Demand for crude oil products had risen by 17.4 per cent from 1954 to 1955, and was expected to continue to show increases of this magnitude in the following years.[1] Thus, by the beginning of the period under review, it seemed more apparent than ever to both Britain and America that if the economies of Western Europe were to sustain their post-war recovery access to abundant, cheap Middle Eastern oil was a vital strategic interest. Protecting this interest was at the heart of all notions of Middle Eastern defence.

However, 'defence' could be conceived of on two levels. The first and the most obvious level was the simple matter of organizing military assistance to friendly regimes in the area. This involved the promotion of organizations designed to ensure cooperation between strategically important states in the region, and the apportioning of appropriate quantities of Western arms and military advice. This form of 'defence' essentially looked outwards towards the direct threat believed to be posed by the Red Army across the Soviet southern border. On another level, however, 'defence' was more of a political concept. Since a state could equally well be subverted from within by the establishment of a regime inimical to Western interests, 'defence' came to imply the maintenance of influence over important governments in the area. This, of course, was a mode of operation much favoured by the British, and which had been at the heart of the maintenance of 'informal empire' in the region since the First World War.

While this form of 'internal defence' had the benefit of guaranteeing interests without the need for unsustainable military expenditure, it could justly be described as a form of colonialism. In particular, since it was by definition a more insidious method, it tended to complicate the question of interests. Thus, while the Americans and British might be at one over the need for some form of military organization backed by the West to assist Middle Eastern states in resisting any direct Soviet aggression, the Americans, with their suspicion of anything which smacked of British colonialism, tended to baulk at the British penchant for informal methods of control. They suspected that these might be a cover for Britain's attempts to secure her own rather more selfish imperial and commercial interests. This consideration is of vital importance to any discussion of Western schemes for Middle East defence in the 1950s.

In fact, the antecedents of the Baghdad Pact in terms of Western plans for Middle Eastern defence can be traced to the British and American schemes for a Middle East Command. By the late 1940s the British base in the Suez Canal Zone had taken on a special strategic significance for the US as a potential airbase from which operations could be launched against the southern Soviet Union.[2] This significance was reinforced by the outbreak of the Korean War. The problem for the Americans was that it was equally clear that any continuation of the British occupation of Egyptian territory would be unacceptable to local nationalists. What they ideally sought, therefore, was the retention of the Canal Zone Base as an asset to Western defence of the region under the auspices of an arrangement which might make it appear to be something other than a continued colonialist occupation of the country. The best way to achieve this end appeared to be to replace the existing Anglo-Egyptian Treaty with a new agreement which would provide for the incorporation of the Canal Zone into a broader regional security system, and which would include Egypt and other Arab states as partners with the Western powers.

At a series of meetings in June and July 1951 British and American negotiators reached agreement on the basic structure of such a system. The 'Middle East Command' (MEC) would have a British Supreme Commander, and a staff of officers from the United States, France, Turkey, Egypt, South Africa, Australia and New Zealand, together with close but informal links with NATO. The plan was intended to supersede the Treaty of 1936, and required the British to withdraw all of their troops not assigned to the Command and surrender their base in the Canal Zone to the Egyptians, provided that the Egyptians assigned the base to the MEC, maintained it in peacetime, and permitted the new organization to establish its headquarters on Egyptian soil. In the event or imminent contingency of war, Egypt was required to guarantee the Command access to all necessary facilities including ports and airfields.

It seems incredible that British and American officials should have believed that the Command would be acceptable to Egyptian nationalist opinion. In the event the Egyptian Prime Minister Nahas scuppered the plan by announcing, first, on 8 October 1951, the unilateral abrogation of the 1936 Treaty, and second, a week later, through his Foreign Minister, Egypt's rejection of the MEC. Although the British continued to pursue schemes for Middle East defence founded on the Canal Zone Base, developing plans for a Middle East Defence Organization, the significance of the Middle East Command was that it taught the US that Anglo-American defence efforts based on British assets in Egypt were likely to founder on the rock of nationalist opposition. Some alternative method would have to be sought to defend the region against the Soviets.

With the advent of the Eisenhower Administration, and the appointment of John Foster Dulles as Secretary of State, the shape of the US's alternative defence structure became clearer. The 'Northern Tier' concept of defence seized on by Dulles originated in the traditional British imperial notion of using troops from the Indian subcontinent to defend the Middle East.[3] While the British were anxious not to take sides in the dispute between India and Pakistan over Kashmir, believing that the best hope of perpetuating the role of the subcontinent in the defence of the region was to seek reconciliation between the two post-partition states, the Americans were not so squeamish. In August 1950, Secretary of State Acheson had first formally mooted the idea of an 'outer ring' collective defence organization, involving Turkey, Iran, and Iraq, linked to an equivalent South Asian regional organization.[4] This approach was given new impetus by the National Security Council's special report on US policy towards south Asia, which recommended that the US should press India and Pakistan to bring to bear their large resources of manpower on the side of the United States. This recommendation apparently ignored or made light of the deep-seated hostility between the two states.[5] An official policy statement from the State Department of July 1951 followed similar lines, arguing that the Pakistani army, properly equipped, could be expected to 'send troops to Iran's assistance', thus fulfilling 'one of the traditional functions of British-Indian troops in past wars'.[6]

The US apparently continued to flirt with ideas of bringing the Pakistanis into the Middle East during the period of discussions over the MEC with the British outlined above. This in spite of British hostility in view of the likely alienation of India.[7] Thus, when Dulles took over at the State Department, American defence strategy for the Middle East was at something of a crossroads. There appeared to be little to be gained from the continued pursuit of the Suez Base as the foundation of future arrangements. Dulles's pioneering visit to the region during May 1953 served to confirm that the route the US wanted to take was based on the 'Northern Tier' strategy, bringing to bear the manpower resources of Pakistan in defence of Iran, and linking the two to Turkey. Dulles's enthusiasm was particularly fired by his visit to Karachi, with the result that later that year the Pakistani Army Commander-in-Chief on a trip to Washington was promised $25 million in military aid.[8] Dulles's 1953 trip also underlined for him the depth of hostility felt towards Britain in the region. He noted that 'generally in the area . . . we find an intense distrust and dislike for the British', and that 'the days when the Middle East used to relax under the presence of British protection are gone'.[9]

Perhaps unsurprisingly, the British Government for its part remained lukewarm, not to say hostile, to American ideas about the Northern Tier. They stymied its attempts to secure the renewal of some form of Suez Base agreement under the guise of a broader Middle East defence plan, and also complicated matters in the Indian subcontinent, souring relations with India. Nevertheless, the US promotion of Pakistan in the region continued, and the February 1954 announcement of a mutual co-operation agreement between Turkey and Pakistan paved the way for an offer of US aid to Karachi under a formal Mutual Defence Assistance Agreement.

However, despite the apparent reservations of the British about the Northern Tier, a significant degree of controversy surrounds the question of who, in late 1954, was promoting the Northern Tier concept. Ayesha Jalal argues that the impetus towards the formation of the Turko-Iraqi Pact in January 1955 came from Washington. 'The British could see', she contends, 'that the pact was yet another US move to drive them out of an established sphere of influence.' Due to the weakness of their political and military position, 'the British now reconciled themselves to accepting the US lead in the Middle East. . . . By April 1955, the need for Iraq forced Great Britain to become a signatory to the Baghdad Pact.' On the basis of this assessment, she poses the question as to whether the Baghdad Pact marked 'the United States' final victory over Great Britain during the Cold War, a victory which the Suez Crisis of 1956 served to confirm?'[10]

Leaving aside the somewhat controversial implication that the US aimed at some form of victory over Britain as part of its Cold War strategy, Jalal's analysis of the British and American attitudes to the pact raises issues of fundamental importance for the relationship between the two in the Middle East during this period. To begin with, it directly contradicts the analysis of the origins and nature of the pact put forward by Brian Holden Reid, one of the first historians to discuss the organization with reference to British government records.[11] 'In considering the various motives why the British government sought to organize a defensive pact in this region', he argues, 'the attitude of Turkey was crucial.' The essence of his argument is that the Turkish Prime Minister, Menderes, anxious to promote the role of his country in the region, and to prove himself a loyal ally of Britain and, or so he believed, America, set about creating the pact, with the British as the driving force in the background.

The flaw in Brian Holden Reid's argument, however, lies in taking a British gain from the pact, the renewal of the Anglo-Iraqi special agreement, which was not guaranteed until a very late stage of the negotiations, and arguing retrospectively to make this into the successful culmination of a year's patient diplomacy. This is surprising since he acknowledges himself that the original draft of the treaty put forward by Iraq did not even permit the continued use of defence facilities by Britain. Brian Holden Reid is not alone in believing that the impetus for the formation of the pact came from the British Government. Keith Kyle, too, argues that Eden picked up Dulles's Northern Tier initiative in the latter part of 1954, and was instrumental in promoting the Turko-Iraqi agreement.[12]

In fact, as will be seen, it was Britain's opportunism that allowed the government to captialize on the Turco-Iraqi pact. The British Government turned the Northern Tier concept, something about which it had been decidedly lukewarm due to the probable opposition of Egypt, into a vehicle for the renewal of one of its most important treaty relationships in the area, and more than that, into a potential new regionwide system for the maintenance of British influence. To this extent, Brian Holden Reid errs in the opposite respect to Ayesha Jalal, who argues forward from British hostility towards the American sponsored Northern Tier to conclude that the Baghdad Pact must have been a major setback to the British position in the region. Both appear to misinterpret certain critical events in the period from July 1954 to April 1955, and, in particular, neglect the crucial shift in emphasis in American and British policy during the period January to April 1955.[13]

Returning to July 1954, the first critical event was the Anglo-Egyptian Treaty providing for the staged evacuation of British forces from the Canal Zone Base. This marked the beginning of the end of the British strategy of focusing on the Base as the pivot of Middle Eastern defence. In fact, it had become apparent by the spring of 1954 that the Suez Base was becoming more of a military and political liability to the British than an asset. The hostility of the Egyptian government to the British presence on its soil, which, if anything, had intensified under the regime of Nasser, had combined with the impact of the first test explosion of the H-Bomb to make the concentration of forces at the Base appear militarily obsolete.[14] However, the withdrawal agreement, which still, after all, afforded Britain access to the facilities of the Zone for a further period of seven years should they be required in the event of war, did not immediately turn Britain away from the strategy of building on Egypt for Middle East defence. Too many strong arguments about the strategic importance of Egypt and the Canal had been put forward in the past for the government to sacrifice the opportunity of making Egypt into a pillar of future defence arrangements, an opportunity which might well have been presented by the new cordiality in relations in the wake of the Anglo-Egyptian agreement. In addition, British officials simply did not believe that there could be stability in the region without Egyptian involvement, or at least, acquiescence in new defence arrangements.[15]

However, at the same time as Britain was formally concluding her treaty with Egypt, the September 1954 elections in Iraq brought back to power the Anglophile Nuri Said. This development was bound to stir hopes in Britain that some form of accommodation could be reached between Britain and Iraq to replace the existing Anglo-Iraqi agreement due to expire in 1957. Nuri's policy was characterized by a strong, almost fanatical concern with the threat to Iraq from the Soviet Union.[16] In addition to his leaning in favour of an alliance with the British because of their historical role in breaking the Turkish hold on Arab lands, he was conscious of the fact that Britain was the only great power in the post-war years which was prepared to provide support against the perceived threat from the Soviets. Nuri's concern with the danger from the Soviet Union seems to have had its origins in his early years as an officer in the Ottoman army. The Turkish regions of the Ottoman Empire were always fearful of the possibility of Russian expansion to secure unilateral control of the Straits. In later years Nuri's suspicions were reinforced by the prolonged occupation of northern Iran by Soviet troops, and by Stalin's demands on Turkey for a revision of the Montreux Convention in favour of the Soviet Union. Thus, Nuri's predilection, despite traditional Iraqi fears of the Turks, was for an alliance directed against the Soviet Union.

The problem that the British Government faced, however,

was the unpredictability of Nuri's manoeuvrings. The discussions over the treaty were marked by a good deal of prevarication and Nuri himself was frequently rather vague about the character of the agreement he was seeking to negotiate. 'Nuri is very diffuse, and it is always difficult to see precisely what he is getting at' was apparently a familiar complaint of British officials.[17] Matters therefore became somewhat complicated for the British in the run up to the signature of the Turco-Iraqi pact in February 1955. If we accept that the Turco-Pakistani pact had aroused British resentment in the face of perceived American interference in a British sphere of interest,[18] then there would appear to be grounds to believe that a similar pact between Turkey and Iraq could be viewed by the British government in the same light. This would especially be so if it did not take into account her existing treaty rights in Iraq. What British diplomats wanted to ensure above all in the negotiations between Turkey and Iraq, therefore, was that Nuri would make provision for the renewal of the 1930 Treaty. US encouragement for the Northern Tier, and a fear that Britain might somehow miss the boat if a Turco-Iraqi agreement were reached without due regard for her position, help to explain the urgency with which the British pressed their claims on Nuri, urgency which Brian Holden Reid takes as evidence of British prompting of and enthusiasm for the pact. It could equally well of course be taken as evidence of British concern at the potential deterioration of her position unless Nuri could be persuaded to renew the Anglo-Iraqi relationship.[19]

In addition to worrying about the implications of any pact for its rights in Iraq, the British Government showed rather greater awareness than the US Administration at this point about the influence the pact might have on the region as a whole. The British were not prepared to discount Egypt from the political and military equation in the Middle East at this stage, and were concerned as to Nasser's likely reaction to an alliance between an Arab state and what was regarded as an outside power. The Americans at any rate believed that the British were not showing sufficient enthusiasm for Turkish efforts, an attitude which would be puzzling if, as Brian Holden Reid suggests, it was the British who were driving the Turks onwards, and the Americans who were lukewarm. A communication from the State Department passed to Evelyn Shuckburgh on 11 January 1955 expressed the concern that British thinking on the Northern Tier concept was not as positive as it had been. Although Shuckburgh attempted to allay these US fears in private he acknowledged that 'the fact remains . . . that there is a difference of emphasis between the US and ourselves in this. They are vigorously pressing forward the Northern Tier idea whereas we are not entirely convinced that this is wise having regard to Egyptian objections and the extreme instability of Arab opinion generally.'[20] Shuckburgh went on to point out that it was understandable that Britain should now be less inclined towards the Northern Tier since her relations with Egypt had improved so much in the wake of the Canal Zone agreement. In any case, he argued, no Middle East defence arrangement was likely to have much value unless it enjoyed Egyptian support.

At this stage the State Department appeared to be unconcerned about the potential for any deterioration in relations between Iraq and Egypt, and the consequent heightening of tension in the region which might be brought about by any Northern Tier agreement. Indeed, the Department went so far as to suggest that 'even if such action by Iraq should result in the break-up of the Arab League . . . the Northern Tier would provide an alternative centre of attraction round which the Arab states might group themselves, and this would not in their opinion be a bad thing.' It must be admitted, however, that at no stage did the US make a direct promise to join any Turco-Iraqi pact. At a meeting with State Department officials in Washington on 28 January, Shuckburgh was told that what Dulles favoured was 'eventual US association with the pact provided it was on the same lines as US association with the Manila Pact, i.e. the US would only be involved in the event of aggression from outside the area.'[21]

However, what did happen to the US position in the course of the next three months was a change in emphasis caused by what Dulles was later to describe as the virtual takeover of the pact, and its diversion to their own purposes, by the British. In a crucial phone conversation a year later, occasioned by a renewed dispute within the Administration over whether the US should join the pact, the President and the Secretary of

State reviewed the circumstances surrounding its formation and the US attitude to it:

> [The] President said we were originally strong[ly] in favour of [the] Pact being formed. Dulles agreed, but said we were not in favour of Iraq joining. [The] President emphasized that we were in favour of [a] pact between Pakistan and Turkey. Dulles said that the trouble was that the British had taken it over and run it as an instrument of British policy – that has drawn down upon it a tremendous amount of criticism.[22]

Several important points emerge from this review of the history of the pact. Firstly, there is Dulles's contention that while the US had favoured the Northern Tier concept, it had not wanted Iraq to join. This is flatly contradicted by the evidence of State Department telegrams issued at the time. In a conversation with the Shah of Iran, Assistant Secretary George Allen had noted that: 'while discussing US military aid to Iraq ... we had informed Nuri when we signed [the] military aid agreement last year that [the] extent of our aid would be related to Iraq's support for collective security.'[23] Indeed, this and the second important contention made by the President, that what the US had sought was a Turco-Pakistani Pact, appear to be contradicted by a telegram sent under Assistant Secretary Hoover's signature to Karachi on 18 March 1955, which asserted that:

> we feel [that the] Turco-Iraqi Pact [is a] more suitable vehicle than [the] Turk-Pakistani Pact as [the] basis [for] ME defense because it provides wide latitude for taking defensive measures jointly or among certain of the parties and importantly reflects a more immediate intent to undertake these measures.[24]

However, the final important contention of the conversation, that the British had taken over the pact and used it as an instrument of their policy in the region, helps to provide the clue for the unravelling of these apparent contradictions. What seems to have happened is that Dulles in particular had allowed his conception of how the pact developed to distort his recollection of how the US had responded to it during the various stages of its development. Thus, during the period from the Turco-Iraqi negotiations in January 1955 to the accession of Britain to the pact in April 1955, the Administration had come to realize the depth of opposition to the pact within the region, particularly from Egypt. As it became clear that Nasser would not be prepared to live with the pact, and that, moreover, he was likely to use the Arab–Israeli dispute as a weapon against Iraq, accusing her of being party to a Western plot to turn the Arabs' attention away from their true enemy within, Dulles in particular saw the potential for instability in the area being increased greatly. Also, a sentiment began to emerge that the British, by capitalizing on the Turco-Iraqi agreement to renew their treaty with Iraq, had somehow subverted the Americans' original Northern Tier concept, turning it into a means of maintaining their imperial influence within the Arab world.[25]

Dulles's response to this development was threefold. First, he set about trying to renew the pact as a Northern Tier organization by pressing hard for Pakistani accession. This explains Eisenhower's comment in their phone conversation that what the US was in favour of was a pact between Turkey and Pakistan. Secondly, the US pressed the British to accept a moratorium on any further Arab membership of the pact, in a bid to contain the damage done to relations with Nasser. Finally, the US, in conjunction with Britain, set about seeking a solution to the Arab–Israeli problem through the secret 'Alpha' negotiations. If Arab–Israeli tensions could be defused, then conditions would not be so ripe for Soviet interference in the region, and the Arab states might be more prepared to turn their attention outwards and join a renewed Northern Tier Pact. Of course, with hindsight, it was very easy for Dulles to blame the British for the turn for the worse that events in the region had taken during the course of 1955. If they had not moved to join and promote the Baghdad Pact, then Nasser might not have turned hostile and taken Soviet arms. However, all of this was very much a retrospective reasoning process on Dulles's part. At the time, he was perhaps more surprised than anyone at the depth of Nasser's hostility to the pact. During a conversation with the Lebanese Ambassador, Charles Malik, he noted that: 'he had been surprised at the vehemence of the Egyptian attack on Iraq's action, since he had supposed it had been widely understood throughout the Arab world that the association of Iraq with the "Northern Tier" was a logical and reasonable development.'[26]

However, while the US Administration was having second thoughts about its earlier rather dismissive attitude towards opposition to the pact in the Arab world, British Government sentiments were moving in the opposite direction. Now that the prize of the renewal of the Anglo-Iraqi agreement seemed to be within their grasp, they repented of their earlier diffidence about defence organizations unfavourable to Egypt. Although Anthony Eden, on a visit to Cairo in late February, made no progress in persuading Nasser to accept the pact, he still reported the atmosphere to be 'most friendly especially on all that concerned Anglo-Egyptian relations'.[27] Now it was the British Government which, seduced by the potential prize of the Anglo-Iraqi agreement, began to see Nasser's opposition as less significant and less vehement. Ralph Stevenson, the Ambassador in Cairo, offered one dissenting voice against this trend of opinion. In a far-sighted despatch he argued that 'I personally very much doubt whether there can be much stability in this area until this Egyptian–Iraqi conflict is resolved', and that 'the net advantage to the West is small if Iraqi realism and cooperation are matched by neutralism and irresponsibility in Egypt and the other Arab states'.[28] However, Evelyn Shuckburgh was now in no mood to listen to sentiments with which he himself would probably have been in accord a mere three months earlier. In his reply to Stevenson he argued that:

> As things are, the Turko-Iraqi Pact represents our best hope of building an effective defence system and we cannot afford to let it wither entirely after producing a single bloom in the shape of the Anglo-Iraqi Special Agreement. Our own credit as an acceding state, and our relations with Turkey are deeply engaged.[29]

With regard to Egypt, it could only be hoped that with careful treatment Nasser's opposition would cool, and some means could be worked out of 'hitching' her to the new system.

The key element in British thinking, once the prize of the Anglo-Iraqi Special Agreement had been secured by Britain's accession to the pact in April 1955, was summed up in

Shuckburgh's argument that the Baghdad Pact fitted Britain's 'essential defence requirements in the Middle East'. If we return to the two definitions of defence given at the start of this chapter, it is clear that the pact was now coming to be conceived of as the answer to both requirements. It provided a means of direct defence of the region against the Soviet Union in the north. But, much more importantly, it offered a means for Britain to maintain and renew her political influence throughout the region. If other Arab states could be persuaded to join then Britain might be able to develop the sort of regionwide alliance linked to her which would guarantee all of her essential interests.

Concurrently, however, Dulles had decided that the extent of Egyptian opposition to the pact required a moratorium on new Arab membership. The Northern Tier aspect of the pact was to be stressed by an American drive to secure Pakistani membership of the organization. In addition, in order to remove the source of Arab resentment tapped by Nasser, Dulles ordered that the negotiations over Project Alpha should be given top priority. Reporting these developments towards the end of March 1955, Harold Beeley noted that Dulles had instructed the State Department that nothing was to be done 'to encourage any of Israel's immediate neighbours to enter the Turco-Iraqi Pact at present', and that immediate attention was to be given to the problem of 'finding some means by which Nasser's prestige may be retrieved and his confidence restored'.[30]

The American attitude angered the British Government, with Eden arguing that:

> it would be most unwise to try to help Nasser at the cost of weakening our support for the Turco-Iraqi Pact. Our declared object is to make the Pact the foundation for an effective defence system for the Middle East. If this is to be achieved, Syrian, Lebanese and Jordanian accession will eventually be necessary.

Although Eden was prepared not to press for immediate accessions by Arab states, conceding that the next most likely adherent was Pakistan, he concluded by asking Harold Beeley, Counsellor at the Washington Embassy, to persuade the State

Department that 'they cannot expect to command respect in the Middle East unless they pursue a consistent policy based on their convictions. Their enthusiastic support of the Turkish–Iraqi Pact is too recent in men's minds to enable them to execute a volte-face with safety or dignity.'[31]

The British Foreign Office believed that what it saw as American backsliding from the pact was also the result of pressure from the other side of the Arab–Israeli divide, something which would help to explain the emphasis given by Dulles to an Arab–Israeli accommodation at this time. While the power of the Jewish lobby in Washington was nothing like that which it was to achieve in the post-1967 years, Dulles had already stressed to the British that the Administration had to be wary of arousing its opposition. The week preceding the signature of the Anglo-Iraqi Special Agreement, and Britain's accession to the Baghdad Pact witnessed sharp exchanges between London and Washington over the wording of the Turco-Iraqi Pact. The State Department argued that it contained no clear-cut statement of general peaceful intentions, and that Britain should consider an exchange of notes with the contracting parties making these explicit.[32] Evelyn Shuckburgh minuted that: 'this is becoming an almost blatant piece of Israeli pressure, exercised through the State Department's lawyers.' Sir Ivone Kirkpatrick agreed, arguing that: 'if the Americans anticipate difficulty with Congress over their accession, let them make such a statement.' Eden too was incensed, minuting that: 'they might have thought of this before March 30. It seems to me rather impertinent.'[33]

The point was of course that the Israelis felt themselves to be threatened by a defence organization involving one of the leading Western powers, Britain, and an Arab state, Iraq, which had never agreed peace terms with Israel, or recognized her right to existence. There was the persistent fear that this might open the way to the rearming of Israel's Arab enemies.[34] To this extent, the British decision to join the pact would create difficulties for the Americans not only with Nasser and, incidentally, Saudi Arabia, a product of the long-standing Hashemite–Al Saud rivalry, but also with Israel. These were the roots of the Americans' future objections to joining the pact on the grounds that it complicated inter-Arab and also

Arab–Israeli relations. Still, the last minute American intervention was further evidence to the British Government that they
were 'faltering badly over the Turko-Iraqi Pact'.[35] Although
the Administration backed off in the face of the British reaction, and emphasized that the realization of the Northern Tier
remained of great importance to them,[36] their failure to persuade the British to amend or qualify the pact merely served
to reinforce Dulles's three-pronged strategy of avoiding further Arab membership, emphasizing the pact's Northern Tier
character by working for Pakistani accession, and pursuing
an Arab–Israeli rapprochement through Alpha. It was the latter two elements of this strategy which dominated the US's
manoeuvrings during the summer of 1955.

With regard to the question of Pakistani accession to the pact,
the State Department exerted as much pressure as it was able
on the Pakistani Government to adhere, and welcomed the
government's eventual decision to join in July 1955.[37] Indeed,
at this stage the US was still keen to see Iran join the pact on
the principle that this too would serve to underline its Northern Tier quality. However, as will be seen, matters were to
change dramatically towards the end of September, when the
Egyptian arms deal with the Soviets convinced Dulles that the
approach of trying to insulate the Northern Tier from Arab
politics was not working. Before discussing the impact of the
arms deal on American and British strategy, however, it is necessary to backtrack and outline some of the details of the Alpha
negotiations with Nasser, and his reaction to the Baghdad Pact.

In fact, the timing of the signature of the Turco-Iraqi Pact
had been particularly unfortunate for Western relations with
Egypt, since it had coincided with a large Israeli raid on Gaza.
Indeed, the coincidence of the two events may not have come
about by chance. It would have been entirely in character for
Ben Gurion's *realpolitik* to have led him to conclude that the
development of the Baghdad Pact, something which, as has
been suggested, might offer a long-term threat to Israel, could
best be thwarted by souring the attitude of Egypt.[38] Certainly,
the raid itself was an indication of the return of Ben Gurion
as the driving force behind Israeli security policy. Although he
had temporarily retired from politics during 1954, the handling of Israeli foreign affairs by his successor Moshe Sharett had

caused him great concern.[39] The uncovering of a spy ring in Egypt, led by Avri Elad, and the subsequent resignation of the Defence Minister, Phinas Lavon, had provided him with the opportunity to return to the cabinet. The Gaza raid was intended to make plain that he meant to play a broader political role than that suggested merely by his cabinet brief.

Whatever the politics behind the raid, it had a decisive impact on Nasser's thinking.[40] Nasser now began to move in three directions. He tried to establish a competing anti-Baghdad grouping under the banner of Arab nationalism; he sought membership in the extra-regional grouping of non-aligned nations; and he developed further his contacts with the Soviet Union and other Eastern Bloc countries. 'A distinctly Egyptian brand of neutralism began to emerge.'[41] Egypt's first move to counter the Turco-Iraqi entente had been to summon an emergency meeting of Arab League Prime Ministers in Cairo, a meeting which lasted from 22 January 1955 until 6 February. However, things did not go entirely as Nasser had planned, and he was not able to rally sufficient support for proposals against the pact. Having failed to influence the other Arab states by direct methods, Nasser resorted to a propaganda campaign against the pact intended to influence Syria in particular.

Syria was in many ways the pivotal country in the rivalry for leadership of the Arab world which was developing between Nuri and Nasser. Long-standing Hashemite ambitions for the unity of the Fertile Crescent, comprising Syria, Lebanon, Jordan and Iraq, meant that Nuri would be particularly anxious for a positive response to Iraq's initiative from that source. Syria enjoyed, therefore, 'what amounted to a casting vote in the Baghdad Pact's future: had she applied for membership, other Arab states would have followed; in the event, her hostility "froze" the alliance, isolating its only Arab member, Iraq.'[42] The debate over the Baghdad Pact, conducted against the background of intense Egyptian lobbying, resulted in the fall of the moderate, pro-Iraqi Syrian Government on 6 February. Its replacement by one drawn from the neutralist left was a triumph for Nasser, and a major setback for Nuri. The culmination of Nasser's attempts to establish an anti-Baghdad grouping in the Arab world lay in the Egyptian–Syrian–Saudi alliance of March 1955, which was facilitated by the change in Syria's Government.

Although it was 'never either militarily effective or economically stimulating', these were not its principal intentions. It was 'a diplomatic coup, swiftly conceived and executed, to counter a challenge from Nuri'.[43]

One effect of Nasser's new alliance was to lead him to support, through the propaganda broadcasts of Radio Cairo, Saudi claims to the Buraimi Oasis. These attacks on the British role in the Arabian Peninsula were increasingly to exasperate Prime Minister Anthony Eden during the coming months, and contributed significantly to the souring of Anglo-Egyptian relations. Eden's scribbled comments on press summaries of the Egyptian output ranged from 'this is gross impertinence by those people who are likely to be attacked and destroyed by Israel before long' to 'anything in our power to hurt Egyptians without hurting ourselves?'[44]

As regards the second element of Nasser's new approach, membership in the extra-regional grouping of non-aligned countries, this was given impetus by his attendance of the Bandung Conference in April 1955.[45] In a speech to the conference on 18 April Nasser argued that 'cooperation among the Asiatic-African nations can play a dominant role in the lessening of the present international tension and the promotion of world peace and prosperity.' He concluded his remarks by calling for the liquidation of colonialism wherever it existed.[46] Nasser later described Bandung as 'a turning point in my political understanding', and the point at which he realized that 'the only wise policy for us would be [one] of positive neutralism and nonalignment.'[47]

The culmination of the final strand in Nasser's strategy was the much-vaunted 'Czech' arms deal of September 1955.[48] In the first instance, of course, Nasser only turned to the Eastern Bloc for arms because of the refusal of the Western powers to supply him with his requirements. To this extent, the deal reflected a miscalculation in American policy. Dulles was convinced that the Soviets would not jeopardize the slow improvement in East–West relations simply to gain a foothold in Egypt. Indeed, at the Geneva summit in July 1955, Khrushchev had flatly told him that there would be no arms sales to Egypt. Secure in this knowledge, Dulles ignored or misread the signals coming out of Cairo, and decided to stand firm in the face of pressure from the CIA for some indication of willingness to supply Nasser. The result was that Nasser called the Americans' bluff, and turned to the Soviet Union for assistance.

Although there was much public talk of ultimatums being delivered to Nasser in the wake of the arms deal, in reality the direct US response to the agreement was much less severe than might have been expected. At a news conference on 4 October, Dulles argued that: 'it is difficult to be critical of countries which, feeling themselves endangered, seek the arms which they sincerely believe they need for defense.'[49] William Burns suggests that:

> Nasser was still regarded in the fall of 1955 by many Middle East specialists in the State Department and in the CIA, and to a certain extent by Dulles himself, as a sort of errant protégé, who might still be manoeuvred into leading the Arabs toward a settlement with Israel and into some kind of a loose association with Western defence plans in the Middle East.[50]

Indeed, at a meeting with the British Foreign Secretary, Harold Macmillan, on 3 October, Dulles emphasized that he 'was inclined to temporize regarding Egypt at this stage in order to see how matters developed there . . . we should not take any threatening or drastic step at this time'.[51] However, one implication of this strategy which Dulles did not divulge to Macmillan emerged at what seems to have been quite a stormy National Security Council meeting on 6 October.

Up to this point, it will be recollected, Dulles's approach had been three-pronged: encouraging 'genuine' Northern Tier states such as Pakistan and Iran to join the pact in a bid to isolate it from Arab politics; avoiding further Arab membership of the pact; and working through Project Alpha for an Arab–Israeli accord. The 'Czech' arms deal seemed to be direct evidence that this strategy had not worked. The conclusions which Dulles drew from all of this were laid before the National Security Council. He argued that 'we still have great hopes that the new relationship between the USSR and Egypt can be held to a minimum of significance. Such hopes would be abruptly ended if we should urge Iran to join the Baghdad Pact.'[52] Dulles amplified the implications of his statement by arguing that 'he was disposed to give a negative reply to the request of Iran that the United States approve Iran's announcement of entry into the Baghdad Pact'. Although Dulles presented a supplementary financial argument against support for Iranian entry into the pact, asserting that this would bring with it demands for greatly increased US assistance to Iran, under questioning from Vice President Nixon, he admitted that this was not the main factor in his decision:

> The primary factor was the overall political question; namely, whether United States policy in the Middle East should be directed toward an attempt to insulate the new Soviet–Egyptian relationship or whether United States objectives would be served by seeming to enhance the significance of the Soviet–Egyptian deal by a major counter-move in Iran.

Dulles's shift in policy against even endorsing the expansion of the pact as a Northern Tier concept marked the beginning of the State–Defense split over the organization. There were some sharp exchanges over the matter between Defense Secretary Charles Wilson and Dulles, with Wilson professing himself to be 'much bewildered. Why had we been for so long so eager to get Iran into the Baghdad Pact and now that she was prepared to join, we are opposing the move?' However, it is clear that Dulles's views in this respect carried much more weight with the President than those of the Defense Secretary. Wilson was known for his gruff, combative approach and his habit of chain-smoking his way through meetings.[53] One assumes that at this point he simply lit another cigarette and resigned himself to sitting through another lecture from Dulles.

In addition to rebuffing the Iranians, Dulles continued, the other implication of the need to insulate the arms deal at this stage was the rebuffing of the Iraqis. They had approached Dulles arguing that since they were now clearly the most pro-Western state in the area, any aid previously intended for Egypt should be diverted to them. Also, they had argued, the US should assist them by permitting them 'to interfere in the situation in Syria'. Here again, Dulles believed that the US could not countenance such a development, on the basis that 'if Iraq actually moved on Syria it would cause serious trouble throughout the Middle East'. More importantly, due to Saudi opposition, 'any United States permission to Iraq to move against Syria would gravely affect existing relations between the United States and Saudi Arabia . . .'.

This policy statement by Dulles was to prove to be of the greatest importance for the future of Anglo-American relations in the region. It illustrated that the US was not prepared to place Iraq above Saudi Arabia in its list of Middle East allies, no matter how 'pro-Western' the regime in Baghdad might appear to be. Although the British were now energetically engaged in a strategy of promoting the Baghdad Pact, and through it Iraq as the leader of the Arab world, the US Administration demurred from this approach.

Nevertheless, while agreeing that 'up to March 1956, the Americans were concerned about the impact of the Fertile Crescent upon their ally Saudi Arabia', William Gorst and W. Scott Lucas have shown that the Egyptian–Syrian–Saudi defence pact signed on 27 October did soften Dulles's attitude somewhat towards Iraqi and British schemes for the subversion of the Syrian government. This was possibly because it showed the extent to which Syria and Egypt might turn Saudi Arabia against the United States.[54] Since the policy of isolating the Soviet–Egyptian alliance, and working to promote Alpha precluded any direct action against Egypt in order to stem this development, Dulles became more prepared to countenance a degree of American involvement, at least at the discussion level, in plans to change the Syrian Government. However, although Dulles was willing to concede to Eden in January 1956 that Syria was 'behaving much like a Soviet Satellite in most issues', he argued that none of the plans put forward to effect change in that country 'had seemed sufficiently sound to warrant our support'.[55] This was to remain the case at least until after March 1956, and the reorientation of British and American policy in the region.

The softening of Dulles's opposition to British and Iraqi schemes for Syria in the wake of the 27 October agreement also seems to have extended to the question of Iranian entry to the Baghdad Pact, for Dulles did not openly oppose Iran's ensuing accession to the organization. However, the decision seems to have been a very close-run thing. According to the later account of one State Department official, Dulles drafted a telegram on the evening of 31 October to the US Ambassador in Tehran instructing him to advise against Iranian adherence to the pact.[56] The reason cited on this occasion was the proximity of the decision to the scheduled four-power meeting in Geneva and the damage likely to be done to US–Soviet relations. He was only persuaded to soften the tone of his despatch by the insistence of his advisers that the Iranian Government would be destabilized by US opposition to its joining the pact. Although the US Administration publicly welcomed the Iranian move, therefore, Dulles's equivocal attitude was reflected in his refusal to grant the Shah any of the sweeteners in the form of military and economic aid for which he had been pressing.

As has been suggested, the other side of the American attempt to limit the effects of the Egyptian–Soviet arms deal was the added impetus given to the efforts to promote Project Alpha. These were to be coupled with an inducement to Nasser to cooperate in the shape of the Anglo-American offer to assist with the financing of the Aswan Dam, a pet project of his. In these two respects, British and American strategy at this stage was still in accord.[57] Of course it was in the interests of both powers to see a lessening of Arab–Israeli tensions. For one thing, it was thought that this would reduce the chances of the Soviet Union gaining influence in the area as a supporter of, and supplier of arms to, the disillusioned Arab countries. This was a particular concern of the United States. Nasser's 'Czech' arms deal only reinforced Dulles's conviction that this, the root cause of the Arabs' desire to arm themselves, had to be taken away.

The British, too, viewed the prospect of Soviet involvement in the region with trepidation. However, they were also convinced that the maintenance of their political influence in the Middle East would be bound up with their success in securing some settlement of a problem for which they, as the power to whom Palestine had been mandated, were viewed as being largely responsible. Furthermore, once they had opted for a regional strategy of maintaining their influence through the Baghdad Pact, it was essential that they try to remove this internal source of tension. Otherwise Nasser would continue to portray Iraq as a pariah nation, attempting to turn the Arabs' attention away from their true struggle with Israel. Indeed, the first practical schemes for the Alpha Project were British in origin, although their general parameters had earlier been agreed with the Americans. As early as December 1954, Evelyn Shuckburgh had drafted 'Notes on the Arab–Israeli Dispute', which concentrated on the two principal issues which were to form the core of the Alpha Plan, boundaries and refugees.[58] The essence of the plan as it developed was to trade off concessions by Israel in the form of territory, and compensation for the Palestinian refugees, in exchange for recognition from the neighbouring Arab states, and guarantees of security from the Western powers.

Unfortunately, in several respects the Alpha proposals were rather naive. In particular, the proposals with regard to a territorial settlement in the Negev were given almost the air of pantomime by Nasser when they were put to him. The idea was that Israel should cede two converging triangles of territory to the neighbouring Arab states. These would meet in the middle where they would be joined by an East–West Arab overpass, and a North–South Israeli underpass. This looked too much like an ivory-tower planner's solution to the intellectual problem of maintaining communications for both parties. Nasser pointed out that in practice it could hardly be expected to work, exclaiming, tongue in cheek, that 'if an Arab on the upper level had to relieve himself and accidentally hit an Israeli, it would mean war!'[59] In addition, the planners overestimated the chances of persuading the Israelis to trade territory for peace. Neither the State Department nor the Foreign Office seem to have understood the intensity of the Israeli opposition both literally and metaphorically to giving ground.[60]

Nevertheless, the American and British Governments worked to promote the plans throughout 1955, exerting as much pressure as they could on both Nasser and Ben Gurion to come to the negotiating table. In the wake of the arms deal, Anthony Eden, in a speech delivered at the Guildhall on 9 November, made a public appeal to both parties. 'If some arrangement could be reached between Israel and her Arab neighbours about their boundaries,' he argued, 'the United States and Britain, and perhaps other powers also, would be prepared to give a formal guarantee to both sides.'[61] In fact, Eden's remarks were well received in the Arab world, because of his references to a possible compromise between the 1947 UN partition boundaries in Palestine and the 1949 armistice lines.

In Israel, however, any thought of going back to the 1947 plan was rejected out of hand. Eden's speech was received angrily here not only because of its implications for Israel's borders, but also because of long-standing mistrust of the British, and of Eden personally, who was viewed as having been unfriendly to Zionism in the 1930s and 1940s.[62]

However, as will be seen in the next chapter, the Alpha Project was never to advance to the stage of direct negotiations between Egypt and Israel. It foundered on the British side in the wake of King Hussein of Jordan's dismissal of General Glubb, and on the American side once Robert Anderson's missions to the region had made it clear to the Administration that Nasser was unwilling to cooperate.

The other aspect of Anglo-American attempts to wean Nasser away from further cooperation with the Soviets was the promotion of the Western offer to assist in the financing of the Aswan Dam. This offer had been tabled before the arms deal, but, in its aftermath, both Dulles and Macmillan had agreed that it could be used as an inducement to Nasser not to move further away from the Western camp. The British pushed the plan particularly hard in November and December because of intelligence information reaching them from Egypt that if the West did not regain the initiative soon, Nasser might opt for a permanent Soviet alliance.[63] Again, though, enthusiasm for the project was to wane once it was decided that Nasser could not be trusted.

Thus, the circumstances surrounding the formation and development of the Baghdad Pact are instructive as to the course that relations between Britain and America over the Middle East were to take for the next three years, and, in some respects, beyond this. An initial British lack of enthusiasm for the pact, on the grounds that it would invoke the hostility of Egypt and destabilize the region, was soon forgotten once it became clear that it could be the instrument for the renewal of her treaty rights in Iraq and, more importantly, a potential vehicle for the maintenance of her influence throughout the area. From the formation of the pact stemmed the British strategy of building up Iraq as the leader of the Arab world, a strategy that transcended the Suez crisis, and was only broken down by the Iraqi Revolution of July 1958. Similarly, on the American side, the creation of the pact had a major impact on strategy. Although the American Government had been behind much of the pressure for a Northern Tier pact, the development of an organization which rapidly seemed to become prey not only to the Arab–Israeli rivalry, but also, seemingly, to all of the tensions of the Arab world, led to a distinct cooling off in US enthusiasm during the period leading up to the 'Czech' arms deal. Although, after the deal, the Americans could cooperate with the British over attempts to isolate the Soviet–Egyptian agreement, cracks in the common front between the two were not hard to find. There was increasing British exasperation at the United States' unwillingness to accede to the pact and at their refusal to fall in with the strategy of building up Iraq.[64] The Administration's continuing concern for Saudi attitudes pointed forward towards the schemes which Eisenhower and Dulles were to develop the following year for the promotion of King Saud, rather than the preferred British choice of Nuri Said, as Nasser's rival for the leadership of the Arab world.

4 March 1956 and the Break with Nasser

The two events which were to change the British attitude towards Nasser from one of continuing if rather more suspicious accommodation in the wake of the arms deal, to one of open and unremitting hostility, took place in Jordan. First came the failure of the December 1955 mission of General Sir Gerald Templer, Chief of the Imperial General Staff, to secure Jordanian accession to the Baghdad Pact. Hard on the heels of this humiliation, at the beginning of March 1956, came the sudden dismissal of General Sir John Bagot Glubb, commander of the Jordanian Arab Legion. Both events were bitter blows to British prestige in the Middle East and contributed to a major reorientation of British policy.

Viewed from the British perspective, Jordan had seemed to be the most likely candidate for the position of first Arab state after Iraq to accede to the Baghdad Pact. Not only did Britain have an existing defence treaty with the country, but her role was prominent in officering and leading the Jordanian Arab Legion. Although Eden had agreed with the Americans in March 1955 that there was no imminent likelihood of an Arab nation joining the pact, he did not envisage an indefinite moratorium on Arab membership. This was especially so since, as the pact developed, it came to be viewed in London as the most promising vehicle for the maintenance of British influence throughout the region.

According to one scholar, from late 1953 onwards, after Jordan had agreed to an increase in British troops in the country, Anthony Eden as Foreign Secretary had been working towards the goal of an 'Iraqi–Jordanian axis' as the basis for the British position in the Middle East. An Eden minute of January 1954 argued that 'if we are to have any position in the Middle East, our authority must be based on relations with Jordan and Iraq. If we haver any more, we shall be friendless . . . The chances of [the] Egyptians becoming our friends are slight.'[1] A case can be made for a connection between Eden's thoughts in late 1953 and the policy which was to be adopted from March 1956 onwards of promoting links between Iraq and Jordan. Viewed in this context, the attempts to persuade King Hussein to accede to the Baghdad Pact which this chapter will chronicle would seem to fall into the pattern of Eden's earlier diplomacy.

However, as can be seen from the analysis of British policy towards the pact in the preceding chapter, such arguments draw what is perhaps too neat a link between the policy of January 1954 and March 1956. To begin with, in early 1954, Eden was certainly not in exclusive control of British policy in the region. Churchill's views on the strategic importance of Egypt and the need to maintain the Suez base had to be taken into account. Then came the brief Anglo-Egyptian honeymoon from mid-1954 until February 1955, when Evelyn Shuckburgh for one believed that Egypt could not be neglected in any serious plans for regional defence. The British decision to join the Baghdad Pact which, following this line of argument, would fit into the framework of existing policies designed to promote the regional role of the 'Iraqi–Jordanian axis', was in reality a piece of opportunism on the part of the British Government. From this point onwards, the emphasis was not on building an 'Iraqi–Jordanian axis' but rather exclusively on promoting the role of Iraq. Jordan was very much a sideshow in all of this. To talk of a policy of cementing an 'axis' undoubtedly exaggerates British perceptions of the importance of linking the two countries. The British Government would certainly welcome any Iraqi willingness to assist in the defence of Jordan, which, as the government's precipitous decision to disengage from its relationship with the country in January 1957 showed, came to be regarded as something of a liability. However, this was merely one aspect of promoting Iraqi leadership in the Arab world. It was Iraq, as has been shown, which was now being seen as the most reliable bastion of British influence in the Middle East.

Returning to 1955, the British view by November was that the position of Iraq as the one Arab member of the Baghdad Pact was becoming too isolated. Since the principal plank of policy was to build up the Iraqi role in the Arab world, the Foreign Secretary, Harold Macmillan, who had taken over the office on Eden's assumption of the premiership in April, decided that the time was propitious to secure Jordanian membership of the pact. As he commented later, 'after all, we were paying large subsidies. Why should we continue our support, both financial and military, if they would do nothing in return?'[2] The initial impetus which helped to spur Macmillan into action seems to have come from the Turkish Government. In the wake of the Egyptian arms deal with the Russians, the Turkish Government had gone 'wild with apprehension'.[3] Turkish leaders started to pressurize the British to test the ground in Jordan over accession to the pact, motivated by the fear that they were about to be outflanked by the Russians, a fear reinforced by the Egyptian–Syrian–Saudi agreement of 27 October.

Winthrop Aldrich, the American Ambassador in London, reported that the initial British response to Turkish approaches had been that 'while Jordanian adherence would be favourably regarded by Her Majesty's Government, [the] latter would not press [the] Jordanians to join so long as there [was] any chance regarding gaining Egyptian cooperation.' Anthony Eden, too, displayed some initial hesitation, an attitude which would be puzzling if we accept that he had been pushing forward a policy aimed at promoting an Iraqi–Jordanian axis for the last two years. 'I am somewhat apprehensive that the effect on Egypt of Jordan joining at this time might be unfortunate', Eden minuted on 6 November.[4] However, in the longer term, the British Ambassador in Amman expressed the hope to the Jordanian Government that sensitivity over the response of other Arab countries would not preclude eventual Jordanian accession. Such a move could be accompanied by 'revision [of the] Anglo-Jordanian Treaty along lines followed with Iraq'.[5]

The US Administration's response to the Turkish initiative was that it would 'not advise against Jordanian adherence [to the] Baghdad Pact', but that 'if Jordan adhered prior to [a] settlement [of the] Jordan–Israeli boundary this would create an additional difficulty in connection with possible US adherence . . .'. However, the State Department 'saw no reason why [the] Turkish President should not sound out [the] situation in Amman'.[6] Still, the American reply was rather more favourable than might have been expected in view of the policy pursued by Dulles throughout the summer of 1955 aimed at avoiding additional Arab membership of the pact in order not to antagonize Nasser. Since, as the discussions at the National Security Council meeting on 7 October have shown, Dulles was now pushing even harder for this line of policy, such an attitude is indeed rather surprising.

As a discussion between Ambassador Henry Byroade and Nasser on 3 November shows, Nasser had expressed the hope that the US 'would not apply pressure for new adherents to the northern tier at this stage', to which Byroade had replied 'that this was our position but that others felt strongly otherwise'.[7] Surely, then, any US support for Jordanian adherence would complicate greatly the negotiations with Nasser over Alpha which were being given top priority in the American strategy at this stage? One might dismiss this difficulty in fathoming the Administration's, and particularly Dulles's, approach were it not for a report sent by Macmillan to Eden on 28 October of a discussion with Dulles at a Foreign Ministers' meeting in Geneva. Macmillan noted that:

> Dulles asked me whether we would not bring pressure upon Jordan to join the Baghdad Pact. He thought it would be a fine thing if they did. He regarded Jordan as our affair. He added that he thought we might consider trying to get Jordan to make a unilateral settlement of frontiers with Israel. If this could be done, leaving out Egypt altogether, it would be a great advantage.[8]

On the face of it, Dulles's open encouragement of Macmillan to pursue Jordanian accession to the pact contradicted his policy priority of seeking an Arab–Israeli peace settlement through negotiations with Nasser. Jordan's joining the pact was guaranteed to arouse Nasser's wrath. However, a closer examination of Dulles's comments provides one possible explanation of what was going through his mind. To begin with, his discussion with Macmillan was conducted against the background of the Egyptian–Syrian–Saudi Pact which was announced on 27 October, but which had been an open secret for some days before. This, as has been shown in the previous chapter, seems to have had a major impact on Dulles's thinking, leading him to back away from outright opposition to Iranian accession to the pact, and also to give more credence to British and Iraqi schemes for changing the Syrian Government. Indeed, it was at the same meeting that Macmillan noted that Dulles was 'moving in the direction of being less averse to, if not wholly favouring, a coup d'état by the Iraqis' in Syria. Since the Egyptian–Syrian–Saudi agreement could be regarded as a move which raised the stakes again in the region, Dulles may now have decided that countermoves, such as action in Syria or Jordanian adherence to the pact, were more acceptable than they had been before.

However, the key to Dulles's thinking may well lie in his implied linkage of a Jordanian decision to join the pact with 'a unilateral settlement of frontiers with Israel'. The principal goal of Dulles's strategy at this stage was, after all, an Arab–Israeli rapprochement. The drive to work with Nasser towards this end simply originated in the belief that he was the kind of strong leader who could reach agreement with the Israelis without facing such great risks in terms of internal dissent. Perhaps Dulles believed that any sign of a move towards accommodation with Israel on the part of Jordan might exert pressure on Nasser to try to outbid the Jordanians in this process. Whatever the basis of Dulles's calculations, Macmillan's report of Dulles's approach to him still appears extraordinary in view of the other lines of policy the US was pursuing at this time. Perhaps it was an indication of Dulles's tendency to propose ill thought out policies off-the-cuff on missions abroad, when isolated from his Washington advisers. Of course, Byroade's ignorance of Dulles's initiative with the British is not altogether surprising in view of the picture that Miles Copeland presents of the way US relations were conducted with Nasser at this time.[9]

Whatever Dulles's reasoning, Macmillan seems to have taken his attitude as another signal that the time might be right to pursue Jordanian membership of the pact. Indeed, one scholar has suggested that 'the official documents convey an impression – difficult to substantiate – that it was Macmillan who egged on Eden throughout the crucial weeks of November and December 1955' in pursuit of Jordanian accession.[10] This may have led Macmillan to exaggerate somewhat Dulles's encouragement for this move, in much the same way as he was to misrepresent

Eisenhower's attitude towards military action over Suez a year later. Certainly, the US version of their conversation indicates only Macmillan pushing Jordanian membership of the pact, and makes no mention of Dulles's views.[11] Indeed, US records of a succession of meetings between the two show Macmillan putting pressure on Dulles to support Jordanian and United States' accession to the pact, and a series of negative or at best neutral responses from the Secretary of State.[12] These form the basis of another possible explanation of Dulles's comments in relation to Jordanian accession to the pact: that Macmillan fabricated the remarks. However, in view of Eden's own strong partisanship for the Baghdad Pact, which he had described as 'more important than the attitude of Egypt' at a cabinet meeting on 20 October, Macmillan's gingering of the Prime Minister to act may well have been more of short-term tactical than longer-term strategic importance.[13] The stance of both men since Britain's entry into the pact had been that its development ultimately superseded in significance any other problem in the region.

Nevertheless, Macmillan was content to wait for the Turkish initiative to progress, aware that a positive outcome was more likely to be secured if Amman took the first step in approaching London. Although King Hussein appeared to have been won over by a Turkish state visit in early November, he still had doubts about the wisdom of joining the pact in view of the attitude of other Arab states, especially Egypt. When it became known that the Egyptian Major General Amer was planning a visit to Jordan, perhaps to undo all the good work of the Turks, Macmillan decided on a spectacular gesture.[14] The result was the sending to Amman of General Sir Gerald Templer, Chief of the Imperial General Staff, in order to 'push Jordan over the brink'.[15] It is clear that, by this stage, the US Administration had reverted to what might be termed its expected attitude towards attempts to secure Jordanian accession to the pact. On 9 November, Dulles had told Macmillan that unless Lebanon, Syria and Jordan were ready to make peace with Israel (which he doubted), he rather wondered whether it was wise to bring them in.[16] This indeed casts further doubt on the veracity of Macmillan's earlier report of Dulles's encouragement for Jordanian accession to the pact.

With regard to the Templer Mission itself, Dulles informed Macmillan that the US would not lend its support on the grounds that 'an immediate move to extend the Baghdad Pact would probably deny us Nasser's cooperation' in an Arab–Israeli settlement.[17] In any event, Templer presented to the Jordanian Government an eight-point draft agreement stipulating that Jordan should accede to the Baghdad Pact, with the Anglo-Jordanian Treaty being replaced by a special agreement under the terms of article one of the pact. In return, Britain would agree to reinforce the Jordanian Army and help in organizing the Air Force. King Hussein was initially disposed to accept the British terms.[18] In the wake of Templer's departure on 14 December, however, dissent within the Cabinet of Prime Minister Mufti led to his resignation, and replacement by Haza Majali, the minister of the interior, a known partisan of Iraq who was keen to secure pact membership.[19] Nevertheless, the new Prime Minister had scant opportunity to develop his plans for, on 17 December, anti-pact agitation broke out throughout the country. The scale of the disturbances was such that on the evening of 19 December Hussein called in the British Ambassador, Charles Duke, to tell him that Jordanian accession to the pact had now become impossible.[20]

The following day Majali resigned as Prime Minister, and elections were called. The appointment of Samir Rifai on 9 January 1956, together with his statement that the country would not participate in any alliances, served to calm the internal situation in the country. Eisenhower noted in his Diary the following day: 'We tried to make the British see the danger of . . . pressuring Jordan to join the Northern Tier Pact. They went blindly ahead and only recently have been suffering one of the most severe diplomatic defeats Britain has taken in many years.'[21] The anti-pact riots were widely ascribed to the influence of Egyptian propaganda delivered via the 'Voice of the Arabs' radio station, and Saudi funding.[22] Certainly the significance of the Egyptian role in blocking the extension of the pact was not lost on the British Government, and contributed to the continued souring of relations between the two countries.

One significant domestic political development in Britain which took place during the crisis in Jordan, was Prime Minister Eden's decision to reshuffle his cabinet. Harold Macmillan was replaced at the Foreign Office by Selwyn Lloyd, and moved by Eden to the Exchequer. This change has conventionally been represented in terms of Eden's desire to have a rather more malleable figure in the Foreign Office who would not seek to challenge his authority or develop independent lines of policy.[23] It may well be that, although Eden had not disagreed with the attempt to push forward Jordanian membership of the Baghdad Pact, he had been unhappy at the independent initiative Macmillan had displayed in implementing the policy. The change in incumbent at the highest level, however, did not affect the growing disenchantment of the Foreign Office at lower levels with the policy of conciliating Nasser. At a meeting with State Department officials in Washington on 13 January, Shuckburgh wondered whether 'we should be able to reach an understanding with Nasser without paying him too high a price'.[24] He questioned the State Department's disposition to favour a long-term policy of encouraging Arab unity under Egyptian leadership, arguing that this would be difficult to reconcile with 'the need to stick to our positions and demonstrate our loyalty to the Baghdad Pact'.

Later in the month, during discussions with Eisenhower and Dulles in Washington, Prime Minister Eden himself made a similar point, asking 'how long we could continue to cooperate with Nasser?'[25] Dulles agreed that the policy of seeking reconciliation with Nasser did not appear to be yielding dividends, and that 'the outcome of Nasser's present talks with Mr Eugene Black of the International Bank about the Aswan Dam and of other talks would indicate whether Nasser was willing to work with us or not. If not, we might have to change our policy towards him.' In fact, the 'other talks' referred to by Dulles were a private US initiative, conducted with only the minimum of Anglo-American consultation, to give the peace negotiations new momentum. Indeed, despite all of the declarations at the Washington meeting about the need for close cooperation in the Middle East, 'Eisenhower had in fact set out on a course of his own.'[26] Eisenhower's initiative had involved the despatch of his personal representative, Robert Anderson, to Cairo and Tel Aviv for discussions with Nasser and Ben Gurion. Although Dulles had informed British Ambassador Makins in a general way of the American intention to bring in a covert mediator to advance Alpha, he did not share with him the name of the man chosen nor any details of his mission. He merely assured him that 'the operation would of course be in the framework of our agreed Alpha policy'.[27]

The mission had in fact been arranged in the deepest secrecy by Allen Dulles, head of the CIA, with the logistical planning being handled principally by the intelligence agency. Eisenhower had chosen Anderson for what he regarded as this vital role because he held his negotiating ability in the highest regard, even going so far as to argue that if he had to hand his office over to anyone, Robert Anderson would be his favoured choice.[28] At a meeting between Eisenhower, Dulles and Anderson on 11 January it had been agreed that two key inducements should be emphasized to Nasser in a bid to secure his cooperation. The first was the established offer of assistance with the Aswan Dam. The second was US support in the prevention of the extension of Arab membership of the Baghdad Pact. Dulles asserted that '. . . Nasser would be willing to pay a considerable price to get the support of the US in limiting the Baghdad Pact to its present Arab membership with concentration on the peril from the north, with Egypt maintaining its hegemony of the Arab countries.'[29]

Of course, Dulles recognized that linking Alpha to the Baghdad Pact would be a delicate operation given the need to placate the British Government.[30] In fact, this US offer would look like a natural outgrowth of the strategy of trying to insulate the pact from Arab politics which Dulles had pursued during the previous summer, were it not for Macmillan's report of the encouragement he had given to the British in seeking Jordanian accession to the pact in October 1955. This casts further doubt on the veracity of Macmillan's account. Whatever the explanation, any offer by the US Administration to prevent further Arab membership of the pact, coming on top of its refusal to adhere itself, repeated at the January meetings with Eden,[31] would be bound to cause a great deal of Anglo-American tension.

Another flaw in Dulles's strategy of offering US assistance in preventing Arab accession to the pact was that the one lesson Nasser had presumably learned from the crisis in Jordan was that his influence was such that he could in any case block, or at least make extremely difficult, any attempt by another Arab government to join the pact even without US help. Finally, the other element of the approach to Nasser, the linking of the offer to finance the Aswan Dam to progress on Alpha and hence the veiled threat that non-cooperation could result in the withdrawal of the offer, was perilous. Apart from anything else, it ignored the fact that in October 1955 the Soviet Ambassador in Cairo had claimed that the Soviet Union would be prepared to finance the dam. Although this was regarded as a piece of propaganda by the Americans, Dulles's approach did not allow for the possibility that Nasser might have an alternative to Western funding for the project.

In the event, neither Anderson's first visit to the region in the latter part of January 1956, nor his second in the first part of March, was to produce any significant progress on Alpha. Although the initial indications from Nasser seemed positive, as is witnessed by the flurry of telegrams between Dulles and Anderson during the latter's first visit to Cairo in mid-January,[32] the lack of progress on Anderson's second trip served only to confirm the intransigence of the two sides. Anderson's failure was the result of unpropitious timing, the unacceptability of mediation to Israel, and a decline in the motivation of the Administration as it became clear that progress was not being made.[33] During the months in which Anderson undertook his mission the positions of the parties involved actually moved further apart rather than closer. This was due to a combination of Israeli fears and increasing Egyptian confidence in the wake of the arrival of Soviet arms.

In the meantime, events in Jordan had had a major impact on British strategy. On 1 March 1956, King Hussein had announced the dismissal, with immediate effect, of General Glubb, the commander of the Arab Legion. The news had a profound impact in London where, because of the importance of the Legion as a touchstone of British prestige in the region, Hussein's move was viewed as being a major setback. Although the news came like a thunderbolt to the government, it should have been prepared. Reports from Amman throughout 1954 and 1955 had mentioned repeatedly the tensions between Glubb and Hussein, and speculations regarding Glubb's possible replacement.[34] Indeed, it was indicative of the state of developing hysteria over the intentions of Nasser, that Glubb's dismissal was immediately taken by almost all British Government sources as a Nasser-inspired move.[35] In fact, its origins were indigenous. Tension had been developing both within the Legion, and between the commanders of the Legion and political leaders, over the twin problems of officer promotion and defence plans. Many of the aspiring junior officers felt that the promotion structure in the Legion was too rigid and slow, making it difficult for native Jordanians to progress. In addition, controversy surrounded the question of Legion expansion, a matter fundamental to the drafting of future defence plans. Glubb wanted to keep the Legion as a mobile long-enlistment regular force, a strategy which he deemed essential for the protection of the country's long frontiers. Others wanted a much larger conscript force, not for sound military reasons, but in order to outdo the Israelis in sheer numbers.[36]

At the same time as these tensions were coming to a head, the King was under great pressure from his principal aide-de-camp, Ali Abu Nuwar, to move away from the alliance with Britain and towards the nationalist camp of Arab states being developed by Nasser. To this extent, the sacrifice of Glubb appeared to the King to be the sort of symbolic gesture which would both remove a potential internal challenger to his authority, and appease the Arab nationalists in the short term, affording him time to reconsider his country's position. If it was accompanied by protestations of a desire for continuing friendly relations with Britain, it might enable him to have the best of both worlds.

The severity of the initial British response, however, may well have taken Hussein by surprise. Its explanation had three sources. The first was concerned with the manner of Glubb's dismissal, which was deemed particularly humiliating and ungrateful. As Evelyn Shuckburgh commented, 'the King has done it, and Glubb leaves in the morning for Cyprus. It is a monstrous piece of ingratitude . . .'.[37] The second reason, closely linked to this, was the impact of the dismissal on British prestige throughout the region. As Charles Duke reported on 2 March, 'it is my firm conviction that if we are to retain any credit in Jordan, and perhaps throughout the Middle East, HMG must react speedily, publicly and effectively against Glubb's removal.'[38] The final and most important reason was the conviction that the events in Jordan formed part of a broader strategy, orchestrated by Nasser, to undermine the British position throughout the region. Although it seems certain that Nasser did not persuade Hussein to dismiss Glubb, and he may indeed have been as surprised as everybody else,[39] Eden and Lloyd both assumed that Nasser had been behind the King's actions.

On 5 March Eden wrote to Eisenhower arguing that 'there is no doubt that the Russians are resolved to liquidate the Baghdad Pact. In this undertaking Nasser is supporting them and I suspect that his relations with the Soviets are much closer than he admits to us. Recent events in Jordan are part of this pattern.'[40] In private, Eden's anger knew no bounds. Shuckburgh comments that 'he was quite emphatic that Nasser must be got rid of. "It's either him or us, don't forget that." '[41] The dismissal of Glubb was to mark the point at which the British Government abandoned the strategy of trying to work with Nasser, and adopted an approach based on open hostility to him. However, before this decision was taken, tempers cooled somewhat in the specific respect of how to respond in Jordan. Glubb himself played an important part in this process, arguing in a meeting with Shuckburgh on 4 March that it would not be right to take severe action against Jordan, and that the King was sincere in his desire to maintain friendly relations with Britain. Ambassador Duke also repented of his initial fury, asking, on 4 March, whether 'on further reflection ... our regard for General Glubb's great personal qualities and services in Jordan and resentment at the ignoble manner of his dismissal have not led us to take a more tragic view than is justified of the significance of this episode for Anglo-Jordan relations generally'.[42]

In the event, the protestations from the King of his continuing desire for good relations, together with Glubb's entreaties, gave Shuckburgh, with the backing at Cabinet level of Macmillan, the opportunity to forestall the drive by Lord Salisbury and Rab Butler to end the treaty with Jordan. Instead, Shuckburgh began to press for an alternative strategy involving the promotion of closer links between Jordan and Iraq, which might eventually lead to Jordanian accession to the Baghdad Pact, and would fall in with the existing approach of building up the regional role of Iraq.[43] It is significant that this initiative originated within the Foreign Office, and was promoted by Macmillan in the Cabinet. Surely, if this new approach was linked to Eden's earlier suggestions of building an 'Iraqi–Jordanian axis', then it would not have been necessary for Shuckburgh and Macmillan to struggle so hard for the acceptance of the policy at Cabinet level? In reality it appears to have been a short-term tactical ploy by the Foreign Office to prevent Eden precipitously abandoning what was left of the British position in Jordan, and not part of some longer-term strategy designed to forge an 'Iraqi–Jordanian axis'.[44]

As to the broader questions of Middle East strategy in the wake of the Glubb affair, the new strongly anti-Egyptian line was agreed at a Cabinet meeting on 21 March. The essence of it was Selwyn Lloyd's contention that 'instead of seeking to conciliate or support Colonel Nasser, we should do our utmost to counter Egyptian policy and to uphold our true friends in the Middle East'. This would involve, in addition to the strengthening of Iraqi–Jordanian ties, increased military, diplomatic and economic support for the Baghdad Pact, an effort to promote US accession to the organization, and to detach Saudi Arabia from Egypt.[45] It is important to note that from this point onwards the guiding tenet of British strategy in the Middle East, a tenet which transcended the defeat at Suez, and even endured beyond the collapse of the Anglophile regime in Iraq in July 1958, was that Nasser was Britain's principal enemy. The subtleties of Nasser's relations with the Soviet Union, something on which the Americans were to focus much more attention, did not greatly concern the governments of both Anthony Eden and Harold Macmillan. Whatever he might say or do, Nasser was Britain's enemy, and he must be opposed at all costs. Any gain for him, as far as they were concerned, would ultimately benefit the Soviets in any case. Nasser dominated their perception of threat in the region.

However, their attempts to persuade the US that the only means of thwarting this threat was to build on Iraq and the Baghdad Pact were to meet with failure, now and at repeated intervals in the next three years. One of the problems in this approach was that although the Americans were to come to the same conclusion as to the inadvisability of continuing to work with Nasser they did so for different reasons. Moreover, since throughout the period under examination, the Soviet Union dominated the US's perception of threat in the region, the Americans were more inclined to treat Nasser pragmatically, if suspiciously, and to base their attitude to him on current evaluations of his closeness to the Soviets. However, in March 1956, all of this was very much in the future. In the short term, the Administration had to deal with pressing British requests to join the Baghdad Pact and to fall in with the approach of opposing Nasser. In Eden's telegram to Eisenhower on 5 March, he had argued that 'I feel that we can no longer wait on Nasser. Indeed if the US now joined the Baghdad Pact this would impress him more than all our attempts to cajole him have yet done.'

In fact, Eden's telegram arrived at a point when the President had not yet entirely given up hope of some success from the second mission of his special representative Robert Anderson to the region. Although Eisenhower was very sceptical as to the possibilities of positive results, as witnessed by his diary entry on 8 March which suggested that 'we have reached the point where it looks as if Egypt, under Nasser, is going to make no move whatsoever',[46] he was not prepared to commit himself to any new course of action without a thorough review of the alternatives. Already, however, his diary revealed the seeds of a new strategy which he and Dulles were to build on during the coming two years. He commented that 'it would begin to appear that our efforts should be directed toward separating the Saudi Arabians from the Egyptians.' As has been indicated, one of the principal US objections to the Baghdad Pact, in addition to the complications it introduced into Arab–Israeli relations, was the inter-Arab hostilities it aroused. The US had pointed not only to Egyptian–Iraqi tension, about which, in the wake of any abandonment of Nasser, she might not be so concerned, but also to Iraqi–Saudi tension. Saudi opposition to the pact stemmed both from the traditional rivalry of the Hashemites and the al-Saud family, the latter having deprived the former of the Kingdom of the Hejaz in 1925, and also from Saudi anger with Britain over the Buraimi Oasis dispute. The recent problems over Buraimi had begun in 1952 when Saudi Arabia had occupied the oasis, located in the south-eastern tip of the

Arabian Peninsula, and then jointly controlled by the British client states of Abu Dhabi and Muscat and Oman. The Saudis were encouraged to act by the Arabian American Oil Company (ARAMCO), whose management believed that Buraimi might contain vast oil reserves.

The Saudi action was taken by the British as a challenge to their position in the Persian Gulf, and, despite Churchill's agreement to negotiations at the June 1954 summit with Eisenhower, alleged Saudi violations of this agreement led the British to reoccupy the oasis forcibly in October 1955.[47] Buraimi thus became one of the major topics of discussion at the meetings between Eisenhower, Dulles, Eden and Lloyd in Washington at the end of January 1956 alluded to above.[48] The British position against taking the dispute to arbitration was based on the fact that the Saudis had already indulged in bribery of the members of the previous tribunal. In addition, they had been further angered by the use of Saudi money in helping to fund the anti-pact riots in Jordan. However, the essence of the British attitude was summed up by Eden who argued that 'the British position in the Persian Gulf was of the greatest importance for the United Kingdom. We depended on it for our life. If we retreated once more over the Buraimi affair our position in the Gulf would be untenable'.[49] Dulles summed up the American position, arguing that 'the United States had a big stake in the area, which was part of the assets of the Western world. There were large oil reserves and the Dhahran air base. The agreement about this base expired this year and the Americans did not wish to have to give up the base.' To this extent, it would cause the US great difficulties if Britain did not move to placate the Saudis. Still, despite great pressure from the American side, the British would not give ground, and both parties had for the present to agree to differ.

Thus, the British request to the Administration to consider accession to the Baghdad Pact early in March 1956 seemed to Dulles and Eisenhower destined to draw them into conflict with their Saudi allies. Indeed, when Eden called in the US Ambassador, Winthrop Aldrich, on 6 March to discuss his appeal to Eisenhower, Aldrich noted that 'I took occasion again to press what I regard as the equal urgency of Britain reaching a solution of outstanding problems with Saudi Arabia with a view to establishing UK-Saudi relations on a basis which would also influence and deter Nasser.'[50] Dulles also took the opportunity to stress to Selwyn Lloyd that the US could not consider adherence to the pact at this time, although he chose to emphasize the difficulties posed by the probable need for a corresponding security guarantee to Israel. He also refused to rule out the possibility that Nasser might yet take a more constructive attitude towards peace with Israel.[51]

In reality, however, despite their efforts to hold the British at bay, Eisenhower and Dulles now instigated their own review of Middle East policy. During the course of this review one of the key elements taken into account was the attitude of King Saud, who had urged the US not to join the Baghdad Pact.[52] Indeed, the policy document produced by Dulles for the crucial conference with the President on 28 March, the so-called 'Omega' memorandum, laid great emphasis on the importance of strengthening the US position in Saudi Arabia, both by assuring Saud that his military needs would be met, and by putting pressure on the British to 'undertake a generous agreement on the Buraimi issue'.[53] During discussion of the document, Eisenhower himself again referred to the possibility of promoting 'King Saud as a figure with sufficient prestige to offset Nasser',[54] and dictated his own memorandum after the meeting suggesting that Saud's position as a spiritual leader of the Muslim world could first be built up, after which 'we might begin to urge his right to political leadership'.[55]

However, the main plank of the new approach concerned Nasser himself, its goal being to make him realize that 'he cannot cooperate as he is doing with the Soviet Union and at the same time enjoy most-favoured nation treatment from the United States'. In order to bring this fact home to him a series of economic and propaganda counter-measures were proposed, the most significant of which was that the US and UK should 'continue to delay the conclusion of current negotiations on the High Aswan Dam'. There was, however, one important qualification in the new US policy towards Nasser. Dulles's paper stated that: 'we would want for the time being to avoid any open break which would throw Nasser irrevocably into a Soviet satellite status and we would want to leave Nasser a bridge back to good relations with the West if he so desires.'

While the Administration may have given up hope of securing Nasser's cooperation in the short term, it still realized the extent of his influence in the region. If, at any stage in the future, Nasser could be persuaded to exert this influence against what the US perceived to be Soviet-inspired moves in the area, then he might yet be a potent anti-Communist force. No such qualification was present in the new British estimation of Nasser.

As regards the Baghdad Pact, Dulles's conclusion was that the US should give it 'increased support . . . without actually adhering . . . or announcing our intention of doing so'. In fact, Anthony Gorst and Scott Lucas argue that the decision not to adhere to the pact was the only respect in which Dulles's new approach differed from that favoured by his British counterpart, Lloyd. The precise phrase employed is that the policies of the two were 'broadly similar'.[56] However, as always, it was the differences that these broad similarities masked which were to prove to be of the greatest significance. Light is shed on the hidden reason why the US was unwilling to join the pact by a phone conversation between Eisenhower and Dulles on 7 April, referred to in the previous chapter. During discussion of an attempt by Defence Secretary Wilson to have the question of the US joining the pact put on the NSC agenda, Eisenhower and Dulles turned to an examination of the broader reasons why they did not favour US accession:

> [The] President said we were originally strong[ly] in favor of [the] Pact being formed. Dulles agreed, but said we were not in favor of Iraq joining. [The] President emphasized that we were in favor of [a] pact between Pakistan and Turkey. Dulles said that the trouble was that the British have taken it over and run it as an instrument of British policy – that has drawn down upon it a tremendous amount of criticism.[57]

Dulles made these criticisms explicit in discussions with congressional leaders on 10 April:

> The original concept . . . has . . . been exploited by the British for their own purpose . . . The UK has a great interest in Iraq . . . [and] UK adherence to the [Baghdad] Pact provided a new basis for their relationship with Iraq . . . The UK has used the Baghdad Pact to build up the Iraqi and to try to spread Iraqi and British influence to the south. The British

pushed the Pact rapidly and in some instances without con-
sulting the US. It brought Iran into the Pact against our
advice. The US has not consented to join the Pact, in spite
of British pressure, for a variety of reasons, but primarily
because the Pact is not now primarily an instrument for collective defense against the Soviet Union but has become an
instrument of Arab intrigue. The Iraqi[s] are using their
position in the Pact in their efforts to build up influence in
the Arab world, and to challenge Egyptian leadership.[58]

Despite a great deal of pressure from the Joint Chiefs of
Staff and the Defense Department, Dulles believed that the
political objections to the US joining the pact far outweighed
the military benefits which might be derived.[59] Dulles's unwillingness to sanction US accession to the pact represented therefore not just a minor tactical disagreement with the British but
a major disaffection with British strategy in the area. While the
alternative strategy of promoting Saudi leadership of the Arab
world was not yet being pushed hard by the Administration, in
the way in which it was to be in the wake of Suez, the seeds of
the new approach were already there. Indeed, a memorandum
by Norman Brook, the British Cabinet Secretary, on 14 April
seems to have been intended as a direct critique of the new
American policy. In it, he suggested that Nasser was making a
revolutionary bid for the leadership of the Arab world, and,

> if we try to counter Nasser's move by stiffening feudal author-
> ity which is already regarded as reactionary, I fear that we
> may find we have backed the losing horse. We should be
> on a certain loser if we tried, as the Americans seem to be
> tempted to do, to build up King Saud as the leader of the
> Arab world.[60]

Of course, one implication of Brook's argument which he
does not seem to have taken up, is that it could equally well
be argued on this basis that to try to promote Iraq, which also
had a monarchical regime, even though it was perhaps less
'feudal' in character, might prove to be similarly fruitless. Even
leaving aside the question of the development of the Saudi
alternative, however, Dulles's reasons for not wanting to join
the pact signalled his refusal to fall in with the British strategy
of building up Iraq as a rival leader of the Arab world to Egypt.

It is important to note this difference, because it remained a constant source of tension in the Anglo-American relationship in the Middle East at least until the Iraqi Revolution.

The final point of divergence between the two countries was over Nasser himself. While it is true that both governments had now decided not to cooperate with him, the British seem to have gone further than the Americans in regarding Nasser as their inveterate enemy. Dulles still talked of allowing Nasser a bridge back to good relations with the West. All talk of conciliation had now left the vocabulary of British policy-makers. It is too easy to dismiss this difference as a function of Eden's hysteria infecting the government in the run up to Suez. It was to remain a constant source of tension in Anglo-American dealings through to the end of the 1950s, and lay behind many of the differences of opinion which were to emerge between the two countries.

Dulles's exasperation with British policy in the Middle East was made plain in a speech delivered to US foreign service personnel on 21 April. He described the British as 'just desperately grasping at straws to find something that will restore their prestige and influence in the world'.[61] He went on to criticize virtually every aspect of British Government policy in the region over the previous year, cataloguing what he described as 'a series of very grave errors'. Firstly, on Buraimi, he accused the British Government of developing a state of undeclared war with Saudi Arabia, the consequence of which was that Saudi money was being spent throughout the region to fight the British. Dulles's view of this was blunt: 'you can't have a war and seize property arbitrarily like that from the Saudis and then call on us to save you from the consequences of that.'

Then, on the Baghdad Pact, Dulles recollected that although it was true he had expressed the view that a northern tier grouping would be desirable, 'the British, in an effort to bolster their position in Iraq, got Iraq into the Pact without any knowledge on our part'. They then followed this, in Dulles's account, by pressing Iran to join the pact, 'against my advice'. Finally, in Dulles's words, 'when they came to talk about Jordan in the Pact, I said: "You're crazy to try to get Jordan in the Pact. Already Iraq's being in the Pact makes the Pact not something which is primarily against the Soviet threat, but you are

right in the middle of Arab politics." ' Dulles's bitterness at
British policy was summed up in his comments on the failure
in Jordan. 'Then when the British get into any kind of a mess,
they say: "well, you must be true allies and back us up in
everything we have done, and if you don't it's terrible." '

Dulles did hint, however, that an attempt was under way
to try and bring the strategies of the two countries somewhat
closer together in the Middle East. 'They are hoping their
policy is somewhat more into line,' he commented, 'although
on some things they have done without our knowledge and
against our advice it isn't going to be an easy task.' What he
seems to be referring to is the 'Omega' plan, outlined above,
which was an endeavour to paper over the widening cracks in
the Anglo-American common front in the region.[62] The principal elements of cooperation involved in Omega seem to have
been letting the Aswan Dam offer wither, preparing for a coup
in Syria, and longer-term economic measures to bring pressure to bear on Nasser. Although, on the British side, MI6 was
working somewhat beyond the bounds of Foreign Office policy,
and presenting Eden with schemes for the overthrow of Nasser,
one scholar has presented a picture of two governments still
fundamentally in step until the radical shift in British policy in
late July.[63] However, although there were elements of cooperation in the approach of the two governments, the conflicts
outlined above were not resolved. While the Foreign Office
line may have been more moderate over Nasser than that of
Eden or of MI6, Nasser was still regarded as a dangerous foe.
The British approach in all quarters was now without the pragmatism which continued to inform that of the US Administration. This, rather than any revolutionary change in outlook
after the nationalization of the Canal, forms the essential background to the different policies adopted by the two governments during the forthcoming crisis.

Although it is important, therefore, to emphasize that the
two countries were still capable of close cooperation in the
region when their interests coincided, as in the case of Syria,
divisions over Nasser, Buraimi and the Baghdad Pact were not
resolved. These divisions form the essential background to the
breakdown in relations between the two countries which was
to result from Nasser's nationalization of the Suez Canal.

5 The Suez Crisis

The main point about the nationalization of the Suez Canal was that it was an issue perfectly formulated to drive a wedge between the United States and Britain in the wake of their respective reorientations of policy in March 1956. As has been suggested, aside from the broader strategic divergence between the two over the question of the promotion of the Baghdad Pact and of Iraqi leadership of the Arab world, they had come to subtly, but significantly, different assessments of the new approach to be adopted towards Nasser. British opposition to him was trenchant. Nasser was Britain's enemy, and his designs had to be thwarted. If not, he would subvert Britain's position in the Middle East, an area which, because of the importance of its oil supplies, was vital to national survival. The US, on the other hand, did not see Nasser threatening anything so vital. Certainly, his influence in the region was inimical, and his actions seemed to be profiting the Soviet Union. However, an important element of pragmatism still remained in the US approach to dealing with him.

Thus, the issue of the nationalization of the Suez Canal was one which fell in perfectly with the British paranoia that Nasser might attempt to stifle Britain economically by controlling her access to the oil supplies of the Gulf. The significance of the Canal as the principal mode of transport for these supplies can be gauged by the statistic that, in 1955, 62 million tonnes of crude oil, and another five million tonnes of oil products, passed northwards through the waterway. Of this, 20 million tonnes were headed for Britain. The defence of the Canal then, was an issue over which Britain was prepared to fight her apocalyptic 'last battle' in the Middle East.[1] To the United States, on the other hand, Nasser's move was an unfavourable development, but certainly not an issue of life and death. This difference in analysis lay at the heart of the divergence in response of the two countries.

However, before looking at the circumstances surrounding Nasser's decision to nationalize the Canal, and the response of the British Government, it is necessary to pick up the thread of Anglo-American consultation during the summer of 1956 over covert operations in Syria. This may be termed the other side of the coin of Anglo-American relations in the Middle East. The fundamental point about the planning for 'Operation Straggle' in Syria in 1956, and indeed, about the close consultation established between the two countries during the Syrian crisis of the following August, is that it shows how well the relationship between the two could work when their interests coincided. This did not necessarily require them to have the same view of the threats that they were working to counter, or, indeed, of the ends they wished to achieve. It simply meant that when they both perceived a certain existing situation or potential development to be inimical then they were capable of the closest collaboration in working to undermine or subvert it.

So, on Syria, Dulles had expressed the view to Eden and Lloyd at their meeting in Washington in January 1956 that 'Syria was perhaps the most dangerous country in the area: the Syrians behaved like a Soviet satellite.'[2] The danger that Syria might somehow be ripe for direct takeover by the Communists never seems to have been far from the forefront of American thinking about the country. Since the threat of the Soviet Union establishing a client state in the heart of the region was of paramount concern to the Administration, Dulles appears to have been prepared to run certain risks over Syria that he was not prepared to take over other issues in the Middle East.

The British for their part were also aware of the great strategic significance of Syria. Apart from anything else, the Iraqi Petroleum Company pipelines ran through the country on their way to Mediterranean terminals. With an unfavourable regime in control of the other main supply route to the West via the Suez Canal, the potential for a stranglehold to be exerted over oil supplies by any hostile power controlling these two countries seemed very real. In addition, in order to build on the alliance with Iraq, the government had to pay a measure of lip service to Iraqi designs for the formation of the 'Fertile Crescent', which would link Jordan and Syria to Iraq.

Although, prior to March 1956, it is clear that the US Administration was particularly sensitive to any plans for political change in Syria backed by Iraq, on the basis that this might be perceived as the promotion of the Fertile Crescent which would arouse the hostility of Egypt and Saudi Arabia,[3] after March 1956 the emphasis shifted somewhat. Egyptian sensitivities were obviously not now important. If the US could work with Britain to prevent what was perceived to be a leftwards drift in Syria, while at the same time blocking any plans which might involve a direct Iraqi takeover, she might be able to have the best of both worlds. She could deal with the principal threat she perceived in the region, that of the advancement of Soviet influence, while at the same time reassuring the Saudis that she was working to limit Iraqi ambitions. This was precisely the strategy employed from March 1956 until the Suez Crisis scotched Anglo-American plans.[4]

The British, on the other hand, although unwilling to disavow the Iraqi aims for the Fertile Crescent, tacitly accepted the American conditions for joint planning when they acquiesced in the CIA-sponsored removal of the Iraqi-backed former Syrian President Shishakli from his position in waiting in Lebanon. The most important thing after all was to secure a compliant regime in Damascus which would pose no threat to the closer ties between Iraq and Jordan which Britain still hoped to promote. There was a much greater chance of achieving this end if the Americans were to cooperate. Indeed, the timing of the proposed Syrian coup for 29 October 1956 may well have been no coincidence. It may have been part of a British strategy to coordinate the toppling of the governments of Egypt and Syria and regroup the states of the region around Iraq. However, if this was so, it displayed an extraordinary naivety on the British part as to the likely effect of the Israeli attack on Egypt on opinion in the Arab world. Perhaps this is a good instance of a bifurcation in British policy between the Foreign Office and MI6. MI6 not surprisingly displayed rather less understanding of the ramifications of its activities in Syria for the rest of the region than did the Foreign Office. Sure enough, the news of the Israeli offensive in Sinai led the Anglo-American sponsored plotters in Syria to disperse, with a number being arrested and tried by the authorities.[5]

Having thus outlined one respect in which American and British strategies in the Middle East converged from March to October 1956, it is important to turn to another in which they diverged: the handling of Nasser, and the response to his announcement of the nationalization of the Suez Canal Company on 26 July. As will be recollected, it had been decided by both countries as a result of their reviews of policy in March 1956 that the Aswan Dam offer should be allowed to wither on the vine. Some controversy, however, surrounds the question as to whether the British were consulted by Dulles before his withdrawal of the offer on 19 July. Despite claims that they had been caught unaware by the US action, it does appear that the British were 'kept fairly well informed about American thinking on the Aswan issue'.[6] Selwyn Lloyd had anticipated Dulles's decision at a cabinet meeting on 17 July, reporting that 'the United States were likely to share our view that the offer of financial aid for the building of the High Dam at Aswan should now be withdrawn'. When the actual announcement was made, the Foreign Office commented that: 'Mr Dulles has taken the decision for us. We were not absolutely in step at the last moment but the difference between us was no more than a nuance.'[7]

Of course at a later date the British tried to magnify the importance of this nuance, with Harold Caccia, the new ambassador in Washington, claiming in a meeting with Assistant Secretary Hoover on 23 November that 'the present crisis over the Suez Canal had been occasioned by the action of the US Government, in the way in which the Aswan Dam project had been turned down in July'.[8] While it is true that the British felt the matter could have been handled more diplomatically by Dulles, they were neither unaware of his impending decision, nor out of sympathy with it. The most convincing explanation of later claims by Macmillan, Lloyd, Eden and US Ambassador Aldrich as to the lack of consultation, is that they allowed their recollection of events to become clouded by their resentment of Dulles's role in the ensuing Suez Crisis.[9]

In fact, Dulles's actions were determined by two considerations, one of which was the hostility of Congress to the Aswan project, with which the British had been kept up to date.[10] In order to prevent any indirect funding of the Dam utilizing the untargeted portions of the 1957 foreign aid appropriations, the Senate Appropriations Committee included the following passage in its report on the 1957 aid bill, released on 16 July:

the Committee directs that none of the funds provided for in this act shall be used for assistance in connection with the construction of the Aswan Dam, nor shall any of the funds heretofore provided under the Mutual Security Act as amended be used on this Dam without prior approval of the Committee on Appropriations.[11]

The implications of this statement for the Executive–Legislative relationship greatly concerned both Eisenhower and Dulles. In effect, the Committee's action implied the existence of a Congressional veto over White House use of untargeted aid funds, thus setting what the Administration would regard as a dangerous precedent. Dulles's precipitous move to withdraw the Aswan offer thus appears, on the one hand, as an attempt to pre-empt such action by the Committee. The other explanation of Dulles's behaviour lay in his desire 'to cancel the offer in a fashion that would illustrate pointedly to Third World governments that the US would not reward developing countries with aid if they refused to cooperate with the West and tried to use Cold War rivalry for their own ends'.[12] Indeed, one of the principal American frustrations with Nasser was that his equivocal stance, and the offers of aid as inducements to cooperation which it elicited, seemed to be active demonstrations to others that neutralism yielded greater dividends than partisanship.[13] The problem with this form of demonstration was that it challenged directly Nasser's own notion of 'dignity'. This was a guiding tenet of his actions, and one which emphasized the importance of uniting the Arab world by freeing it from external domination.[14] The withdrawal of the Aswan Dam offer was particularly galling in this respect, especially since it was delivered while Nasser was attending a meeting in Yugoslavia with Tito and Nehru. The decision to respond by nationalizing the Canal seems to have been Nasser's own personal initiative.

Eden's immediate response, as shown by notes he scribbled on the back of an envelope at the dinner he was attending in honour of King Feisal of Iraq, was to contemplate military action to secure the Canal.[15] At a cabinet meeting the following day it was agreed that, even 'in default of assistance from the United States and France', Britain should be prepared to take military action alone.[16] At the same time, the newly constituted Egypt Committee, consisting of Eden, Lloyd, Macmillan, Salisbury, Home and Monckton, agreed that 'while our ultimate purpose was to place the Canal under international control, our immediate objective was to bring about the downfall of the present Egyptian government'.[17]

The intention to depose Nasser in addition to reversing Egyptian control of the Canal caused the military planners, who were now required to prepare for action in Egypt, significant difficulties. It was almost universally agreed that any attempt to occupy Cairo would be unacceptable. On the other hand, merely seizing the Canal carried with it no guarantee of bringing about Nasser's overthrow. The first version of the invasion plan, 'Musketeer', which provided for landings at Port Said followed by an occupation of the Canal, was regarded as unsatisfactory both by the man designated force commander, General Stockwell, and by the politicians. Macmillan commented: 'I think it is doubtful whether the purpose of the plan is the right one. The object of the exercise, if we have to embark upon it, is surely to bring about the fall of Nasser and create a government in Egypt which will work satisfactorily with us and the other powers.'[18]

The political and military disaffection with the first version of 'Musketeer' led to its replacement by an entirely new plan presented by General Stockwell on 8 August. This involved an amphibious assault on Alexandria, followed by the advance of 80 000 men via Cairo to the Suez Canal. It carried with it a much stronger guarantee of ousting Nasser. The emphasis laid on the objective of unseating Nasser is not, of course, surprising in view of the hostility of the British Government towards him even before the nationalization of the Canal. The Americans, however, with their differing perception of Nasser's importance as an enemy, attached much greater weight to the need to seek a solution of the specific question of international control of the Canal.

This difference was made apparent in Eisenhower's first communication to Eden on the subject in which he warned him that American public opinion would be outraged should there be a failure to exhaust all reasonable efforts at negotiation over the Canal issue before resorting to force. Dulles emphasized Eisenhower's point by indicating in a covering note that the President was referring 'not to the going through the motions of having an intermediate conference but to the use of intermediate steps as a genuine and sincere effort to settle the problem and avoid the use of force'.[19] In his reply to Eisenhower, Eden stressed that as to the question of setting up an international regime for the Canal, he did not believe that they disagreed. However, he made explicit the more immediate aim of the British Government, stating that 'the removal of Nasser and the installation in Egypt of a regime less hostile to the West, must . . . also rank high among our objectives'.[20]

From this point onwards, the preferred American strategy was one of prevarication in the hope that as time passed, public opinion in Britain would move against the use of force, and pressure the Government into seeking compromise. The British on the other hand, aware that any military operation could not take place until the middle of September at the earliest, pursued negotiations more as an expedient to pass the time while forces were built up.[21] After all, the downfall of Nasser was very unlikely to be secured by negotiation. There was no more than the slimmest of chances that Nasser might accept a settlement sufficiently humiliating to undermine his position at home without being compelled to do so by force.

The first of the American-inspired initiatives to negotiate a settlement of the dispute was the London Conference convened on 14 August, and attended by the eight surviving signatories of the 1888 Suez Convention, together with 16 other countries with an interest in the running of the Canal. In the countdown to the conference, Dulles had managed to dissuade Eisenhower from attending in person, an approach which the President had favoured as a possible method of securing Nasser's attendance. The core of the debates at the conference was over what kind of international body should be created to help Egypt to operate the Canal. With the Egyptians refusing to attend, Robert Menzies, the Australian Prime Minister, was deputed to take to Cairo a proposal, hatched by Dulles, for an Executive International Authority to run the Canal, agreed to at the conference by 18 of the countries present. Unfortunately, the speech with which Dulles had introduced his resolution may well have contributed to a misperception of the

American position on the part of the British and French. 'His words read like a first-class lawyer's recital of the Anglo-French case; his identification with that case and all its implications was henceforth assumed, in the face of much evidence to the contrary, to represent the "real, underlying" American position.'[22]

Nevertheless, whatever comfort the British may have drawn from Dulles's words, the discussions had done little to break the impasse over the Canal. Although passions had been dampened somewhat in Europe, Nasser had given no indication that he might be willing to accept the plan conveyed to him by Menzies. While the Australian Prime Minister was received politely enough in Cairo, Nasser showed little interest in the proposals he brought with him. Crucially, Britain and France had failed to persuade the other maritime countries represented at the conference to stop paying canal dues to Egypt. They were thus deprived of what might have been the best available method short of force to put pressure on Nasser.[23]

Even before the failure of the Menzies mission had become clear, however, Eisenhower wrote to Eden emphasizing that their views diverged on the use of force. 'I must tell you frankly', he asserted, 'that American public opinion flatly rejects the thought of using force, particularly when it does not seem that every possible peaceful means of protecting our vital interests has been exhausted.'[24] However, Eden does not seem to have grasped the significance of Eisenhower's comments, and perhaps operated on the assumption that Eisenhower was in some way isolated from the policy being pursued by Dulles. He evidently clung to an earlier comment of Dulles's about Nasser being made to 'disgorge' the Canal, and noted on his copy of the President's telegram 'Foster advocated going in'.

In the wake of the failure of the Menzies mission, Dulles had come up with his own scheme to establish a Suez Canal Users' Association (SCUA) to run the Canal. From his point of view, the proposal fell in perfectly with the policy of spinning out the crisis until tempers cooled and the use of force became politically impossible. This was the explanation for the complexity and studied ambiguity of the plan.[25] Eden seized on the same characteristics of the scheme but for different reasons. On 18 August, Selwyn Lloyd had reported to the Egypt Committee as to which actions by the Egyptian Government might provide a pretext for military operations over the Canal dispute.[26] The most likely occasion for armed intervention would be if the Egyptians refused to let a British ship transit the Canal for non-payment of dues. SCUA, by setting up an alternative body to collect such dues, appeared to hold out the prospect of such a dispute, and one in which, moreover, the US might be involved alongside the British.[27]

Although the decision was a close one, because of lingering British doubts about the intentions of the Americans, Eden decided that rather than referring the dispute to the United Nations Security Council, a move that was widely expected in Parliament and the country, he would opt instead for SCUA. However, not only did the move arouse a storm of protest in the ensuing debate in the House of Commons, leading to the collapse of the initial bipartisan consensus over Suez, Eden also had the ground cut from under him by the author of the plan himself, Dulles. As the debate was winding up in the House, news arrived of a press conference in which Dulles had emphasized that American ships would not shoot their way through the Canal. So much for SCUA as a pretext for the use of force.

An even bigger blow to the British in the search for pretexts was administered by the failure of Operation Pile-Up, the government-sponsored attempt to clog up the Canal with so much traffic that the Egyptians would be shown to be incapable of running it effectively. The removal of the French and British pilots on 15 September was followed by the arrival of 50 ships at Port Said on the following day. But, as Nasser loudly trumpeted, the Egyptians themselves, without the aid of the foreign pilots, had proven able to see the ships safely through the Canal. Although the Canal Users' Conference was convened in London soon after this incident on 19 September, and the association formally established on 2 October, Dulles himself by this stage, had already gone even further in killing off his 'foster child'. At another press conference on 1 October, he had exclaimed, 'there is talk about teeth being pulled out of the plan, but I know of no teeth in it, so far as I am aware.'[28]

By this point, however, the Prime Minister's misapprehension as to American intentions had already been reinforced by the visit of Macmillan to Washington on 25 September. From his conversation with Eisenhower, he reported to Eden that the 'feeling I had was that Ike is really determined, somehow or another, to bring Nasser down'.[29] Macmillan gained a similar impression from an ensuing discussion with Dulles, telling Eden Dulles had observed that 'he quite realized that we might have to act by force'.[30] Of course, in view of the attitude that the Administration had already expressed, and the stance that it was to take in the crisis itself, Macmillan's reports appear paradoxical in the extreme. Indeed, it is even more important to seek an explanation for them in view of the fact that Macmillan's outlook was to shape the conduct of British policy in the region after Eden's resignation.

In fact, the attitude of Macmillan throughout the crisis had been among the most 'hawkish' of any British cabinet minister. He had been the first, for instance, to suggest, at an Egypt Committee meeting on 28 July, that collaboration with the Israelis might prove to be beneficial in military operations against Nasser.[31] Macmillan went further, and, at a meeting at 11 Downing Street on 3 August, discussed with, among others, Salisbury and Gladwyn Jebb, the Ambassador to France, the possible shape of any post-Nasser Middle East. Proposals aired included the creation of the Fertile Crescent and the expansion of the Baghdad Pact.[32] Although Eden discouraged Macmillan's initiatives, they were illustrative of an attempt on his part to set out a radical and distinctive stall on Middle Eastern issues.

David Carlton has suggested that Macmillan's radicalism was machiavellian. He argues that Macmillan realized that Eden was vulnerable on Middle Eastern questions, and deliberately positioned himself to the right of him to take advantage of any weakness or vacillation he might display to step into the breach as Prime Minister.[33] With Macmillan, he argues, 'we may be dealing with nothing more than the cynical machinations of an opportunist intent on creating conditions in which he might have a chance to seize the premiership'.[34] On closer inspection, however, Carlton's argument appears flimsy. To begin with, he makes the mistake of investing Macmillan with an insight into the course events were likely to take during 1956 which could really only have been gained with hindsight. More importantly, he neglects the elements of continuity in his thinking. Macmillan had taken what could be described as a radical stance on the Middle East during his time as Foreign Secretary in 1955, and was to continue to hold the same opinions on Nasser after assuming the premiership. Indeed, as will be seen, the only difference between Eden's and Macmillan's handling of the region was that after Suez Macmillan realized the need to wait for the opportunity to confront Nasser, this time with American assistance. Whatever else Macmillan can be accused of, it is certainly not of inconsistency in his outlook on British strategy in the Middle East. 'Radicalism' was not something which he assumed or cast off for the purposes of political opportunism.

Returning to the specific question of the explanation of Macmillan's reports to Eden, therefore, they appear to have been conditioned by his own mind-set on the Suez problem. Roger Makins has referred to a 'failure of communication' over the meeting with Eisenhower.[35] Macmillan appears to have built Eisenhower's willingness to see Nasser put down at some stage into a tacit acceptance of the use of military action to settle the Suez dispute. The charitable interpretation of this is Alistair Horne's suggestion that 'the highly sensitive antennae of Macmillan let him down'.[36] The less charitable explanation, and the one which justifies a charge of machiavellianism, although on other grounds than those suggested by David Carlton, is that Macmillan deliberately distorted his reports to Eden in a bid to stiffen his resolve to stand up to Nasser militarily. Given Macmillan's hawkish stance throughout and after the crisis, elements of both of these interpretations may be needed to explain his actions on this occasion.

Macmillan's conversation with Dulles, in which the latter seems to have managed both to encourage and discourage British designs in the same breath, fell in with the pattern of the rest of Dulles's diplomacy during the crisis. With SCUA undermined as a pretext for war, the British, much to Dulles's chagrin,[37] turned back to the United Nations Security Council at the beginning of October. Apart from the continuing search for pretexts, the idea behind the British involvement of the UN was to try to persuade the Americans to see the dispute in cold war terms. This was the philosophy which underpinned a contemporaneous telegram from Eden to Eisenhower. In it he argued: 'there is no doubt that Nasser, whether he likes it or not, is now effectively in Russian hands, just as Mussolini was in Hitler's.'[38]

Some controversy, however, surrounds the prospects which may have existed for a negotiated settlement to the crisis between Selwyn Lloyd and Mahmoud Fawzi, the Egyptian Foreign Minister, behind the scenes at the United Nations at this point. Anthony Nutting suggests that the negotiations could have succeeded, while Selwyn Lloyd maintains that little was accomplished.[39] In a later interview Nasser argued that at this juncture, 'I got the impression they were willing to reach agreement.'[40] Fawzi's account, too, suggests that some progress was made.[41] All had vested interests in their own versions of the story. Nevertheless, it may well be that Eden was at his most receptive to any chance of a negotiated settlement at this point, before the possibility of collusion with the Israelis and French had emerged.[42]

Indeed, a telegram from Eden to Lloyd on 14 October appeared to encourage further negotiations with the Egyptians. In it, the Prime Minister asked:

> Should not we and the French now approach the Egyptians and ask them whether they are prepared to meet and discuss in confidence with us on the basis of the second half of the resolution which the Russians vetoed? If they say yes, then it is for consideration whether we and the French meet them somewhere, e.g. Geneva. If they say no, then they will be in defiance of the view of nine members of the Security Council and a new situation will arise.[43]

It is clear that at this juncture the British, from the point of view of taking military action to settle the dispute, were being backed into a corner. The military plan which was viewed as most practical politically, the so-called 'Musketeer Revise', involved an amphibious assault on Port Said at the mouth of the Suez Canal. This had been adopted in mid-September when it was decided that the bombardment of Alexandria envisaged in the earlier plan 'Musketeer' would cause an unacceptable level of civilian casualties. The Chiefs of Staff, however, had made it clear that deteriorating weather conditions in November would necessitate a new operational concept for any assault on Egypt. The 'Winter Plan' submitted by the Chiefs on 12 October envisaged a two-week timetable for operations, and emphasized that after 15 November sea conditions would preclude landings on open beaches. Eden was anxious to avoid having to fall back on this plan, and was well aware that his 'window of opportunity' was narrowing. It is arguable, therefore, that pressure from Washington had now helped to delay British action long enough to prevent conflict, and that for the present, the Suez crisis was over.[44] The vexed question of how to start a war with Egypt had finally defeated Eden.

However, possibly from as early as 3 October, when Macmillan's diary entries cease altogether, the idea of making use of Israel in some respect had begun to be considered again.[45] One of the factors which precipitated British contacts with the Israelis was, paradoxically, the need to restrain Israeli pressure on Jordan.[46] Since Britain was bound by the Anglo-Jordanian Treaty to come to Jordan's defence were she to be attacked, the Chiefs of Staff were put in the position of having to consider the ramifications of a possible simultaneous war with Israel and Egypt. Forestalling an Israeli attack on Jordan therefore became an important concern for Eden. His over-riding priority, however, continued to be finding a pretext for attacking Nasser.[47] This was reinforced by the bellicose mood exhibited in the foreign affairs debate of the Conservative Party Conference at Llandudno on 13 October.

Faced with this situation, Eden seized on the possibility of a way out afforded by the visit to Chequers of the French acting Foreign Minister, Albert Gazier, and the Deputy Air Force Chief of Staff, General Maurice Challe on the afternoon of 14 October. Challe outlined a scenario involving an attack on Egypt by Israel through Sinai threatening the Suez Canal. Britain and France would then intervene, demanding that the belligerents withdraw from the Canal and allow their forces to move in to protect it.[48] This seemed both to offer the opportunity to deflect an Israeli attack on Jordan, and to provide the much sought after pretext for attacking Nasser. To Scott Lucas, the decisive factor in leading Eden to take up the French plan was the need to protect the 'Iraqi–Jordanian axis'. This, he argues, was what made Eden abandon his earlier objections to acting with the Israelis.[49] However, Eden's eagerness may equally well be explained by the fact that the other pretexts, which had previously seemed to offer much less politically reckless expedients for the assault, had now all been exhausted. We do not need to construct ingenious arguments about Israeli exploitation of British fears over Jordan to explain Eden's actions. The Prime Minister had been backed into a corner. Any escape route, no matter how dangerous, was now welcome.

Eden moved quickly and, together with Lloyd, visited Paris on 16 October. Here they met the French Prime Minister Mollet and Foreign Minister Pineau and agreed on the Challe plan. The French then communicated the plan to the Israelis. At an ensuing tripartite meeting near Paris between 22 and 24 October the Israelis agreed not to attack Jordan, and set the date for their attack on Egypt for 29 October. While the Israelis were glad of the opportunity to attack Nasser, with Western support, before his army had had time to assimilate the large quantities of Russian arms purchased the previous year, Prime Minister David Ben Gurion, for one, was very suspicious of British motives. There was a great deal of haggling at the Sèvres meetings over the length of the delay between the Israeli invasion of the Sinai, the Anglo-French ultimatum, and the beginning of bombing operations against the Egyptian airfields. Although a compromise was eventually reached which satisfied minimum British concerns for international propriety, Ben Gurion remained worried by the threat to Israeli cities from air raids during this period.

Suspicions were to continue to be rife between the three new allies. Ben Gurion always referred to the Challe plan as 'the British' or 'the English plan', and regarded it as an example of British hypocrisy. In his diary on 17 October he had noted: 'the English plot, I imagine, is to get us involved with Nasser and bring about the occupation of Jordan by Iraq.'[50] Indeed, 'distrust of Britain's motives and policies was one of the features that brought the French and Israelis together.'[51] All the same, for their own reasons, all three countries now found it expedient to cooperate to defeat Nasser.

Eden gave his first indication of the way events were moving to the full British Cabinet on 23 October, when he noted that:

> when the Cabinet had last discussed the Suez situation on 18 October, there had been reason to believe that the issue

might be brought rapidly to a head as a result of military action by Israel against Egypt. From secret conversations which had been held in Paris with representatives of the Israeli Government, it now appeared that the Israelis would not alone launch a full-scale attack against Egypt.[52]

However, he refrained from bringing the Cabinet completely into his confidence regarding collusion, and on 25 October presented the Challe plan to them as though it were an Anglo-French contingency plan formed in the absence of certain information as to the Israelis' intentions. He went so far as to rebut explicitly the charge of collusion which he acknowledged might be brought against the British and French should these circumstances arise.[53] Only a very small circle had any idea of the precise direction of policy at this point, a matter which caused Eden himself some difficulties. He was evidently very uncomfortable about UK representative Pierson Dixon's attack on the Israelis at the UN on 19 October in the wake of the Qalqilya raid on Jordan. Dixon, of course, was not to realize that he was ruffling the feathers of projected allies.[54]

It is still unclear, however, how Eden hoped to deflect the allegations of collusion that were bound to be voiced once operations actually started. Eden's biographer acknowledges that the plan was 'plainly, as he knew, a pretext for achieving the destruction of Nasser; but it was so obvious a pretext that one still wonders why he believed it would not be seen as such'.[55] Harold Macmillan later admitted that it was a 'bad plan', but at the time he had no qualms about supporting it. 'The plan of October 25th sounded alright,' he later remarked, 'especially to a harassed Cabinet. . . . Collusion would not have been disreputable if Anthony hadn't said it wasn't true.'[56] The truth of the matter probably was that Eden and Macmillan alike were now so desperate for an expedient to attack Nasser before the opportunity passed, that they pushed any doubts about the British–French–Israeli plan to the back of their minds. They perhaps hoped that, if the operations were conducted quickly and successfully, the euphoria of victory would sweep away any concerns, in Britain at any rate, about the basis of their actions.

The one imponderable factor in all of this was the attitude

of the Americans, who had effectively been kept in the dark about British and French intentions from the beginning of October onwards. In fact the Administration's attention was distracted during the crucial weeks, firstly by the final stages of Eisenhower's re-election campaign, and secondly by the crisis in Hungary which erupted in the final days of the month. It was to be the concurrence of the Anglo-French operation in support of the Israelis with these two events which contributed to the strong sense of personal betrayal felt by Eisenhower.

In the final days before the mounting of the operation, then, it was mainly concern over the American response to the Anglo-French action which led Eden to insist on strict adherence to the cover story on the part of those who were aware of the true plan. The need to feign surprise at Israeli operations, and to make the Anglo-French ultimatum appear genuine, dictated that no obvious military preparations should be made before 29 October. Had Eden felt able to discard this crippling cover story, and position his forces to take immediate advantage of the Israeli action, the course of the crisis might have run very differently. As Eisenhower later commented, 'had they done it quickly, we would have accepted it, and waited to see . . .'[57] In this respect, a week was to prove to be far too long a time in politics.

The Israeli assault opened on schedule on 29 October, and was greeted initially by a silence in London and Paris which the US Administration could only regard as ominous. The following day saw the issuing of the Anglo-French ultimatum to the combatants, and the use of the vetoes of the two countries against a ceasefire resolution introduced in the United Nations Security Council by the US. With the expiry of the ultimatum, Anglo-French bombing raids began on Egyptian airfields late on 31 October. At the same time, the huge amphibious task force assembled in Malta set sail, harassed on its way by the US Sixth Fleet. Realizing that the British and French were serious about attacking Egypt, Nasser began to withdraw forces from the battle with Israel in the Sinai, in order to defend the Egyptian heartland.

Meanwhile, events in Hungary had come to a climax, with representatives of the Nagy Government first apparently receiving a sympathetic hearing from two Soviet Politburo representatives on 30 October, only for the Soviet leadership to take the decision to overthrow Nagy the following day. The coincidence of this date with the Anglo-French ultimatum contributed to the sense that the Soviets were seizing the opportunity presented by Anglo-French excesses in the Middle East to conduct their own excesses in Eastern Europe.

The full outline of the collusion between Britain, France and Israel had become clear to the US Administration by 1 November as the minutes of a National Security Council meeting make clear. Dulles told the gathering that:

> apparently . . . the British persuaded the Israelis not to strike at Jordan because to do so would involve the British in the invocation of the Anglo-Jordanian treaty. The result of British persuasion was, accordingly, an agreement that the Israelis would strike south at Egypt. This was a move which the British and French could use as a pretext to intervene to protect the Suez Canal.[58]

The meeting concluded that the whole world was looking to the US for leadership on this issue, and that she could not be seen to favour the side of the 'colonialist' powers, otherwise she would surrender the leadership of the developing world to the Soviet Union. Whatever the danger to her ties with Britain and France, therefore, it was imperative for the US to block their actions in this case by all available means short of force. The most immediate expression of this policy was the American move to have the debate over a ceasefire resolution transferred from the Security Council where the British and French vetoes had already blocked action, to the General Assembly, where it was passed overwhelmingly on 2 November. Although, with the fighting between Israel and Egypt virtually concluded, there were moves to forestall the Anglo-French landings within the British Cabinet on 4 November, the Cabinet voted to press ahead. Paratroop operations began on 5 November, and the huge amphibious invasion force, despite harassment on the way to its positions by the US Sixth Fleet, was ready for action on 6 November. However, by now American pressure of a different kind was beginning to have an effect.

As Diane Kunz has pointed out, 'sterling was dependent on the dollar as Britain was dependent on the US. Neither the currency nor the country could go it alone.'[59] The Anglo-French intervention had triggered a run on the pound which, because of the decision to opt for de facto convertibility of sterling 18 months earlier, and because of the Bank of England's advice to Macmillan not to follow the French in applying for a standby draw from the International Monetary Fund before the outbreak of war, could only be stemmed with American assistance. This assistance was to prove to be forthcoming only on the most rigorous terms. Although there is little doubt that dollar reserves were draining at a rapid rate, with losses of $85 million up to 6 November when the decision was taken to halt military operations,[60] some controversy surrounds the question as to whether this was the decisive factor in the cabinet's calculations. The attitude of Macmillan seems to be crucial here, for the Cabinet was likely to take his advice on financial matters.

Although he was more pressingly aware than anyone else of the difficulties of the pound, the single most important factor to sway his judgement was the severity of the American response.[61] A telephone call from Macmillan to Washington early on the morning of 6 November to ask for assistance in seeking aid from the IMF met with rebuff. Only if a ceasefire were forthcoming by midnight that night would the Americans consider the request.[62] If Britain could not go on without American financial assistance, it was even more the case that she could not continue in the face of such open American political hostility. All the same, considering Macmillan's earlier position, this was undoubtedly a sensational loss of nerve.[63]

Following a meeting on 6 November in which Macmillan, Lord Salisbury and Rab Butler all advocated a ceasefire, Eden telephoned Paris and Washington to announce Britain's intentions. However, although it might now have been expected that the US Administration would accede to British requests for financial assistance, the Americans drove a hard bargain. This seems to have been principally the result of the incapacitation of Dulles, who was hospitalized for much of November, and the influence exerted over US policy by Assistant Secretary of State Hoover and Treasury Secretary Humphrey during the weeks following the ceasefire. Firstly, Hoover reversed Eisenhower's initial inclination for a meeting with Eden, and then held in check his instinct for reconciliation.[64] Eden was virtually ostracized by the Americans from the day after the announcement of the ceasefire until his departure to Jamaica for health reasons on 23 November. Furthermore, both Hoover and Humphrey were determined that the British should not receive American aid until they had promised to withdraw from Egypt without preconditions. Their attitude was in part a result of concerns about possible Soviet intervention, shared, it should be noted, by Dulles and the President himself, and also, to some degree, of anti-British spleen.[65]

It was only with Eden out of the way in Jamaica, and the Americans satisfied that there was no imminent danger of Soviet action, that Eisenhower was finally able to bypass the State Department's objections, and open a channel of communications through Ambassador Aldrich to Butler and Macmillan. In turn, these two were able to manipulate opinion in the Conservative Party in favour of withdrawal from Suez. Macmillan managed at the same time to cultivate the appearance of reluctance, and to deflect the blame for the British retreat on to Butler.[66] With the hard bargaining completed, Harold Caccia, the new British Ambassador in Washington, conveyed to a recuperated Dulles on 3 December Britain's intention to complete withdrawal from the Canal within 14 days. The Secretary of State then acceded to British requests for immediate financial help. However, in the meantime, as will be seen, the US Administration had begun the process of reviewing its policy in the Middle East which was to result in the promulgation of the Eisenhower Doctrine in January 1957.

Having thus outlined the most significant details of the Suez Crisis, it is important now to assess its broader impact on the Anglo-American relationship in the Middle East, and on British strategy in the region. Alistair Horne argues that 'with the passage of more than three decades, Suez still appears as the historic watershed of the post-1945 era, certainly for Britain'.[67] Anthony Adamthwaite, too, concludes that 'notwithstanding revisionist efforts to play down Suez, it remains a major landmark'.[68] There can be little doubt that Suez was a significant blow to British self-confidence, and to the British capacity for independent action. However, accounts which see Suez as a decisive transition, with America taking over responsibility for the Middle East from Britain, are too revolutionary in their outlook.[69]

They neglect the evolutionary nature of this change throughout the 1950s. Thus, Howard Dooley perhaps goes too far when he asserts that 'when Great Britain slipped at Suez, responsibility for finding an answer to the Eastern Question passed irrevocably to Eisenhower's United States'.[70] It is certainly true that the Eisenhower Doctrine was to assert an increased US desire to assume unilateral responsibility for certain problems that arose in the region. However, as will be seen, the British did not retreat from the maintenance of what they considered to be important positions in the area by force, most notably in Jordan in 1958, and Kuwait in 1961.

Indeed, it seems to be the flaw in all accounts of the British role in the region which take 1956 as their terminal date to overestimate the impact of Suez. For Scott Lucas, for instance, 'Suez was a watershed for British influence, not only in the Middle East but throughout the world'.[71] The problem with defining watersheds, however, is that they impose a certain obligation to research the period subsequent to the event in question to the same degree as that prior to it. Neither Scott Lucas nor Keith Kyle, despite the admirable detail of their work on the crisis itself, bring to bear such evidence to support their sweeping contentions about Suez. The subsequent chapters of this study will show the fallacy of Lucas's statement that after Suez 'Britain paid the price of permanent subservience to American policy'.[72]

To do full justice to Scott Lucas's arguments, however, it must be admitted that if one contends that the basis of British policy was the promotion of the 'Iraqi–Jordanian axis' then Suez does look like more of a watershed. Soon after Suez Britain was to move to pull out of her treaty with Jordan. Nevertheless, when one approaches the period with a broader perspective, and recognizes the fundamental importance of Iraq alone in British strategy, then Suez appears less significant. The defeat of Nasser and the promotion of Iraq were themes of British policy which quite clearly transcended the Suez Crisis. Building up ties between Iraq and Jordan was only really one aspect of this broader strategy, and was, in any case, not wholly abandoned after Suez, as British support of the Arab Union in 1958 was to show.

It will be argued here, therefore, that British strategy in the region changed very little in the wake of Suez. Macmillan was every bit as determined as Eden had been to stop Nasser. Indeed, if as Chancellor Macmillan had been first in and first out of the struggle with Nasser, he was to be first back in as Prime Minister. The only difference between Macmillan and Eden was that Macmillan now laid much greater emphasis on the need to enlist American support to achieve British aims. The policy of promoting Iraqi leadership of the Arab world through the Baghdad Pact was also pursued with just as much vigour after Suez as before it. Despite Iraq's efforts to distance itself from Britain during the crisis, Prime Minister Nuri seems to have taken the decision to lay the blame at the door of the French in its aftermath. In respect of British strategy in the Middle East, therefore, it is the Iraqi Revolution of July 1958 which will emerge as more of a watershed.

The Anglo-American relationship in the area continued both before and after Suez to function on the basis of 'competitive cooperation' involving the maintenance of the respective interests of the two powers.[73] It is this constant thread that will serve to explain both the forthcoming instances of much closer cooperation between the two after Suez, and the instances of disagreement and mistrust. Indeed, the severity of the American response to the British action over Suez seems to have been dictated partly by circumstantial considerations and partly, as will be seen, by the continuing concern with blocking the expansion of Soviet influence in the area. Having decided to act over Suez, neither Dulles nor Eisenhower could understand why the British did not move quickly to seize the Canal and overthrow Nasser. As Dulles told the President, 'the British, having gone in, should not have stopped until they had toppled Nasser. As it was, they now had they worst of both possible worlds. They had received all the onus of making the move and, at the same time, had not accomplished their major purpose.'[74]

The crippling cover story to which Eden had insisted on sticking over Suez meant that the military operation could not begin immediately, however. During the interim the US felt constrained to pre-empt Soviet moves and take the lead in opposing colonialism at the United Nations. Then, after the British decision to halt operations, the unusual influence exerted over the Administration's policy owing to the incapacitation of Dulles, by Hoover and Humphrey, neither of whom had any great sympathy with Britain, dictated the severe conditions attached to American aid. In these respects, Suez was a true indication neither of Britain's ability to act as a world power, nor of the state of the Anglo-American relationship.

Perhaps John Darwin strikes the right note over Suez when stressing that its impact was not 'obvious, simple, clear-cut, or immediate', but rather 'subtle and diffuse'.[75] It highlighted the constraints on British policy, but did not lead to any fundamental shifts in this policy. What it did appear to do, however, was emphasize the importance of the American alliance in achieving its goals.

6 The Eisenhower Doctrine

One aspect of the Suez crisis which has so far gone unremarked in this study, was the Soviet attempt to capitalize on the Anglo-French action by issuing threats of nuclear retaliation against the two should they fail to halt operations. While these warnings were pieces of pure propaganda, they no doubt served to underline in the eyes of the US Administration the extent to which the Soviets might reap the dividends of the discomfiture of the old colonial powers. In fact, the Suez crisis instigated a debate within the Administration as to what US response would be appropriate to prevent the Soviet Union filling what was then perceived to be a power vacuum in the region. The 'Eisenhower Doctrine' or 'Middle East Resolution' which emerged from this process was, however, to prove to be more effective as a piece of cold war rhetoric and posturing than as any meaningful contribution to the furthering of peace or stability in the region.

In respect of its implications in the short term for Anglo-American relations in the Middle East, it is important to note that the internal debate in the US Administration over what course of action to pursue was conducted during November and the early part of December against the background of possibly the worst period of tension between Britain and America in the post-war years. As has been indicated, although Eisenhower had welcomed the British decision to call a cease-fire in the Suez campaign on the evening of 6 November, the financial aid that the British sought was certainly not immediately forthcoming. In addition, Eisenhower's initial agreement to talks with Eden in Washington in the first flush of his electoral triumph was withdrawn when he was advised that this would send the wrong signals about Washington's view of the crisis. It was to take four weeks of hard bargaining and a humiliating commitment to precipitous withdrawal from Egypt before American financial help was secured.

This period was characterized by a series of tense exchanges between the new British Ambassador in Washington, Sir Harold Caccia, and various Administration officials. For instance, when, on 23 November, Caccia broached with Assistant Secretary Hoover the question of renewed Anglo-American consultation on Middle Eastern issues, Hoover was 'somewhat taken . . . aback. On the American side there had been a growing feeling that we wished to avoid frank discussion, particularly over the Middle East'.[1] On the financial question, Caccia commented on 28 November, that: 'we have now passed the point where we are talking to friends. We are negotiating a business deal . . . and we are dealing with an Administration of business executives who rightly or wrongly consider that they are animated by the highest principles.'[2] Selwyn Lloyd too was surprised by the depth of the hostility of US officials, describing the American attitude as 'quite irrational', and even 'temporarily beyond the bounds of reason'.[3] Nevertheless, with terms for a withdrawal agreed between Dulles and Caccia on 3 December, the British sought to seize the opportunity to influence the direction of US policy in the region. The course for which the British pressed was, as might be expected, US adherence to the Baghdad Pact.[4]

In fact, the Administration's review of strategy had already been under way for some weeks by this point. The process appears to have begun with a memorandum circulated by William Burdett of the State Department's Near Eastern section on 13 November. This followed a call by Dulles for Department officials to contribute their thoughts on future Near Eastern policy. Burdett argued that the US needed to create and join some new broadly based organization involving the Afro-Asian countries to replace the Baghdad Pact, which was now tainted by its association with the discredited colonial power of Britain. Although objections were raised as to the effect that this would have on friendly countries which were members of the existing organization, particularly Iran and Turkey, Burdett's proposals indicated that the starting point of the debate, in the opinion of the Near Eastern section at least, was that the Baghdad Pact could never be a suitable vehicle for the promotion of US influence in the Middle East.[5]

As might be expected from the earlier debates on the question of US accession to the pact, however, the Joint Chiefs of Staff and the Defense Department expressed a different view. They felt that the US should now move to join the pact because the collapse of British influence might leave the existing friends of the West in the region militarily and politically isolated. Since the pact was a going concern, it offered the best chance of checking any Soviet aggression in the area. Its collapse would be 'an irretrievable loss to the best interests of the United States in the Middle East'.[6] Pressure was also exerted in favour of pact membership by the US Ambassadors to the respective regional members of the organization. The views of Gallman, the ambassador in Baghdad, are illustrative of the kind of sentiments which were expressed. The pact, in his opinion, was the best way to contain Soviet expansionism in the region. Nothing short of full US membership would be sufficient to stiffen the resolve of its indigenous members to resist Soviet pressure.[7]

However, the Near Eastern section remained unswayed by these appeals. In his reply to Ambassador Gallman, Assistant Secretary William Rountree argued that since the US was currently engaged in attempts to stabilize the region in the wake of Anglo-French military action, the 'US joining [a] Pact in which [the] British [were] a partner would pose [an] especially difficult problem . . .'. Rountree also repeated the complaint about the British role in the organization voiced by Dulles in April 1956 on the occasion of the last British-sponsored attempt to secure US accession, namely that the 'original US concept of [the] "Northern Tier" was one of an indigenous organization. The Baghdad Pact has been regarded by non-member states . . . as Western-inspired and in large part UK-dominated.'[8]

In addition to the internal debate over US adherence to the pact, the Administration was also subject to external pressures both for and against its membership. In the wake of a statement by the State Department on 29 November underlining the US's continued willingness to extend military and economic aid to the indigenous members of the pact, Abba Eban, the Israeli Ambassador in Washington, telephoned Rountree to emphasize the concern with which his government would regard any decision to go further and formally join the organization. Although Israeli influence over the Administration was very limited at this stage, Israeli pressure provided further evidence that the pact remained hostage to the political rivalries of the region.[9]

On the other hand, the indigenous members of the pact,

Turkey, Iran, Iraq and Pakistan, exerted their influence in favour of the US joining their organization. At a meeting with the ambassadors of the four countries on 4 December, in advance of his departure to the NATO conference, Dulles cited the familiar difficulties with Congress which stood in the way of a positive decision.[10] While the US still wanted to 'salvage' the Baghdad Pact, 'one of the problems involved in our adherence was that the Pact had unfortunately become involved in area politics and was not universally viewed as an instrument solely to oppose Communism and Soviet aggression'.[11]

Although there were strong views both for and against the pact within the Administration, instanced by a dossier of documents assembled by Rountree for Dulles before his departure to Paris for the NATO summit,[12] it seems that Dulles and Eisenhower's own inclinations were against joining the pact. The President had already indicated his views in a meeting on 21 November when he had commented that 'if the British get us into the Baghdad Pact – as the matter would appear to the Arabs – we would lose our influence with the Arabs'.[13] A critical factor in Eisenhower's assessment appears to have been the attitude of King Saud towards the pact.[14] As was shown earlier, Eisenhower had been in favour, since March 1956, of building up Saud as a rival to Nasser in the Middle East. In the aftermath of the Suez crisis, he began to push this policy forward with even greater vigour. During the meeting referred to above, he had 'reiterated his feeling that we should work toward building up King Saud as a major figure in the Middle Eastern area'. He again emphasized the importance in this respect of seeking a solution to the Buraimi Oasis dispute between Britain and Saudi Arabia.

While Dulles was away at the NATO summit discussing with Lloyd the possible shape of future US commitments in the Middle East, Eisenhower wrote to him reminding him that:

> I continue to believe, as I think you do, that one of the measures that we must take is to build up an Arab rival of Nasser, and the natural choice would seem to be the man you and I have often talked about. If we could build him up as the individual to capture the imagination of the Arab world, Nasser would not last long.[15]

In fact, by this stage, Dulles had resolved the debate over the US's next move in the region to three broad alternatives. At a meeting with Senator William Knowland, the Senate minority leader, on 8 December, Dulles told him that the choices which faced America were to join the Baghdad Pact, to try to organize a new grouping, or 'to deal on a bilateral basis with some maneuvrability'. The latter choice would involve 'a Congressional resolution authorizing the President to use the Armed Forces and to spend certain sums to bolster the military defense abilities and economies of countries whose governments showed a determination to combat Communist infiltration'. Dulles told Knowland that he had come to the conclusion that this third choice would be the best.[16]

However, Dulles was not yet prepared to acquaint the British with his conclusion. At a meeting with Selwyn Lloyd at the NATO summit on 10 December, he claimed that the US had reached no decision on the Baghdad Pact, although he did outline to the Foreign Secretary the three alternative courses he was considering. He also took the opportunity to stress once again the US view of the importance of Saudi Arabia as a counterpoise to Egypt, and the need for a solution to the Buraimi dispute.[17]

The new strategy was formally agreed at a meeting between Eisenhower, Dulles, Hoover, Wilson and Radford on 20 December.[18] Stressing once again the importance of Saudi objections to the pact in view of the need to build up King Saud as a counterpoise to Nasser, Dulles recommended seeking a Congressional resolution which would incorporate three elements. The first would empower the President to extend economic assistance to countries in the Middle East requesting it. Suez had made Eisenhower particularly aware of the importance of the Third World to the United States.[19] As far as he was concerned, if the US did not engage the Soviet Union in the battle for the hearts and minds of the 'emerging' nations, then she would in future see herself economically stifled through the denial of markets and raw materials. Although he had come to power in his first term on the slogan 'trade not aid', the theme of his second term as he saw it was almost the opposite – 'trade and aid'.

At the same time, therefore, as he was proposing to attach

$200 million of untargeted aid to the Eisenhower Doctrine, he was also negotiating with a largely unreceptive Congress for a much larger $2 billion Development Loan Fund spread over three years for Third World countries. To Eisenhower's way of thinking, comparatively small sums allocated as aid could prove to be much more effective in winning over these nations than much larger sums spent on traditional methods of military defence. The Middle East Resolution drew its inspiration, therefore, on the one hand, from the President's preoccupation with the efficacy of aid as an instrument of foreign policy.

The second provision of the new proposal was to extend American arms aid to countries in the Middle East which might request it. This was intended to provide an alternative to the supply of weaponry from the Soviet Union, although in this respect the US was rather more limited in its scope for manoeuvre by the need to consider the position of the Israelis. However, because of Israel's attack on Egypt during the Suez War, and her continuing refusal to withdraw from land occupied in the Sinai, until her claims regarding the passage of Israeli ships through the Straits of Tiran had been settled, the Israeli lobby in Washington was in a comparatively weak position at this point. Still, the Administration had to tread carefully.

The final element of the new strategy, and that which gained it the greatest prominence, was the assertion that: 'if the President determines the necessity thereof, the United States is prepared to use armed forces to assist any such nation or group of nations [in the Middle East] requesting assistance against armed aggression from any country controlled by international communism.' The intention of this proposal was to serve a direct and public warning to the Soviet Union that the US intended to defend its friends in the region. It was also designed to tap a reliable well of anti-Communist sentiment at home and to 'facilitate the emergence of a new "national consensus" in foreign affairs . . .'.[20] It was intended to be a symbol of executive–legislative agreement over American goals in the Middle East.

Eisenhower briefed legislative leaders as to his new strategy at a meeting on 1 January 1957,[21] the British and French having already been formally notified of American intentions on 29 December.[22] In fact, the British had continued trying up to the last minute to persuade the Americans to opt for pact membership instead.[23] The Middle East Resolution, therefore, was something of a setback for them, especially since it was accompanied by a drive to promote Saudi leadership of the Arab world in rivalry to Egypt rather than that of Iraq. Although Harold Macmillan later represented the Eisenhower Doctrine in his memoirs as 'a gallant effort to shut the stable door after the horse had bolted', and as 'welcome to us', it may be surmised that at the time he was less than pleased at the further rebuff it delivered to British attempts to secure American membership of the Baghdad Pact. Indeed, in a contemporary private letter to Anthony Eden, Macmillan referred to the Eisenhower Doctrine as 'weak ... in many ways'.[24]

In fact, the resolution also ran into substantial difficulties at home in the Senate in particular. Many of the problems surrounded its vagueness.[25] The area it covered, although referred to broadly as the 'Middle East' went undefined. Also, objections were raised as to how one could identify a country 'controlled by international Communism'. As regards the powers granted to the President under the resolution, senators of one persuasion argued that he already had the necessary authority to act, while others asserted that he had requested what amounted to a 'blank check' from Congress, expecting it to approve in advance whatever measures he decided to take. Although it was originally intended as a demonstration of 'national unity' in foreign affairs, in the end the Eisenhower Doctrine itself proved productive of intense partisan controversy.[26]

Ultimately, the Doctrine was only ratified by the Senate on the basis of two considerations. The first, often repeated by Dulles, was that the White House was merely asking for the Congress to express its opposition to Communist expansionism, thereby reaffirming the fundamental continuity in American foreign policy. The second was that congressional repudiation of the President's diplomatic leadership could have damaging consequences for the US's international position.[27] These two considerations underline the extent to which the Doctrine should really be seen as a form of rhetorical deterrent directed towards the Soviet Union, 'an abstract, inflatable ideological device'.[28] Unfortunately, as the Administration was to discover, rhetoric was to prove to be an unsound basis for practical intervention in the region.

For instance, the operation in Lebanon in July 1958, often cited as the prime instance of the Doctrine in action, in fact served to reveal its weaknesses in application. During the course of the crisis preceding the American landings, Dulles argued that:

> he did not see how we could invoke the provisions of the Middle East Doctrine relating to the use of United States forces specifically, since that would entail a finding that the United Arab Republic had attacked Lebanon and that the United Arab Republic was under the control of international Communism.[29]

Dulles preferred to regard the Lebanese crisis as a case in which the US could act 'in accordance with the rules of the game as set forth in the Charter of the United Nations'. The Eisenhower Doctrine provided little more than ideological window-dressing for American action in this case.

The hearings over the resolution were also the occasion for a series of anti-British comments by Dulles which underlined the continuing gulf between the two powers at this stage over future policy in the Middle East. Comments such as 'I cannot think of anything that would more surely turn the area over to international communism than for us to go in there hand in hand with the British and French' caused a great deal of private resentment on the British side. Although Harold Caccia pointed out that the most charitable interpretation was that Dulles was being led by his lawyer's instinct to try all means to win his case, others were not so understanding. Dulles's attitude was stigmatized by William Morris, the First Secretary at the Washington Embassy, as a 'sanctimonious, subjective moral judgement'.[30]

All the same, from the British point of view there was little sense in trying to oppose the Doctrine. The best course seemed to be to work with it and attempt to divert any assistance it provided towards purposes favoured by Britain. As a Cabinet discussion document acknowledged:

> Benefits under the doctrine are not to be limited to allies; they are also available for 'countries dedicated to the maintenance of their national independence.' But benefits, by this

definition, should not go to those who are actively collaborating in the pursuit of Soviet aims. In practice this should produce the sort of grouping of well-disposed countries which is our aim.[31]

Nevertheless, the implication of the American refusal to join the pact was that Britain would have to devote even more resources to its maintenance and support. The Baghdad Pact was 'now more than ever the lynch-pin' of Britain's position in the region.[32] It should be employed as 'a means of retaining a measure of influence in the Middle East'.[33]

A double blow, however, was administered at this point to British hopes of persuading the Americans to fall in with the strategy of promoting Iraqi leadership of the Arab world. In addition to its refusal to join the Baghdad Pact, the Administration seized the opportunity to grant King Saud's request for a visit to the United States at the end of January 1957, so that Eisenhower could assess face to face the possibility of advancing him as an Arab rival to Nasser. According to his own account, Eisenhower found Saud 'introspective and shy'.[34] He was also evidently rather shocked by what he termed the King's medievalism, epitomized by his repeated references to 'my people'. Nevertheless, he secured his grudging support for the Eisenhower Doctrine. Saud's character hardly qualified him to be a rival to Nasser, but, since the President felt there was no other suitable candidate, he decided that 'Saud would be "the person we tie to." '[35]

In fact, a whole number of additional reasons made Saud an unsuitable choice for the role which Eisenhower sought to thrust upon him. Although Dulles had acknowledged in his discussion with Selwyn Lloyd in Paris that Saud 'was not the master in his own house',[36] both he and Eisenhower evidently hoped that Saud would become so in the near future. In reality, their hopes were to prove ill-founded.[37] Saud's rampant corruption and, more importantly, his mishandling of politics at home, made him a particularly unsuitable leader even of his own country, never mind the whole Arab world. His long-standing rivalry with his brother Feisal was far from resolved, and as Saud alienated more and more of the influential princes, his position became progressively weaker.[38] One could argue that Eisenhower and Dulles could not have been expected to see the course events would take up to the palace coup in March 1958. What could have been expected, however, is that they should have seen the folly of resting such hopes on a man who was demonstrably unsuited to fulfilling them.

In fact, the whole notion of promoting Saud as Nasser's rival showed how shallow the American understanding of the Arab nationalist movement was. Simply because, as Eisenhower stressed, Saud held a position of spiritual respect in the Arab world as custodian of the Muslim Holy Places, he could not be expected to command similar esteem in a political context. Politics was much more a question of charisma, which Saud lacked and Nasser possessed. Perhaps too by suggesting that the Arab nationalist movement could be channelled into directions more favourable to the West simply by replacing one leader with another, Eisenhower neglected some of the deeper sentiments which Nasser had tapped. There was a genuine desire to cast off what was seen as the yoke of external domination which, because of the recent history of the region, was particularly associated with the Western powers.

Whatever the weaknesses of the new strategy, however, Eisenhower determined to pursue it. The promotion of Saud, together with the promulgation of the Eisenhower Doctrine, were certainly evidence of greater American activity in the Middle East. However, we should be wary of arguing that the US somehow now picked up the mantle of power cast off by the British after Suez. As has been indicated, the British were resolved to pursue the promotion of their interests through the Baghdad Pact with even greater vigour after the Suez debacle, and were certainly not ready to cast off any mantle. Moreover, while the Eisenhower Doctrine was evidence of a more systematic American desire to take on responsibilities, it did not indicate any sudden shift in the balance between the two powers in the region. Although the Americans were to act independently of the British when their interests demanded in the aftermath of its promulgation, the Anderson mission a year earlier, for instance, had shown that they had been prepared to act in this way before Suez.

Furthermore, the policy of promoting Saud which was now pursued had been conceived as early as March 1956 and, although Suez gave it added impetus, it was not responsible for its inception. The period after the passing of the Middle East resolution early in March 1957, therefore, was to be characterized by a similar patchwork as had gone before of cooperation and conflict on the basis of perceptions of threat and of interest between Britain and America.

7 The Bermuda Conference and the April 1957 Crisis in Jordan

Following the decision to halt operations on the Suez Canal on 6 November, British politics had been in ferment. It was Anthony Eden's misfortune at this point to be obliged, under doctor's advice, to take a complete break from work. Accordingly, on 23 November, he flew out of London bound for Jamaica. On his return, although he evidently believed that he could resume his position as Prime Minister, his reception in the House of Commons showed that he certainly could not command majority support, even within his own party. Although some scholars argue that his continuing bad health was the explanation for his swift decision to resign on 9 January, it is difficult to believe that the weakness of his political position did not have a bearing on that decision.[1]

Indeed, while he had been away, a good deal of politicking had been taking place, with the US Administration itself implicated in behind the scenes communications with both Rab Butler and Harold Macmillan.[2] However, it was Macmillan's superior public performances during the period of Eden's absence, together with long-standing doubts about Butler entertained by the Tory hierarchy, stemming from pre-Second World War days, that helped to tip the balance of succession in the Chancellor's favour. One of Macmillan's primary goals was to restore at least some measure of understanding to Anglo-American relations; indeed, this was the sentiment which was to underpin the forthcoming Bermuda conference of March 1957. However, first, like the American President, he was anxious to see the unblocking of the Suez Canal so that oil supplies could resume to Western Europe by that route. In addition to this, Eisenhower was determined to secure a negotiated end to

114

the continuing Israeli occupation of the Gaza Strip, which Prime Minister Ben Gurion was evidently intent on using as a bargaining chip to guarantee Israel's free passage through the Straits of Tiran.

Ben Gurion was determined that Israel should not emerge from the Suez crisis empty-handed. Israel had originally launched her attack for three reasons: to defeat Nasser before his army could assimilate the newly purchased Soviet weaponry; to end the Fedayeen raids from the Gaza Strip; and to secure passage through the Straits of Tiran to allow for the development of the port of Eilat. Although it could be argued that the successes of the Israeli forces in the war had in part achieved the first purpose, Ben Gurion and his principal advisers, Moshe Dayan and Shimon Peres at the Defence Ministry, and Golda Meir at the Foreign Office, were determined that the other objectives should not be abandoned.

Eisenhower, it seems, did not grasp the strategic considerations which lay behind the Israeli determination to hold fast over Gaza and Sharm-el-Sheikh. Discussing the question with Dulles on 12 January, he declared himself confused. Since it had no natural resources, who would want the Gaza Strip?[3] In endeavouring to maintain its hold on Gaza and Sharm-el-Sheikh, the Israeli Government was able to enlist the support of powerful allies within the US. A press campaign orchestrated by the Israeli Embassy had some success, with most of the major newspapers arguing that the restoration of the antebellum status quo was unrealistic. The political difficulties which Israeli sympathizers could cause for the President in Congress were evidenced by the fact that 41 Republicans and 75 Democrats supported Israel's demand that any withdrawal from Gaza should be contingent on direct peace negotiations with Egypt.[4]

Nevertheless, the Administration continued to exert public and private pressure on Israel to withdraw, with Dulles mentioning the possibility of sanctions in a press conference of 19 February. This caused a further furore in Congress and did not seem to diminish Israeli intransigence. However, patient diplomacy involving the French Foreign Minister Christian Pineau moved matters forward towards the end of the month, and on 1 March Golda Meir, the Israeli Foreign Minister, announced to the United Nations General Assembly

Israel's intention to withdraw. The last Israeli troops left the Gaza Strip on 11 March. Ben Gurion's diary entry for the previous day suggests three explanations as to why the Israeli Government had eventually chosen to abandon the Strip. Firstly, French offers of diplomatic, economic and military aid including, in all probability, help with the Israeli nuclear research programme. Secondly, the costs of occupying Gaza about which Ben Gurion, unlike some of his colleagues, had always been concerned. He had earlier noted that 'if our enemies were clever they would surrender Gaza to us and withdraw all of the UN agencies'.[5] Finally, the threat of United Nations sanctions, potentially supported by the United States.[6]

The Israeli decision opened the way to an agreement for the clearing of the Suez Canal by the Egyptians, thus satisfying one of the principal concerns of the British Government. However, unlike the French, the British had played very little role in the negotiations to secure Israeli withdrawal. Macmillan's priorities now lay not in determining the finer points of the UN presence in Gaza, but in consolidating his position at home and restoring some measure of cordiality in Anglo-American relations.

The initiative for the Bermuda conference taken against the background of these events, however, seems to have come from the American side in the shape of a private message from Eisenhower to Macmillan on 22 January. This suggested discussions between the two leaders on British territory at Bermuda during March.[7] Although the Administration was not prepared to concede that it had in any way betrayed the British over Suez, it recognized the pressing need to put relations on a sounder footing in view of the importance to the US of British positions around the world. As a State Department background briefing paper for the conference acknowledged:

> the US needs the alliance for much the same reasons as does Britain. We rely on British help, both material and psychological, to implement our policies towards the Commonwealth, Eastern Europe, South Asia and some areas of the Far East. . . . In addition, we rely heavily on Britain in the military field. Their contribution, next to our own, forms the largest national component in NATO . . .[8]

Eisenhower's approach delighted Macmillan. Although he had made it his principal purpose to seek a reconciliation in Anglo-American relations, the Prime Minister had resolved not to play the role of suitor in order to underline the British sense of hurt at being 'let down' over Suez.[9]

While the Bermuda meeting had a very public purpose to accomplish in terms of demonstrating the renewed friendliness between the two countries, personified in the relationship between Eisenhower and Macmillan, the records of the conference reveal that in private there was a good deal of hard bargaining over Middle Eastern problems. Matters were dominated by the questions of what attitude to adopt towards Nasser, and how to deal with the Buraimi Oasis dispute between Britain and Saudi Arabia.

On Nasser, Eisenhower's own account in his memoirs reveals that:

> Foster and I at first found it difficult to talk constructively with our British colleagues about Suez because of the blinding bitterness they felt toward Nasser. Prime Minister Harold Macmillan and Foreign Minister Selwyn Lloyd were so obsessed with the possibilities of getting rid of Nasser that they were handicapped in searching, objectively, for any realistic method of operating the Canal.[10]

In fact a State Department briefing paper prepared for the conference under the title 'Long Range Policy toward Egypt', emphasized the continuity in the US attitude on Nasser with that established in the policy review a year earlier. While recognizing that the present policies of the Egyptian Government were 'inimical to the interests of the West', it stressed that the US would 'not become involved in attempts to unseat the Nasser regime'. It referred instead to the need to isolate Egypt politically from the rest of the region, while working in the longer term for a more favourable orientation of Egyptian policy. America's broader objectives with regard to Egypt were: 'the restoration of close relations with an Egypt which lives up to her international obligations, recognizes the advantages of close relations with the West and is prepared to curtail her relationships with the USSR.'[11]

In all of this, there was no specific exclusion of the possibility that a future, more cooperative, Egypt might still be governed by Nasser. Indeed, while recognizing his responsibility for the negative trend which Egyptian policy had taken up to that point, the paper stressed the strength of his internal position, thus implying that Nasser was the leader who would have to be dealt with for the foreseeable future. This mirrored the earlier policy, established in March 1956, of working to isolate Nasser in the short term, while still allowing him a bridge back to better relations with the West should he seek them in the longer term.

The same paper correctly anticipated that the British attitude would be that it was 'virtually impossible to do business with Nasser'. In fact the British copy of Macmillan's draft peroration to the conference on the Middle East confirms this supposition, arguing that: 'in Egypt it seems altogether unlikely that Nasser himself can or will change to a policy of cooperating with the West on any terms which we can offer him.'[12] Eisenhower noted that:

> early in the conversation, Lloyd launched into a denunciation of Nasser, condemning his motives, plans, and trustworthiness. He feared that Nasser, in pursuing his soaring ambitions, would probably become the stooge of the Kremlin, just as Mussolini had become the stooge of Hitler.[13]

Thus, the same difference in outlook towards Nasser which had emerged following the review of policy in the Middle East by both countries in March 1956, and which was to endure at least until the end of the 1950s, was evident at Bermuda.

In general, of course, both governments could agree about the need to isolate Nasser in the short term by working to promote alternative Arab leaders. However, here again, differences emerged on the more specific question of who should take on this role. Eisenhower and Dulles chose Bermuda to launch their most vigorous attempt to date to induce the British to settle the Buraimi Oasis dispute with Saudi Arabia, so as to facilitate the advancement of King Saud as a rival to Nasser. Dulles argued that:

> Nasser's prestige seemed to be descending, and we should try to promote King Saud as a rival Arab leader, the main

trouble being the Buraimi issue. Thus, if the UK could find a solution to this problem, we might promote an evolution in this area which would eventually help sidetrack Nasser.[14]

British accounts too confirm that both Eisenhower and Dulles 'continued for some time on the importance of building up King Saud as the best means of diminishing Nasser'.[15] However, Macmillan and Lloyd refused to give ground. They argued that the British position in the Persian Gulf was a vital national interest, and that their ability to defend the area hinged on protecting the rights of the rulers of Abu Dhabi and Muscat and Oman over Buraimi. Furthermore, they did not believe that Saud's own position was sufficiently secure at home to enable him to play the broader role in the Arab world which the Americans envisaged for him. Still, at Eisenhower's instigation it was agreed to set up a Joint Planning Staff to look at the differences between the two over the Middle East to which each country would assign one permanent representative. It was hoped by this means at least to lay the foundations for closer consultation between the two over policy in the region by addressing problems such as Buraimi.[16]

Thus, no real progress was made at the meeting in settling the differences between Britain and America over strategy in the Middle East. As the *New York Times* reported, 'Administration officials privately said it would be unwise to overlook the importance of points on which differences remained or on which decisions were left open.'[17] The only mildly positive development in this respect from the British point of view was the Americans' announcement that they would be prepared to join the military committee of the Baghdad Pact. However, too much should not be made of this development since it did nothing to bridge the divide between the two over a regional policy based on Saudi Arabia or one based on Iraq. As a telegram from Selwyn Lloyd to Harold Caccia at the end of January had stressed, membership of the military committee was 'very much a second best and no substitute for full accession to the pact'.[18] Indeed the US move served, if anything, to underline the political rift between the two over the pact, since by joining the military committee and refusing to accede to the pact itself, the Administration stressed that it was only prepared to associate itself with the military goals of the organization, and wanted to dissociate itself from its politics.

To underline the limitations of the progress made on consultation between the two countries at Bermuda, we need look no further than the Americans' response to the crisis which broke out in Jordan early in April 1957, immediately after the conference. This was occasioned by King Hussein's decision to dismiss the pro-Nasserite Prime Minister Suleiman Nabulsi who had come to power on a wave of popular sentiment in elections conducted against the background of the Suez crisis in October 1956. Although Nabulsi and the King had agreed over their response to the British–French–Israeli offensive in Egypt, with the King having expressed his readiness to extend armed assistance to Nasser,[19] and also over the negotiations for the termination of the Anglo-Jordanian Treaty and its replacement by an Arab Solidarity Agreement with Syria, Saudi Arabia and Egypt, thereafter their paths diverged. The Eisenhower Doctrine helped to drive a wedge between them, with the King suggesting that American aid would be welcome if it was offered without political strings.[20]

In the initial stages of the April crisis, US records indicate that there was an agreement with the British to discuss together developments in Jordan.[21] However, as events gathered pace, the joint assessment on the ground in Jordan was abandoned. Contacts were to be continued at the level of the State Department and the British Embassy in Washington.[22] Nevertheless, the consultative process was effectively bypassed by Eisenhower, who, impressed by the King's demonstration of resolve in putting down the army mutiny at Zerqa which followed his dismissal of Nabulsi, ordered the sending of the Sixth Fleet to a forward position in the Eastern Mediterranean as a high profile gesture of support for Hussein.[23]

Although it was agreed in the British Cabinet that 'it would be politically desirable to indicate that the UK had been informed in advance of the recent action by the US Government in support of King Hussein, in order to show that there was effective Anglo-American cooperation in the Middle East', this conclusion was somewhat machiavellian.[24] US documents show that Lloyd had approached Ambassador Whitney during the previous weekend at Chequers, asking 'whether any US–UK consultation has taken place or is contemplated [in] Washington re [the] US naval deployment [in the] Eastern Mediterranean'.[25] His purpose was evidently to prepare himself to field critical parliamentary questions over the extent of the government's knowledge of the US Administration's plans. Dulles's comment to Lloyd in Bonn the following week that 'he had mentioned to Caccia that [the] move was one of several we were making in support of King Hussein',[26] hardly looks like 'effective Anglo-American cooperation'.

Although the British Government was not directly critical of the unilateral US action, the military was not so reticent. The British Commander in the Eastern Mediterranean 'complained bitterly', in what his interlocutor described as 'salty language', about the lack of consultation over the movements of the Sixth Fleet.[27]

Thus, although the Bermuda conference provided the opportunity for Eisenhower and Macmillan to stress their strong personal friendship,[28] and to express good intentions about the need for closer coordination of strategy in the Middle East, the Jordan crisis showed that, as before, the Americans were willing to take their own initiatives in the region. It also indicated, somewhat ominously for the British, that the Eisenhower Doctrine was perhaps best suited to the role of a rhetorical justification for unilateral US demonstrations of resolve in support of friendly regimes in the area.

8 The Syrian Crisis and the October 1957 Talks

The crucial events which were to bring about much closer Anglo-American consultation over the Middle East took place in Syria. The main point about the Syrian crisis which began early in August 1957 was that in its initial stages it appeared to present a challenge which incorporated both of the different primary threats which concerned the two powers in the region. In other words, during the months of August to October 1957, it seemed to the American government that the Soviet Union, acting at first in conjunction with Nasser, was fermenting an anti-Western coup in Syria with the object of establishing a Soviet satellite state in the heart of the Middle East. The British were similarly concerned that Nasser, acting as the Soviets' agent, might gain control of Syria in alliance with the indigenous Communists and create a superstate which would straddle the oil supply routes via the Suez Canal and the Iraqi Petroleum Company pipelines.

In the months from the close of the Bermuda conference until the outbreak of the Syrian crisis a series of contacts had taken place between British and American officials aimed at narrowing the gap between the two countries over various Middle Eastern issues. As might be expected from the substance of the Bermuda discussions, the principal issues on which the meetings concentrated were the future of the British position in the Persian Gulf, with particular reference to the question of the Buraimi Oasis, and the policy to be adopted towards Egypt. Broadening out from this base, however, the discussions also touched on the issue of the maintenance of oil supplies from the Gulf.

Reporting on the framework for these discussions established at Bermuda to the Cabinet Official Committee on the Middle East, Harold Beeley noted that the President's initial proposal for a joint planning operation to work out a common Middle East policy, with the apparent object of bridging the gap over the promotion of King Saud, 'had subsequently been somewhat diluted by Dulles who was anxious to maintain the US position in out-bidding the Russians for the support of the uncommitted countries, in which he felt that too close association with the UK would not be of assistance.'[1]

Nevertheless, despite Dulles's downgrading of the consultation process, talks took place in April and again in July between British and American representatives in Washington. Although there were some minor shifts in the stance of both countries little real progress was made in narrowing the gap over Saudi Arabia and Buraimi. The British gained some small satisfaction in persuading the Americans to drop their reference to 'elements of weakness' in their position in the Persian Gulf.[2] However, the degree of American pressure exerted over Buraimi remained out of all proportion to the significance of the problem itself.[3] In fact, the speed with which the Buraimi dispute was to lapse into obscurity after the collapse of American attempts to build up Saud early in 1958 shows the extent to which it had only assumed importance at this stage as an impediment that Saud was putting in the way of closer cooperation in US plans.[4]

A further test of Anglo-American cooperation in the Gulf was posed by the outbreak of civil strife in Oman in July 1957. An earlier round of conflict at the end of 1955 between the Sultan, backed by the British, and the Imam, supported by the Saudis, had seen the Sultan emerge victorious. However, the return of the Imam's brother Talib from exile in Saudi Arabia precipitated renewed hostilities. Although Saudi involvement was less clear-cut than in the earlier round of fighting,[5] the Americans were nevertheless very concerned by the British decision to accede to the Sultan's request to intervene in his support.

American concerns were heightened still further when, despite earlier British claims that their intervention would only be at the level of air support, ground forces had to be deployed in support of the Sultan. Dulles expressed his fear to the President that the tensions caused by this development would be such that: 'we would be caught between our desire to maintain an influence in some of the Arab countries, notably Saudi Arabia, and our desire to maintain good ties with the UK. A small scale Suez might be in the making.'[6] However – fortunately, from the point of view of Anglo-American relations – the operation was concluded quickly and successfully without exciting the anticipated tensions with Saudi Arabia. Still, from the British standpoint, it was viewed as having provided further evidence of what was believed to be Nasser's ability to incite trouble for them throughout the region, even in the Persian Gulf.

On Nasser himself, a Foreign Office memorandum of 10 May described the difference between Britain and America as 'manageably small'.[7] The Americans, it was reported, had concurred with the British view that Egypt would 'remain for a long time the centre of discontent and revolutionary tendencies in the Arab world . . .', and that Nasser was 'hardly likely to change to sincere cooperation with the West' on any terms which might be offered to him. However, despite what the British represented as a meeting of minds, the underlying difference between the two over Nasser remained. There was still a vital element of pragmatism in the US approach to Nasser which was to show through during the later stages of the Syrian crisis and after the formation of the United Arab Republic. The fact that the Americans did not regard Nasser as an inveterate enemy in the same way as did the British helps to explain the US Administration's continued refusal to fall in with British schemes for the subversion of his regime.

Thus the British suggestion, apparently put forward at the April meeting with the Americans, that the two countries should 'work out and hold in readiness a programme of support for an alternative government' and 'agree upon the psychological moment and the means for making the existence of such a programme appropriately known in Egypt' does not appear to have been taken up by the US side. In fact the whole scheme on the British part seems to have been based on some rather wishful thinking as to the extent of opposition to Nasser within Egypt, which the US certainly did not share.[8]

It was, as has been suggested, force of circumstance rather than ivory tower planning which brought the British and American Governments much closer together over the Middle East during the autumn of 1957. The Americans had already shown themselves to be preoccupied by the possibility of a Communist takeover in Syria, instanced by their involvement in the planning for 'Operation Straggle' in the previous year.

Syria had also been the first Arab state openly to condemn the Eisenhower Doctrine in a statement issued by the government on 10 January, and had likewise censured America's attempts to bolster King Hussein during the April crisis in Jordan.

Three key events during August brought Syria to the forefront of American concerns. The first was the signature in Moscow on 6 August of a wide-ranging economic and technical agreement between Syria and the Soviet Union. This was followed on 13 August by the expulsion of three American diplomats accused of plotting to overthrow the Syrian regime. Finally came the retirement of the Army Commander-in-Chief, Nizam al-Din, and his replacement on 17 August by Afif al-Bizri, an officer of suspected Soviet sympathies. His appointment was accompanied by the purging of a dozen other senior officers.[9]

It may well be that the agreement with Moscow was simply the natural climax of a process of cooperation that had been continuing over a period of two years, that there was in fact strong evidence to support the claim that the expelled American diplomats had been engaged in spying activities, and that Bizri was appointed merely as an uncontroversial figure within the army to bypass the feuding of the general staff.[10] However, to Washington, primed for the probability of Soviet moves to subvert the Middle East, a sudden and dramatic coup appeared to be in the making. Although Dulles advised the President on 20 August not to declare that Syria was now 'controlled by international Communism', since this would involve the invocation of the Middle East Resolution, he similarly counselled him to 'avoid any statement that it is *not* so controlled'. The reason for this was that owing to the virtual blockade of the US Embassy, 'we cannot yet make a clear political judgment as to the actual extent of Communist penetration'. Indeed, at this stage, Dulles seems to have been unsure how to react. However, events in Syria seemed to fall in with his theory that 'the Middle East . . . has recently become a prime target of Communist aspirations'.[11]

The British too were pessimistic about the prospects in Syria. A cable from the Foreign Office to Ambassador Michael Wright in Baghdad on the same day argued that recent events marked the 'consolidation of real power in the hands of left wing elements in the Army'. It was now 'extremely improbable' that any forces in Syria could reverse the trend towards deeper involvement with the Soviet bloc.[12]

The American response was to despatch Loy Henderson, Deputy Under-Secretary of State for Administration, on a mission to the region to seek the views of Syria's neighbours on developments there, and to coordinate countermeasures.[13] Already, however, Dulles was referring to the possibility that in Syria 'we must be prepared to take some serious risks to avoid even greater risks and dangers later on'.[14] Henderson's was certainly a high profile mission, and one which 'seemed guaranteed to cause the maximum hostile fuss, to sacrifice the possible advantages of secret diplomacy and to yield no hard, unbiased information on the situation inside Syria', which he did not visit.[15] The first stop on his tour was Ankara, where he conferred with Turkish Prime Minister Menderes, and also King Hussein of Jordan and King Feisal of Iraq, who had travelled there to meet him. From there he flew to Lebanon to meet President Chamoun and then back to Ankara for further talks with Menderes and the Crown Prince of Iraq together with his Chief of Staff.

Henderson's initial contacts in Ankara appear to have convinced him that a Soviet satellite was in the making for, during his meetings in Beirut, he told the Lebanese Foreign Minister Charles Malik, and Prime Minister Sami Solh that:

> if [the] present Syrian regime remained in power, it [was] almost inevitable that in [a] relatively short time Syria would be converted into [a] Soviet satellite which would serve as [a] heavily armed Communist fortress in [the] Middle East ... [the] continuation of [the] process now working in Syria would mean [the] loss of [the] Middle East to [the] free world and [a] threat to world peace.[16]

Henderson seems to have persuaded a receptive Dulles that the situation was extremely serious: on 30 August, Dulles called in Senator Knowland, the Republican minority leader, to tell him 'very privately and confidentially, that there were possibilities of hostilities in the Middle East'.[17] The US Administration was particularly concerned that the Israelis might decide to launch a pre-emptive strike on Syria, and sought to restrain them with every means at their disposal.[18] Dulles also felt that America would have to honour its commitments to Turkey under both NATO and the Middle East Resolution should they be called upon.

On the British side, Harold Macmillan, sensing the possibility that the US viewed developments in Syria with sufficient seriousness to consider broader plans to alter the situation in the region, capitalized on Dulles's fears to instigate a secret correspondence. This was designed to explore the possibility of the subversion of the Syrian regime. The Syrian crisis brought to the fore the 'hawkish' views on the Middle East which Macmillan had held consistently over the previous two years. In Cabinet on 27 August, he had argued that: 'the Soviet Government had substantially increased their hold over Syria and there was a serious risk that the country would soon fall wholly within the influence of the Soviet Union.' This was a particularly dangerous development in view of the fact that the pipelines passing through Syria could handle 25 million tons of Iraqi oil a year, and a further 12 million tons from Saudi Arabia. In view of this,

> it was . . . important that no action should be taken which might provoke Syria to cut these pipelines unless it formed part of a considered plan, which the United States Government were prepared to carry through, for restoring the whole position in the Middle East in favour of the Western Powers. It should not be overlooked that action which led the Syrians to interfere with the pipelines might also cause the Egyptian Government to restrict the passage of oil through the Suez Canal . . .[19]

The clear implication of this was that Macmillan saw the Syrian crisis as an opportunity to enlist US support in his cherished ambition of seizing back the initiative in the region from Nasser. If operations were to be contemplated against Syria, then the link he drew between any Syrian decision to close the oil pipelines and the possibility that Egypt might close the Canal suggested that they would also have to be considered against Egypt. This was exactly the sort of language that Macmillan was to use again a year later in the crisis occasioned by the Iraqi Revolution, and which was so to alarm Eisenhower and Dulles.

Although the Americans did not take on board Macmillan's broader plans, Dulles's reception of the idea of an operation to drive Communist influence out of Syria was much more positive. He agreed that the best approach would be for Syria's neighbours to take the initiative, as had been the case with 'Straggle'. Through Ambassador Harold Caccia, he communicated to Macmillan his view that: 'if such an operation started in circumstances which the US approved, the US would feel committed to make sure that it did not fail.' Caccia, however, counselled caution. Although Dulles appeared to him to be 'trying to screw up his courage to act', he warned that 'if anything goes wrong, you may be sure that Mr Dulles will place the blame elsewhere'.[20]

On 7 September the US made public by means of a Presidential statement its conclusion that Syria had become a base for military and subversive actions in the region. Invoking the Eisenhower Doctrine, the President asserted that: 'if any of Syria's Arab neighbours were physically attacked by the Sino-Soviet bloc, the United States, upon request, would be prepared to use its own armed forces to assist any such nation of group of nations against such armed aggression.' The preferred US strategy of dealing with the Syrian problem was to give encouragement to schemes for the subversion of the regime, while at the same time bolstering the resolve of the neighbouring countries through military and other assistance. The announcement of an immediate airlift of arms to Jordan on 5 September, and plans for the reinforcement of Iraq and Lebanon were part of this process.[21]

This strategy seems to have been closely coordinated with the British. In a meeting with the Australian Minister of External Affairs on 11 September, Selwyn Lloyd described the solution of the Syrian problem as a two-stage process. The first stage would involve its containment by the propping up of Lebanon, Jordan and Iraq, instanced by the US supplies of arms to Jordan. Next, 'a retrieving operation would be necessary' by one of Syria's neighbours. Britain, Lloyd asserted, was working in close consultation with America over Syria, although this was hampered somewhat by the fact that the US 'did not wish the closeness of this collaboration to be known'.[22]

In fact, this 'close consultation', which seems to have resulted from the dialogue between Macmillan and Dulles, involved the setting up of what became referred to as the 'Syria Working Group'. This was an extremely significant development in that it provided a forum for the exchange of intelligence, military and diplomatic information between the two countries. It was also to form the model for the broader range of groups established after Macmillan's visit to Washington at the end of October. In contrast to the rather abstract exchanges which had taken place under the joint planning framework established after Bermuda, the Working Group seems to have been a flexible mechanism, reacting to problems as they arose and proposing practical solutions. Certainly Macmillan, admittedly with an ulterior motive in mind, pronounced himself to be 'tremendously impressed' with its work.[23]

The first clue to the Group's existence comes in a telegram from Selwyn Lloyd to Harold Macmillan on 17 September. Reporting on his discussions with Dulles, Lloyd concludes by observing: 'I do not think there is anything more I can do except wait for the Working Group's report which should reach me Thursday evening and which I will discuss fully with Foster on Friday.'[24] One can only speculate as to the contents of the Group's report, but in view of the substance of the exchanges which had already passed between Macmillan and Dulles, it must have covered the possibility both of direct military action against Syria and also covert operations.

Certainly, Macmillan seems to have kept the process from the Cabinet as a whole, as he was to do with the broader structure of Working Groups established after the October talks. However, some clue as to the direction his thoughts were taking was provided by a note, marked 'Top Secret', 'Personal' and 'Not to be shown to the Chiefs of Staff', sent to Defence Minister Duncan Sandys on 29 September, presumably after he had seen the Group's conclusions. In it, he put the question:

> in the event of Iraq finding itself at war with Syria and Egypt attacking Iraq, if Iraq calls upon us under the Treaty to come to her aid, what military measures should we be able to take and what military consequences might be entailed? . . . It would be assumed for this purpose that the

United States would also be bringing help to Iraq and would be taking military measures against Egypt.[25]

Macmillan seems to have envisaged the possibility at this stage of some broader Middle Eastern war, in which the US, as the result of the combined planning for operations against Syria, might be drawn into backing Iraq alongside Britain against Egypt and Syria. This may well have been the sort of 'considered plan' that Macmillan had hoped for at the Cabinet meeting the previous month.

In the event, the Syrian crisis was to be solved as a result of indigenous Arab rather than great power action. Although both the British and American Governments had expected Iraq to take the lead in intervening in Syria, they were to be disappointed. Nuri es-Said had resigned the post of Prime Minister on 8 June 1957. His successor, Ali Jawdat al-Ayubi, who was to hold on to power until December 1957, was more sensitive to public opinion within Iraq, and did not wish to align his country against the forces of Arab nationalism.[26] Consequently, the kind of indigenous action over Syria for which both Britain and America had hoped did not come to pass.

Instead, it was King Saud who intervened to seek a compromise settlement in Syria, an instinct understandable in view of the dilemma which the crisis had presented him. On the one hand he wanted to maintain good relations with Nasser, while on the other he had to satisfy the Americans. His preferred solution was to try to cool tempers by healing the breach between Syria and the more hostile of her neighbours. Beginning in Lebanon on 7 September, Saud moved on to Jordan on 10 September, gaining an assurance from Prime Minister Samir al-Rifai that his country had no intention of interfering in the internal affairs of Syria. Finally, on 25 September, Saud arrived in Damascus itself, where he denounced any attempts at aggression against Syria and stressed the solidarity of the Arab peoples.

The effect of all this activity was that by early October Saud had emerged as 'the leader of a movement to hold the Arabs together against all outside attractions'.[27] To this extent it might be argued that he was beginning to fulfil the kind of role that Eisenhower had envisaged for him, that is, a rival pole of influence in the Arab world to that of Nasser. However, Nasser too was aware of the potential damage to his prestige should Saud be seen to be usurping his position as leader of the Arabs. In one masterstroke he undercut all of Saud's efforts, restoring his own influence, and undermining that of Saud both in the Arab world as a whole, and even within Saudi Arabia.

On 13 October Egyptian troops landed at Latakia to take up positions in northern Syria alongside units of the Syrian army. What was perceived as Nasser's bold and resolute action in support of a fellow Arab state put Saud's efforts at negotiation in the shade. Nasser emerged again as the 'unrivalled champion of Arab rights'.[28] In fact, his intervention was not quite so unexpected as it appeared at the time for, while Saud had concentrated on high-level diplomatic contacts, Nasser had been working through his ambassador in Damascus, Brigadier Mahmud Riyad, to foster closer links between the Egyptian and Syrian High Commands which facilitated the Latakia landings. Still, whatever its origin, Nasser's intervention was seen as an example of Arab solidarity against the threat of outside aggression, in this case believed to come from Turkey.

Soon after this the crisis, which had erupted as a result of the American over-reaction to the events of early August, petered out. Although Syria remained in a state of chronic internal political uncertainty, which was only to be remedied in the short term by the formation of the United Arab Republic in the new year, Syria, to American eyes, no longer appeared to be ripe for a Communist takeover. Of course, one question which resulted from the course that events had taken, was whether, in view of the fact that Nasser's intervention seemed to the Americans to have forestalled the possibility of a Communist-backed coup, he could now be considered to be a potential rival to Soviet influence in the region.

Dulles had discussed this possibility as early as 11 September in a conversation with Senator Mansfield.[29] However, at this stage he was sceptical about the chance of securing Nasser's cooperation, arguing that 'these speculations were based on what people felt Nasser ought to think rather than anything Nasser had said or done'. Dulles maintained this sceptical stance in talks with Selwyn Lloyd in Washington in the middle of the following month, asserting that US policy toward Egypt might be regarded as 'coolly correct'.[30] However, by the end of the month, the course that events in Syria had taken in the wake of Nasser's intervention led to a reassessment of the US stance. The process began when Dulles called for a review of relations with Nasser in the light of 'what Nasser might have learned from the Syrian experience'.[31]

The result was a memorandum from Assistant Secretary William Rountree to Dulles on 4 November which argued that Nasser might 'have qualms that the Soviet Union is seeking to displace him as leader of the area'.[32] Nasser, it was suggested, might be becoming concerned that Egypt was too dependent on the Soviet Union, particularly in the economic field, as well as at the challenge which 'the Soviet-Syrian understanding' posed to his influence there. Rountree argued that:

> restoration of tolerable relations with Egypt would clearly be in our interests, provided that Nasser shows greater aware- ness of the dangers of close association with the Soviet Union and adopts a genuinely neutral position, and provided that the resumption of constructive relations can take place in such a way that Nasser cannot claim a victory for his policies.

However, while the situation was now slightly more favour- able to laying the foundations for better relations with Egypt, it would be necessary to 'proceed most cautiously'. Rountree recommended that there should at present be no basic change in policy, but rather that the US should watch developments to see if there was a chance for improved relations.

The process of review culminated in a frequently cited note from Eisenhower to Dulles on 13 November in which the Pre- sident asked 'do you think there would be any percentage in initiating a drive to attempt to bring back Nasser to our side?'[33] While Eisenhower stressed that he did not 'have in mind any- thing spectacular', he wanted to find out what Nasser 'would be prepared to do in the way of easing tensions in the Mid East if we on our part would resume efforts to help him over some of his difficulties.' The stumbling block in all of this, however, as Dulles emphasized in a subsequent meeting with the President, was the attitude of King Saud, who, as has been seen, had been considerably worsted by Nasser over the Syrian crisis. Despite the obvious failure of Saud's diplomacy, Eisenhower and Dulles remained anxious to build on relations with him. There was a danger, Dulles argued, that Nasser would be prepared to accept nothing less than an American willingness to treat him as leader of the Arab world. In view of this, it was agreed that nothing should be done which might be seen as 'disloyal to King Saud' or which might push Nasser ahead of him in the Arab world.[34]

However, when, early in December 1957, Nasser approached the American Ambassador through an intermediary, asking that the US should 'keep hands off Syria for a maximum period of three months' to enable him to stem the Communist tide in the country, the request was at least given serious consideration in Washington. Although Assistant Secretary Rountree's reply showed understandable caution as to the indirect method of approach taken by the intermediary, and although he stressed that the US could obviously not bind itself not to take action over Syria, he told the ambassador that an 'affirmative response should be given' to the request. He indicated that the Administration 'would welcome action designed [to] impede [the] Communist threat [to the] security of Syria and [the] entire ME [Middle East]', and that 'we wish [to] avoid impeding any Egyptian efforts to bring about change'.[35]

The most important point about all of these discussions was not that they resulted in any immediate or substantial change in policy towards Nasser, but that they showed the element of pragmatism in the American attitude to him which separated the US approach from that of the British. It was simply inconceivable to the British that Nasser could be wooed back on to the side of the West. This division between the two countries, which was to surface even more clearly in their response to the formation of the United Arab Republic, was the source of much of the tension in their relationship in the region in the late 1950s.

However, despite this longer-term difference, in the short term, the Syrian crisis had served to bring Britain and America closer together in planning for and cooperation over problems in the region than had been the case at any stage since the formation of the Baghdad Pact. True, this consensus had not had to stand the severe test of a crisis of the magnitude of

Suez, or of that which was to be posed by the Iraqi Revolution the following year, but from the British perspective it was at least a promising beginning.

The relationship between the two was now to be cemented further by the impact that the launch of the Sputnik satellite on 4 October had on American thinking about its relationships with its allies worldwide. Sputnik not only opened up the debate within America about the implications of ICBM technology which appeared to make the American continent vulnerable to attack in a way it had not been since the early years of the war, it also 'swept away certain basic American assumptions and caused a crisis in self-confidence'.[36] Americans could no longer take for granted the fact that they were the best educated and most technologically advanced nation in the world.

Harold Macmillan seems to have sensed this change in outlook almost immediately, for on 10 October he wrote to Eisenhower in what seems to have been a bid to capitalize on this new American sense of vulnerability in order to promote still further the Anglo-American relationship.[37] The thrust of his argument was that Sputnik had served to bring home 'what formidable people' the Russians were, and the magnitude of the threat they presented to the free world. In view of this, the question should now be asked as to whether the time had come 'when we could go further towards pooling our efforts and decide how best to use them for the common good'. One obvious application of this principle would be in the field of nuclear weapons research. However, in the broader sense of 'counter-propaganda of all kinds', Macmillan professed himself to have been:

> tremendously impressed by the work our people have been doing together on the Syrian problem. Here is quiet efficient business-like cooperation such as has not existed since the war. I believe that here we have the key to a great new venture. I would like to see this sort of cooperation continued with a view to our working out together the role of the free countries in the struggle against communist Russia.

The opening Macmillan had been hoping for was signalled by Selwyn Lloyd following a meeting with Dulles on 15 October.[38]

During the course of a discussion on Syria, Dulles indicated that he felt that the whole pattern of Western cooperation should now be subjected to a major re-examination. The Anglo-American relationship, Lloyd reported, should be at the core of this, but it should spill out into NATO and SEATO. The President was now anxious to discuss these matters with Macmillan personally.

Macmillan, acting on Lloyd's conclusion that the Administration now had major changes in mind, and that he should 'come over and strike while the iron is hot', cabled Eisenhower that he was willing to come to Washington as soon as possible, with the object of devising 'some new approach to all of these inter-connected problems'.[39] In Cabinet on 21 October, Macmillan indicated that two objectives would be paramount during his talks with the President. The first would be to work towards the repeal of the McMahon Act to facilitate the sharing of nuclear weapons technology. The second would be to:

> endeavour to establish, unobtrusively and without provoking the suspicion of existing international organisations, a basis on which joint Anglo-American machinery might be created for the implementation of an agreed policy towards the political, military and economic issues which confronted both governments, particularly in the Middle East.[40]

However, on the American side, while the importance of the Anglo-American relationship as the starting point for a broader effort to invigorate the United States' alliances world-wide was acknowledged, the ultimate purpose was to 'create a more effective community of effort in the free world' as a whole.[41] There could be no question of Anglo-American exclusivity. It should be planned 'to project any new collaborative elements' into a broader framework.[42]

This emphasis in the American approach appears to have originated with Dulles. Briefing the President in advance of his meeting with Macmillan he underlined that: 'there are some differences in purpose between ourselves and the British regarding the meeting. They wish to stress their special relationship with us. From our standpoint whatever is issued must demonstrate our interest in all of our allies.'[43] Dulles also indicated to Deputy Defense Secretary Quarles, Admiral Strauss and

General Twining that Macmillan had pointed towards the need for a greater sense of intimate cooperation between the two countries. He himself had 'extended this to the need for a greater sense of unity in all of our alliances'.[44]

During the October talks, there was some discussion of the Syrian situation which was rapidly becoming less tense. However, by far the most important development outside the sphere of nuclear collaboration is not minuted in any of the released records of the conference. What was agreed by way of the establishment of Anglo-American Working Groups across a range of problems can only be deduced from a handful of isolated references in subsequent papers. These Groups seem to have been given the highest possible security classification, at the Americans' instigation, presumably because of fears about the response of other allies to what might be seen as an example of Anglo-American exclusivity.

A memorandum circulated by Norman Brook, the Cabinet Secretary, to the heads of the Foreign Office Departments in March 1959, refers back to an earlier letter of 31 October 1957, in which he had informed them of the decision to set up a number of Working Groups, mainly in Washington, 'to concert policy for countering Soviet encroachment'.[45] In this earlier letter he had explained that 'in pursuance of an undertaking we had given to the Americans', the British Government had agreed to do its utmost to prevent any disclosure of the decision to establish the Groups:

> We did not wish to give our other friends and allies the impression that we and the Americans had set up machinery to consider and dispose of all the world's problems and it was for this reason that I asked you . . . to keep within the smallest possible circle of knowledge that a method of consultation by joint Working Groups was being applied systematically over a wide range of questions.

The explanation for Brook's decision to circulate this memorandum in March 1959 was that this security policy had been so effectively applied that there were officials in departments concerned with the work of the Groups who were unaware of their existence, and who, if they were made aware, might be able to contribute usefully to their work. However, although internal security arrangements within the departments were to be relaxed, Brook still cautioned that particular care should be taken not to disclose knowledge of the existence of the system as a whole.

Two further documents have so far come to light, one from an American and one from a British source, which give some clue as to the subjects addressed by the Working Groups. A memorandum of 29 October from Assistant Secretary Elbrick of the Western Europe Desk to Dulles reports that Lord Hood, the Minister at the British Embassy, had called on him to review the action required in setting up a number of committees to implement the plans discussed by Eisenhower and Macmillan.[46] Hood had told Elbrick that the ambassador, Harold Caccia, would name himself or one of his staff as the focal point on the British side for supervising the work of the committees.

Hood's understanding was that nine committees had been agreed. These can be further subdivided into three broad groups. The first group concerned nuclear matters, and comprised, first, a committee of technical experts to report on the types of cooperation which might be achieved in scientific areas. This was to be an outgrowth of the Strauss-Plowden talks. Next was a committee intended to study the question of whether the Combined Policy Committee should be revived or some other mechanism created to perform the same functions. Finally there was to be a study group to develop plans for the control of the dissemination of information on nuclear weapons, designed to ensure that nuclear technology was not misused. The second collection of committees, and that which more directly bears on the present study, was the regional Working Groups. These were to coordinate policy on Syria, which was later to be broadened into the 'Middle East' as a whole, Algeria, and Hong Kong. The final collection of committees concerned broad cold war countermeasures. There was to be a group to study psychological warfare problems, another to determine the criteria for strategic controls on trade, and finally one to study economic warfare measures.

A British Chiefs of Staff Committee discussion on the same day also makes reference to the establishment of the regional and cold war countermeasure Working Groups.[47] Here, the 'Syria' Working Group is referred to as the 'Middle East' Working Group. However, in outlining the new structure of consultation, Sir Richard Powell, the Ministry of Defence representative on the committee, cautioned that:

> the agreements reached were only a first step and it remained to be seen to what extent really close cooperation could be achieved on lower levels in the Pentagon. In this respect we should probably need to tread carefully and not try to do too much at once. Nevertheless, there was no doubt of the desire on the part of those at the top to cooperate with us.

In his summing up of the achievements of the visit to the Cabinet, however, Macmillan was expansive. He argued that the 'declaration of common purpose' issued at the end of the talks 'was, in effect, a declaration of inter-dependence'.[48] This was a theme to which Macmillan was to return repeatedly in the coming months, particularly in his dealings with Washington. However, on the broader issue of the Working Groups, in keeping with the agreements about secrecy made with the US Administration, he chose not to divulge their existence to the Cabinet, although he did cover much of the ground over which they were intended to operate. He indicated that 'the two governments would in future take steps to concert a common policy for countering Soviet encroachment, not only by military preparations but also by political, economic, and propaganda measures'. The US Administration had agreed to the pooling of resources in the field of the research and development of new weapons, and had undertaken to ask Congress to amend the McMahon Act. All that Britain had had to give in return, Macmillan asserted, was an assurance that while the present government was in office, she would not press for any change in the representation of China at the United Nations without American consent.

Alistair Horne, who does not mention the new institutional arrangements beyond the committees on weapons and nuclear cooperation, has suggested that the direct quid pro quo for this concession by the British was American agreement to regard Hong Kong as a joint defence problem.[49] He also notes that when Macmillan presented the fourth volume of his memoirs to the Secretary of the Cabinet in 1970 for vetting 'he had his knuckles mildly rapped' for the inclusion of this information and was requested to remove it. In fact, the Hong Kong arrangement was part of the broader structure of Working Groups set up in Washington, which, as has been suggested, was regarded as a matter of the utmost secrecy. This may well have been part of the explanation for the sensitivity of the Cabinet Secretary to Macmillan's reference.

Thus, in the wake of the Syrian crisis and the Sputnik launch, the British seemed to have succeeded in gaining at least the first stage of their objective of a much closer two-country relationship with America.[50] However, as will be seen, although the new institutional framework provided a valuable forum for the coordination of planning for contingencies in the Middle East, there was often a gap between theory and practice. In particular, the Iraqi Revolution in July of the following year was to provide a test of Anglo-American cooperation which was to expose many of its continuing limitations.

Although the Syrian crisis brought the two powers much closer together over strategy in the Middle East than could have been expected in view of the suspicions generated by Suez, basic differences remained both over the promotion of Iraq and the Baghdad Pact versus the promotion of Saudi Arabia, and the approach to be adopted towards Nasser in the longer term. Indeed, it should be noted in passing that an earlier period of coordinated action over Syria, instanced by the plans for 'Operation Straggle' the previous year, had not prevented the major breakdown in Anglo-American relations during the Suez Crisis.

9 The Formation of the United Arab Republic

'By the late summer of 1957 Syria was on the verge of disintegration as an organized political community.'[1] Although Nasser's intervention had served to defuse what might be termed the great-power crisis there, many Syrians had lost confidence in the future of their country as an independent state. The fact that it had required the deployment of Egyptian troops to stabilize the situation in the country had merely served to reinforce this sentiment. Syria had become the object of competition not only between rival Arab states, but also between the superpowers, and the rival poles of attraction seemed to be pulling the country apart.

In the face of this onslaught both the ideological and institutional foundations of the Syrian state seemed insecure. The rise of pan-Arabism during the 1950s, instanced both by the advance of the Baath Party and of Nasser's regime in Egypt had a particular impact in Syria where the appeal of Arab unity was especially strong.[2] Against this powerful external appeal, the internal institutions which should have held the nation together, particularly the army, seemed weak and riven by dissent. It was to be the coincidence of the aims of the two powerful pan-Arab forces of Nasser and the Baath Party, therefore, which were to draw Syria into union with Egypt early in the new year of 1958.

There was in fact something of an ideological gulf between the outlook of Nasser and that of the Baath. Nasser and his principal colleagues were all military men who had something of a distaste for intellectual theorizing.[3] Nasser's initial ideology was 'primitive and general', and merely stressed opposition to corruption, social oppression and imperialism. Political parties were objects of distrust simply because in pre-revolutionary Egypt they had been the preserve of the corrupt oligarchy. 'Socialism' in Egypt had evolved during the 1950s, therefore, more as a series of improvised programmes than as a predetermined ideology. State planning and ownership only began to emerge slowly after the political decision to nationalize the Canal had left the Government in control of a number of sequestered French and British enterprises. What Nasser brought to the union of Egypt and Syria, therefore, was 'not a radical ideology but a talent for leadership'.[4]

In view of Nasser's political inclinations, the alliance with the Baath Party in Syria was an improbable one. The Baath, which had its ideological roots in the revolutionary socialism of Michel 'Aflaq and Salah al-Din al-Bitar, drew its practical political instincts from the opportunism of Akram al-Hawrani. Although the party to this extent had something of a dual character, 'thanks to 'Aflaq and Bitar, and despite Hawrani's unconcern, it was an avowedly doctrinaire party with a specifically revolutionary, socialist, pan-Arabist creed'.[5] In this respect, it differed greatly in character from the regime of Nasser at the time of the formation of the United Arab Republic.

Until the summer of 1957, the Baath, Nasser and the Syrian Communists, backed by the Soviet Union, had been able to work together towards the goal of eliminating Iraqi influence in Syria, and blocking the attempts at subversion sponsored by the Western powers. However, when it came to the question of forming positive plans for the future of the Syrian state, it was only the Baath who had a clearly defined idea of their longer term goals. The party had been actively promoting the concept of unity with Egypt throughout 1956 and 1957 on the basis that this was the essential first step on the road to a broader Arab union. Nasser, on the other hand, while pleased to see the party championing his cause, did not share its fervour for union between the two countries. He foresaw many practical political difficulties in the way of such a development. All Nasser really sought was control of Syrian foreign policy. He wanted to avoid the administrative quagmire of attempting to bring together the Syrian and Egyptian Governments.

The Syrian Communists, while devoted in the longer run to the cause of revolution in Syria, were constrained in the short term by the fact that their Soviet backers wanted to maintain good relations with Nasser. They were therefore not prepared to support any full-blooded Communist takeover in Syria. However, the growth in party membership during the summer of 1957, against the background of the American 'conspiracy' against Syria, and such conspicuous successes for the Soviet Union as the launch of the Sputnik satellite, made the local Communists, led by Khalid Baqdash, ever more assertive. This placed great strains on their alliance with the Baath.

It is not clear whether the Baath actually believed that the Communists were planning a direct takeover in Syria at the beginning of 1958.[6] However, even the possibility that they might try pointed towards two equally unpalatable outcomes. On the one hand, if they were successful, then the immediate possibility of any union with Egypt would have been thwarted. On the other, should they fail, then a right wing, Iraqi and Western-sponsored backlash might equally well cut the ground from under their plans. To this extent, the renewed urgency with which the Baath pressed for union with Egypt at the end of 1957 was as much an expression of the increasing weakness of its own position as the strength of its ideological conviction.[7]

The upsurge in Baath–Communist rivalry coincided with a period of increased tension within the Syrian army. Of course, the regime in Egypt was in any case particularly appealing to the army high command, being a military junta itself. In the circumstances prevailing at the end of 1957, therefore, when rivalries within the army had reduced it to a number of competing factions which were little short of private armies, it was little wonder that the Baathist leader, Bitar, was able to persuade a group of officers to go to Cairo to seek Nasser's mediation of their differences. The result was that on 12 January 1958 a party led by the Chief of Staff, Afif al-Bizri left for Cairo, leaving behind a note which amounted to a virtual ultimatum to the civilian administration. This complained that the country was on the verge of collapse, that Communism was gaining ground, and that only Nasser could provide a remedy. Although the role of Bizri, who, as was suggested earlier, had links with the Communists, was somewhat ambiguous, he appears for reasons of opportunism to thrown his weight behind the Baathist schemes for union with Egypt.[8]

The deputation, and its impassioned pleas for unity, presented Nasser with something of a dilemma.[9] All he had sought in Syria was control over the direction of foreign policy. Now he was being asked to assume responsibility for the whole government. However, the consequences of rejecting the opportunity must have seemed worse than the potential dangers of seizing it. If he had declined the officers' offer, then his credentials as an Arab nationalist would have been called into question, and his prestige in Syria and the Arab world as a whole would have been seriously dented. His solution was to accept union, but only on his terms. These involved the dissolution of all Syrian political parties, and the concentration of power and decision-making in Cairo.[10] The Baath evidently hoped that once the union came into being their privileged position as Nasser's allies would allow the rules on parties to be bent in their favour, eliminating their rivals, especially the Communists. The Communists themselves were opposed to union on the terms Nasser offered but had little choice but to swim with the tide. The result was that on 1 February 1958 the United Arab Republic of Syria and Egypt was proclaimed.

The effect of the announcement on the politics of the region was dramatic. To begin with, it was evidence that Egypt had outflanked Iraq in the struggle for Syria and the Fertile Crescent. To this extent, and to the extent that it consolidated the ascendancy of Nasser over the Arab world, it was a development which was wholly unfavourable in British eyes, and one which had to be countered quickly by supporting whatever rival organization the Iraqis might seek to promote.

The American response, however, was rather more complex. The news of the formation of the UAR broke while Dulles was attending a Baghdad Pact council meeting in Ankara. The Secretary's arrival at the meeting itself, had been somewhat dramatic. A snowstorm had forced two unsuccessful passes by his aircraft over the runway at Ankara, and Dulles himself had intervened to persuade the pilot to make one more attempt to land at 5pm in the evening. Having touched down safely, the fatigued Secretary then managed to sleep through the commotion caused around midnight by two attempts to blow up the American Embassy Chancery and the American Library. These, according to Turkish Prime Minister Menderes, were a Communist demonstration against the Baghdad Pact and Dulles himself.[11]

During a specially restricted session of the council, called at Dulles's request, he expressed the opinion that the union was almost certainly backed by the Soviets, and would 'be dangerous to all of our interests'.[12] Although the US could not take the lead in opposing it, it would be prepared to support any Arab state which was willing to take such an initiative. Dulles made it explicit to Nuri that he felt that Iraq was best suited for this role.[13]

However, it appears that Dulles acted in haste at the pact meeting, more on the basis of his instincts as to the forces behind the union than on any hard evidence. Already, on the evening of 29 January a measure of doubt as to the Soviet role in the formation of the UAR had crept into his communications with Eisenhower, to whom he wrote that it was not entirely clear whether the development was 'promoted by the Communists or whether the Communists are going along with Nasser's ambitions to unify the Arab world under his leadership'.[14] Still, Dulles's gut reaction was to suspect the unseen Soviet hand behind the move, and to put pressure on Iraq to act as the indigenous country best placed to oppose it.

Dulles, however, was out of step with his own State Department. A memorandum sent by Stuart Rockwell to Assistant Secretary William Rountree on 21 January had already emphasized that there might be short-term advantages to the US in an Egyptian–Syrian union if this served to curb the influence of the Soviet Union in Syria.[15] Although there would be longer-term disadvantages in the aggrandizement of Egypt at the expense of Iraq and Saudi Arabia, these could be outweighed by the short-term gains if the union were accompanied by measures to eliminate the influence of the Syrian Communist Party.

While Dulles was in Ankara, intelligence reports received in Washington had emphasized that the union had come about as a result of a Syrian initiative, and that it was designed to forestall an imminent coup led by Communist elements in the army. Nasser had been reluctant to accede to the wishes of his Syrian petitioners, but had done so in order to preserve his prestige and position in the country. Although the Soviets might welcome the union in public, in private they were opposed to it.[16] This information led the State Department to proceed very cautiously in its response to the UAR. Instructions sent out to

US ambassadors in the region on 1 February were couched in much more guarded terms than those used by Dulles, and merely asked for information about the intentions of the Arab states, rather than urging that they take early action in response to the union.

The contradiction between this approach and that of Dulles confused the British, and led Ambassador Harold Caccia to resort to the framework for consultation between the two countries established after the October talks by calling a meeting of the Syria Working Group.[17] His conclusion was that the US representatives on the Group could only have had an incomplete account of the proceedings at Ankara, because they were unaware of the encouragement Dulles had given to an early initiative by the Iraqis. However, as the British were to discover, it was the cautious instincts of the State Department in Washington which were to prevail in this case. On Dulles's return, and after a briefing as to the background and likely ramifications of the union, he retreated from his earlier position. Indeed, his explanation to the National Security Council of his behaviour at Ankara has almost the flavour of an apology.[18] He indicated that 'there had been practically no solid intelligence at Ankara as to how this union had actually come about', and that 'the US delegation accordingly felt very isolated and very much in the dark'. Further, 'there had been strong pressure on the United States to speak out against the union'. Dulles was now to place even greater emphasis on the argument that the US could not take any initiative in response to the union.

This passive approach of waiting on developments in the region was to dominate US policy from the news of the formation of the UAR at the end of January until the outbreak of the Lebanese crisis early in May 1958. Stephen Ambrose argues that Eisenhower was waiting for an opportunity 'to demonstrate, unequivocally, America's readiness for action and its determination to use force to prevent the domination of the area by anti-Western pan-Arab nationalism'.[19] If Nasser maintained his alliance with the Soviet Union and succeeded in overthrowing pro-Western regimes in the region, then the US would have to act to prevent Khrushchev gaining a stranglehold on the world's basic energy source.

In fact, US policy seems to have been rather more complicated in its inspiration than this analysis might suggest. Its essence seems to have been an amalgam both of the approach outlined by Ambrose of waiting for the Soviets to show their hand by attempting the subversion of one of the 'pro-Western' regimes in the area, and also of an attempt to analyse empirically Nasser's relationship with the Soviet Union. In other words, because intelligence reports about the formation of the UAR such as that delivered by General Cabell indicated that it might portend the beginnings of some form of competition for influence in the region between Nasser and the Soviets, the Administration decided to wait and see which way Nasser would turn in a future crisis. If he supported what was seen as Soviet-inspired subversion of one of the pro-Western regimes, then the US would take strong action against him. If he equivocated, then this would be further practical evidence of the potential wedge which could be driven between him and the Soviet Union.

In practice, this produced a policy of conciliation in public over the United States' relations with Nasser, and also an unwillingness to give direct support to the Iraqi counter-initiative taken by Nuri, with Dulles's initial blessing, in the shape of the creation of the Arab Union of the Hashemite Kingdoms of Iraq and Jordan. This initiative stemmed overwhelmingly from the Iraqi concern with the regional balance of power in the wake of the formation of the UAR.[20] However, it was not popular in either country, with Arab nationalists tending to look to Nasser as the standard-bearer of their aspirations. In addition, problems were to emerge at the governmental level, with the Jordanians baulking at the Iraqi desire to control all of the significant offices of the new union.

Although the British admitted that the Arab Union lacked indigenous support in both Iraq and Jordan,[21] they were confused and chagrined by the US approach towards it and the general question of relations with Nasser. This confusion was made even worse by the fact that in private Dulles maintained a hard line towards Nasser in discussions with British officials. By 8 March, Harold Caccia was urging Selwyn Lloyd that 'it would be most helpful if you could discuss support of the Iraq/ Jordan Union with Dulles . . .'. He reported that his impression was that the State Department had been:

taking too much comfort from the apparent elimination of Communism from a position of influence in Syria, and insufficiently appreciated the threat to the Iraq/Jordan Union and to Western interests presented by the dynamism of Nasser's policy. The idea that it may be possible to get Nasser to play a game of 'live and let live' has gained some currency.[22]

Lloyd's stopover in Baghdad on his way to the SEATO conference in Manila reinforced the British impression that the Arab Union needed bolstering. Prophetically, Lloyd reported to Dulles that the Iraqi leaders were in 'a very jittery state and acting as though they expected to be gone in six months'.[23] Dulles's response to Lloyd's representations over support for the Arab Union was to perform a delicate diplomatic balancing act. Mindful of his initial encouragement to the Iraqis, he could not distance himself too far from the Arab Union or be too positive about the United Arab Republic. Thus, in private, he continued to inveigh against Nasser, even telling Caccia in a meeting on 20 March that 'it seemed to him that Nasser was following in Hitler's footsteps and was embarking on the policy of expansion outlined in his book'.[24] In public, however, he needed to maintain a more flexible position to allow for the possibility that the friction created between Egypt and the Soviet Union over the formation of the UAR might yet provide the opportunity to begin to woo Nasser away from the Soviets. This would be a major diplomatic coup, and would further the Administration's fundamental aim of containing the Russian threat, and preventing the Soviets from using the Arab nationalist movement as a means to undermine the interests of the West in the region. This serves to explain his comment at a press conference that the US was 'getting along with Nasser'.[25]

This, of course, provoked outrage in the Foreign Office, both because it contradicted Dulles's private statements, and because it flew in the face of the guiding tenet of British policy in the region which was that Nasser was an inveterate enemy with whom it was impossible to do business. Comments on Dulles's remark ranged from: 'how's this for a statement of US policy in the Middle East?', to 'Dulles sounds as though he is looking down the wrong end of a telescope to a Nasser far

far away who seems to be quite happy with the Americans. You can't actually see the un-American look on his face at that distance.'

In a telegram to Caccia at the end of March, William Hayter, Deputy Under-Secretary at the Foreign Office, had already referred to 'a slough of despond' into which American policy in the region seemed to have fallen.[26] He was at a loss to explain why the Americans seemed to be unable or unwilling to act on matters such as the supply of fighter aircraft to Iraq. The explanation, as has been suggested, seems to have lain in the Administration's adoption in the short term of a policy of equivocation towards the UAR and Arab Union, and a desire to avoid antagonizing Nasser needlessly.[27]

However, the collapse of the position of King Saud in Saudi Arabia may also have contributed to the Administration's unwillingness to adopt a forward strategy. Since Saud had been Eisenhower and Dulles's favoured choice as alternative leader of Arab nationalism to Nasser, the palace coup which culminated in Saud having to sign a decree on 22 March giving full control over domestic and foreign affairs to his brother Faisal was a major blow. Although Saud had not been deposed, the affair was a 'severe warning' to him.[28] The fact that one of the major precipitant factors for the move against him had been Nasser's accusation that Saud was conspiring against him, implied that even had Faisal been willing to take on the sort of role Eisenhower and Dulles had envisaged for Saud, he would not in any case have had the domestic room for manoeuvre to act.

Thus, in the months immediately preceding the outbreak of the Lebanese crisis, the US Administration had essentially lapsed into a policy of waiting on developments in the Middle East. The Syrian problem of the previous summer and now the formation of the United Arab Republic both suggested that there might be some possibility that Nasser could be split from the Soviets. However, the Administration remained suspicious as to his aims, and intended to judge him on the basis of his response to future crises in the area. This was also a period of some tension in Anglo-American relations with the British at a loss to explain how Dulles could, on the one hand, have encouraged Nuri to take some initiative to counter the formation of the UAR, while on the other refusing to put American weight behind the Arab Union. Also, the gap between Dulles's public and private statements on US relations with Nasser produced a great deal of bad feeling in the Foreign Office.

In practice, it seems to have been another example of Dulles's predilection for running with the hare and hunting with the hounds. Since the Soviet threat was his priority, he was prepared to say one thing in private to the British and another in public until it became clear whether Nasser would support the Soviets in their next anticipated move in the region. Also, in the wake of the collapse of Saud's position, and in view of the often-stated objections to falling in with the British strategy of promoting Iraq and the Baghdad Pact as an alternative to Nasser's leadership, the US Administration was temporarily without a positive policy to pursue in the area. The British Government, on the other hand, stuck firmly to its strategy of opposing Nasser. The formation of the UAR merely seemed to underline further the need to combat his expansionist ambitions in the region, and to bolster the cause of the Iraqi regime.

10 The Lebanese Crisis

The origins of the crisis which erupted in the Lebanon early in May 1958 were bound up with the nature of the post-independence Lebanese political system. The 'National Pact', which distributed power and political office on a confessional basis, served both to maintain the balance between the Lebanese sects, and to entrench their differences. The tension between what might be termed the Eastern and Western orientations of the Christian and Muslim sects, which the pact sought to mitigate, was heightened during the mid-1950s under the impact of Nasser's pan-Arabism and the Anglo-French disgrace over the Suez crisis. The fact that Camille Chamoun, President of the country since 1952, refused to sever diplomatic relations with Britain and France in the wake of the crisis as other Arab states had done, enraged those within the country who increasingly looked towards the fulfilment of the pan-Arab ideal as Lebanon's future.

Indeed, Chamoun himself was something of a controversial figure. Seen by some as a Lebanese patriot anxious to preserve the integrity of the Lebanese state against the aggressive designs of her Arab neighbours, especially Syria, he was seen by others as a self-seeking opportunist intent only on maintaining his own personal political position. Thus, the question of his rumoured bid for a second term of office, which went against the spirit of the 'National Pact', and which was the underlying cause of the disturbances which broke out in May 1958, was one which exacerbated the existing divide in Lebanese politics. The parallels with a more recent self-proclaimed saviour of the Lebanese state, General Michel Aoun, are strong.

The promulgation of the Eisenhower Doctrine, and the haste with which Chamoun moved to accept it, breaking ranks again with the other Arab nations, caused even greater internal difficulties. Within Lebanon, Nasser's Sunni sympathizers were not the only critics of Chamoun's move.[1] Kamal Jumblatt, the leader of the Druze, was hostile, as were many influential voices within the Christian communities themselves.[2] Even the Patriarch of the Maronite Church, Boulos Meochy, was opposed to Lebanon's perceived alignment against Egypt and Syria.

The hostility of both Syria and Egypt to Chamoun's pro-Western policy formed the essential background to the beginnings of Anglo-American planning for possible military operations in support of his government. During the preparations for the meeting in October 1957 between Macmillan and Eisenhower, the military planners of both countries were asked to produce reports on what forces might be available should the governments of Lebanon and Jordan request assistance to combat any insurrection against them sponsored by Syria.[3] This, as Selwyn Lloyd described it, was in accordance with the United States' favoured policy of 'containment plus', whereby the states contingent to a nation prone to imminent Soviet-backed take-over should be bolstered by the direct provision of military aid, and by the promise of Western armed intervention should a coup attempt be mounted.[4] This doctrine was to be paramount in dictating the US Administration's course of action in Lebanon in the wake of the Iraqi Revolution.

After the October talks, in a measure which appears to have been a direct response to Syrian and Egyptian propaganda broadcasts calling for the overthrow of King Hussein of Jordan in early November, Dulles instructed the US Joint Chiefs of Staff to prepare an operational plan for 'possible US–UK military intervention in the event of an imminent or actual coup d'etat in Lebanon and/or Jordan'.[5] The Joint Chiefs were to make use of the new bilateral planning apparatus set up at the October talks by conducting their discussions with the British in the 'Syria' Working Group. At the same time, diplomatically, in response to a request from Chamoun, the British and Americans moved to give him an assurance of support should he be faced with subversion across the Syrian border.[6] To some extent, however, this assurance gave a hostage to fortune. Although both the British and Americans tried to play down their commitment to Chamoun, he was able, during the second stage of the crisis the following May, to exploit Western promises of support to his own advantage in the turmoil surrounding his rumoured bid for a second term of office.

The product of the Working Group's discussions in early December was a report entitled 'Measures to Forestall or Counter an Anti-Western Coup d'Etat in Jordan or the Lebanon'.[7] What this document seems to have shown more effectively than anything else, however, was the deficiencies in the Anglo-American planning process which had produced it. It appears that there was little or no input from either the Foreign Office or the State Department on the diplomatic side, nor MI5 or the CIA on the intelligence side.[8] The result was a plan which simply gave a rough indication of what forces might be deployed and the logistics of any amphibious landing, with no indication of its political ramifications.

On the American side too, doubts were expressed as to the broader regional repercussions of any Anglo-American intervention in the Levant. Indeed, Admiral Burke, the Chief of Naval Operations, pressed strongly for the inclusion of the following passage in the memorandum to the Secretary of Defense on the Anglo-American operational plan:

> The Joint Chiefs of Staff believe that the implementation of such a plan would be politically disastrous to the US position in both the United Nations and with the remainder of the Arab world. This would be a military campaign with political overtones comparable in many respects to the United Kingdom–France–Israeli debacle of 1956 which dropped British–French prestige to an all time low and contributed greatly to advancing the position of the Soviet Union in the Middle East.[9]

The warning from Admiral Burke seems to have anticipated Dulles's own reassessment of the situation in the wake of the formation of the UAR. As has already been suggested, both he and Eisenhower seem then to have adopted a more passive approach in the region which hinged on waiting for whatever they perceived to be the next Soviet-inspired coup against a pro-Western government. In addition, a leakage of information about military planning activities with the British would jeopardize any small prospect of success that Dulles's attempt to separate Nasser from the Soviet Union, in the wake of the formation of the UAR, might have.

The results of this attitude were twofold. Firstly, and significantly in view of the Americans' ultimate unilateral intervention in the Lebanon, the Administration refused to countenance the setting up of an integrated command structure for the projected operation. Despite the repeated protests of the British Chiefs of Staff that this effectively invalidated any joint military plans, the Americans would not move from their position, and insisted on separate national commands.[10] This may well have been the result of a desire to retain the freedom of action in the region which the Eisenhower Doctrine had shown the US to be seeking. It may also have reflected a residual fear, such as that expressed by Admiral Burke, of being dragged into some new Suez-style operation in the Levant by the British.

Secondly, the Administration insisted on the highest possible security classification for the continued activities of the planning group. This had the farcical result that the planners assembled in Washington could not get access to any of the logistical information they needed from both parties to proceed with operational planning because those who could supply it were not security cleared to be aware of the existence of the Working Group. The group was thus thrown into a state of near paralysis for several months, until its activities were concluded early in April at the Americans' request. The US Joint Chiefs gave as the reason for this recommendation to Dulles the fact that: 'the premature dissemination of this sensitive information to the level at which coordinated planning would be conducted might compromise the plan and jeopardize the US and British positions, both in the United Nations and with the remainder of the Arab world.'[11]

The fundamental difficulties which thwarted the development of any practical plan for operations in the Levant at this stage, therefore, revolved around the American fear that the disclosure of these activities would discredit their claim to be the friend of moderate, non-Communist Arab nationalism, undermine their position in the Arab world, and open the way to further Soviet gains. This might have been argued to be true of any form of contingency planning for military intervention in the region, but it was particularly true of joint planning with the British who had so recently been involved in the Suez operation.

It was the intensification of rumours concerning the desire of President Chamoun to flout the National Pact, and seek a second term of office, however, which brought matters to a head in Lebanon in the spring of 1958. The spark required to ignite the volatile mixture of ideological and sectarian tensions which this stirred up was provided by the assassination of a prominent opposition newspaper editor, Nasib Matni, on 8 May. Street fighting and rioting ensued, and the Iraqi Petroleum Company pipeline was cut.

This upsurge of violence produced an immediate Anglo-American diplomatic and military response. On the military side, on 14 May, the US Joint Chiefs of Staff authorized Admiral Holloway, the Commander in Chief US Naval Forces Eastern Atlantic and Mediterranean (CINCNELM), to proceed with detailed Anglo-American operational planning along the lines that had been contemplated in the earlier combined contingency paper.[12] This sudden decision to resume Anglo-American military consultations seems to have resulted from a somewhat confused attempt by the two countries to test their readiness for action by a mobilization of their available forces in the area beginning on 13 May.[13] It appears that in the course of this operation it became clear that the necessary infrastructure was not in place to achieve any meaningful degree of coordination with the British forces in the area.[14]

At a meeting on 16 May attended by CINCNELM (Admiral Holloway), the British Chiefs of Staff were able to discuss an outline operational plan for Anglo-American intervention in the Lebanon, designated Plan 'Blue Bat'. According to Holloway's account, consultations between US and UK staff planners in London had yielded 'a single operational concept... which might be implemented by either one of two forces available – the Army and Air Forces based in Germany (Plan A), or the Sixth Fleet (Plan B), or by both'.[15] In view of the potential political repercussions of Plan A, which involved the need for overflying rights from several European countries, Holloway regarded it as more likely that the US government would favour the use of Plan B.

On the diplomatic front, Chamoun pressed the Americans, British and French for action, repeating his request of the previous November for an assurance that if his regime were to be threatened by external subversion the Western powers would come to his aid. Selwyn Lloyd's initial inclination was that Britain and America should give an affirmative response to

Chamoun's appeal. However, Dulles's attitude would be crucial, he asserted, for Britain could not act alone in the Lebanon.[16]

Dulles, it appears, was keen to play an active role in Lebanon. During a conference with the President on 13 May, he had informed him that although there were grave difficulties in responding to Chamoun's appeal, there were even greater dangers in doing nothing.[17] The Lebanese case, it seemed, fitted in perfectly with Dulles's theories about the rising Communist tide not only in the Middle East, but worldwide, and could be regarded as a test case for American resolve.[18] Despite warnings from McClintock, the US Ambassador in Lebanon,[19] therefore, instructions were sent to Beirut stating that:

> the US is prepared upon [an] appropriate request from [the] President and rpt and [the] GOL to send certain combat forces to Lebanon which would have the dual mission of (a) protecting American life and property and (b) assisting the GOL in its military program for the preservation of the independence and integrity of Lebanon . . .[20]

It appears that these two aims were specified so that any action taken could be regarded in terms of the protection of American nationals abroad and so come under the auspices of the United Nations Charter, rather than the Eisenhower Doctrine. The Lebanese case showed the limitations of the Doctrine to the extent that the President could only invoke it constitutionally if there was clear evidence that the victim had suffered aggression from a country 'controlled by international Communism'.

Dulles's instructions to Ambassador McClintock also informed him that action was being concerted with Britain. However, Dulles argued that the circle of cooperation should not be broadened any further, asserting that 'we are convinced as we believe is the UK that French participation in the military operations would be unproductive'.[21] In fact, the desire to exclude the French was a consistent theme of the Anglo-American response to the Lebanese crisis. On the US side this stemmed principally from the fear of being seen to be too closely associated in the Middle East with a colonial power which was then carrying out a high profile, and internationally controversial, policing action in North Africa.

American sensibilities played a part in determining the British outlook, but the government also probably regarded the French as too unpredictable to be brought within the Anglo-American planning framework. In addition, one may speculate that the British were anxious to protect the newly found intimacy of their relationship with Washington. This could be threatened by anything which served to remind the Americans of the circumstances surrounding the last Anglo-French action in the region. 'The "special relationship" between Britain and the United States never worked so effectively as when it was concerned with excluding the French.'[22]

The French, of course, were far from pleased about their exclusion. Ambassador Middleton noted that the reaction of his French colleague in Beirut was 'extremely sharp'.[23] The ambassador, according to Middleton, was prepared even to go to the lengths of resigning rather than allowing France to be 'unceremoniously thrust aside'. Nevertheless, the Foreign Office pressed ahead with planning on the basis of French exclusion. On 16 May Selwyn Lloyd told Harold Caccia that the best approach would be simply to say nothing about French participation, and to 'keep the French completely in the dark about any military preparations we may be making'.[24] Indeed, Lloyd went so far as to suggest to Sir Michael Wright, the Ambassador in Baghdad, that he should persuade Nuri to pressurize Chamoun not to ask for French assistance.[25]

However, attempts to discourage the French met with little success. By the end of the following month, Lloyd was admitting to Gladwyn Jebb, British Ambassador in Paris, that 'it looks as if at present we should have no chance of persuading the French to agree not to join in'.[26] Lloyd concluded that if it ever came to the question of intervention in the Lebanon, then 'there is just a chance that we and the Americans could frighten the French off if we spoke strongly enough'. In fact, when Chamoun made his request for assistance on 14 July, he included the French. However, although France sent warships to the Eastern Mediterranean she played no active military role in the crisis and Anglo-American blushes were spared.

The crisis in the Lebanon entered a new phase when, on 22 May, the Lebanese Government made a formal complaint to the United Nations Security Council about interference in its internal affairs by the United Arab Republic. This referred to infiltration by armed bands from Syria, the destruction of Lebanese life and property, the supplying of arms to Lebanese rebels, and the waging of a violent radio and press campaign against the established authorities in Lebanon.[27] The Lebanese resort to the Security Council was, however, the subject of some disagreement between the US and the UK which showed the potential vulnerability of their new, closer relationship in the region. Rumours concerning British pressure on the Lebanese Government led to the accusation, from certain quarters of the US Administration, that the British were trying to force America to take a more aggressive line in the Lebanon to further their own ends in the region, and to vindicate their stand against Nasser two years earlier. At a meeting on 19 May, Assistant Secretary Rountree had noted the 'apparent differences with the British as to the circumstances under which [the] US-UK would intervene. From the outset the British have shown an enthusiastic attitude. . . . The British are urging that Lebanon take its case against Syria to the United Nations'. The theme of the meeting was, therefore, 'to find a solution for the internal political problem in Lebanon and to cool down the British on their enthusiasm for immediate action'.[28]

In a phone conversation with Secretary of State Dulles, Henry Cabot Lodge, the US's representative at the United Nations, who was well known for his anti-colonialist attitude, questioned whether America should be giving military guarantees to Chamoun in conjunction with the British.[29] Dulles replied that the Administration was 'trying to cooperate with them all over the world'. He did concede however, that there was some evidence that the British were 'trying to push us in more rapidly than we want to go'. Lodge asserted that the Lebanese representative to the UN had told him that the British were pushing and encouraging the Lebanon to turn to the Security Council because this would 'wipe the slate clean re Suez'.

Dulles raised these suspicions with Harold Caccia over dinner on 21 May, indicating that 'some of our people not just in Washington but elsewhere, had the impression that we were being crowded by our British colleagues into intervention in Lebanon.'[30] Caccia 'rather indignantly' denied that this was the British purpose, and argued that all Britain really wanted was to plan together for such a contingency, a subject on which the US seemed to blow hot and cold.

Nevertheless, the British Government was aware of the need to tread rather carefully throughout the crisis in order to avoid American suspicions as to its broader purpose in the region, which might be fuelled if Britain appeared to be too eager to intervene militarily. Selwyn Lloyd noted that he was particularly anxious to avoid giving the impression that he was trying to push the Americans into an operation.[31] However, the suspicion persisted that the British goal in the Lebanon was to seek vindication for the Suez operation, and to seize the opportunity to confront Nasser. Indeed, in view of Macmillan's initial response to the Iraqi Revolution, this may not have been so entirely unreasonable as Selwyn Lloyd sought to maintain.

Nevertheless, Walworth Barbour, Minister at the US Embassy in London, argued that accusations made by, among others, Ambassador McClintock, that 'Britain and other friendly governments in the Near East . . . would like to seize upon [the] difficulties in Lebanon "as an excuse for fighting Nasser" ' were unfounded.[32] British policies, as he saw them, coincided with those of the US and were to preserve the independence of Lebanon by supporting the legitimate government of the country. The fact that this brought about a conflict with Nasser was merely a result of intervention by the UAR in the affairs of Lebanon, a 'far cry from seeking out [the] opportunity for fighting Nasser or mounting [a] new Suez against Nasser'. Barbour warned of the effect that any drift in US policy towards accommodation with Nasser over the Lebanon would have on Anglo-American relations. Britain had acquiesced in the United States' attempts to normalize its relations with Nasser and to create a 'stand still agreement' with him. However, she was highly sceptical as to the possibilities of success for such an arrangement.

In fact, the US had been conducting, with the knowledge of the UK, a secret attempt to negotiate with Nasser over the Lebanese problem to which Barbour was no doubt making reference. The British Government itself, of course, had lost its diplomatic representation in Egypt as a result of the Suez crisis. On 28 May, the US Ambassador in Cairo had been instructed to raise with Nasser the question of whether he would be prepared

to use his influence with opposition leaders in the Lebanon con-
structively, in view of the fact that the Lebanese Government
had publicly pledged that it would not be a party to any attempts
to amend the constitution. The ambassador was told to state
that his initiative was on a personal basis so as to avoid the
impression that the US was negotiating directly with Nasser
over the Lebanon.[33]

Nasser came up with a three-point plan in response to the
American initiative. This involved Chamoun finishing his term
of office, General Fuad Chehab, the moderate Christian army
commander, succeeding him as President, and an amnesty for
the opposition.[34] Ambassador McClintock was instructed to
approach Chamoun with details of the plan on the understanding that the US did not endorse it, but merely felt that
the government of Lebanon should have the opportunity to
consider it. While this approach took place with the knowledge of the British Government, the implication of Barbour's
report is that they were sceptical as to the prospects for success
of any negotiation with Nasser, and suspicious as to how far
the US was prepared to go in seeking a compromise with him.

In the same vein, the talks between Macmillan and Eisenhower in Washington from 9 to 11 June showed the continuing difference in emphasis over policy towards Nasser. While
Macmillan reported to the Cabinet that the Americans had
agreed that 'for the present, the right course was to support
our friends and to maintain a cool but correct attitude towards
Egypt',[35] a State Department briefing paper for the talks emphasized that:

> although we share many of the UK's doubts regarding
> Nasser's basic objectives and we are under no illusions that
> Nasser will align himself with the West, we nonetheless believe
> that Western interests will be served by placing US-UAR rela-
> tions on a more normal basis so that Nasser may retain an
> alternative to an even closer association with the USSR and
> so that we may exert some degree of influence over United
> Arab Republic policies.[36]

The one qualification to this policy, however, was outlined
in a paper on the Lebanese crisis. Nasser's attitude towards,
and activities in, the other sovereign states in the area would be

'a critical element in determining US and Western policies toward him and the UAR'.[37] Lebanon would be a test case as to whether Nasser supported what the US regarded as a Soviet-inspired attempt to undermine a pro-Western country.

On the public level of diplomacy, the Security Council finally began to discuss the Lebanese complaint on 6 June, following a short delay to allow the Arab League time to seek a compromise between the parties. The US, Britain and France backed the Lebanese charge of UAR interference, while the Soviet Union argued that the threat came from certain Western powers which were preparing for armed intervention in the country. The result of the Council's deliberations was a resolution authorizing the dispatch of a UN observer force to ascertain the validity of the Lebanese Government's charges against the UAR. The duty of carrying out the Security Council's instructions, and setting up the observer force, was to fall on Dag Hammarskjöld, the charismatic and gifted Swedish Secretary General of the United Nations.

The fact that the UAR did not oppose the sending of the group served on the one hand to defuse somewhat American fears as to Nasser's intentions.[38] Eisenhower suggested in his memoirs that this action seemed to fit in with the indications from Cairo that Nasser might be happy to see a temporary end to the struggle in Lebanon.[39] On the other hand, as he told Dulles at the time, now that the United Nations was involved in the Lebanon, 'we would be in a bad spot if we intervened without the UN having first reported that the UN action was ineffective'.[40] As Dulles observed, if Chamoun called on the US to intervene she would have little alternative but to act, because if 'we do not respond, that will be the end of every pro-Western government in the area'. The Administration thus found itself manoeuvred into a corner, with the only way out appearing to be a UN finding that the UAR had interfered in Lebanon on a large scale. This would at least provide some legitimacy for any operations the US might be constrained to undertake.

Indeed, the difficulties of the position exposed something of a split between Secretary Dulles and Henry Cabot Lodge, the United States' representative at the UN. Lodge favoured some form of compromise with Nasser over the Lebanon because of what he regarded as the unacceptable damage which US military action would do to its reputation with the Arab countries. He evidently made this suggestion to Ambassador McClintock who then divulged it to Chamoun. Dulles was angry with both ambassadors, referring to McClintock's act as 'an indiscretion' and telling Lodge that the two of them were 'working a little bit at cross-purposes' over Lebanon.[41]

At the same time, concerns were rising on both sides of the Atlantic that Hammarskjöld would produce a report which whitewashed the UAR's role in the Lebanon. CIA chief Allen Dulles told his brother that Hammarskjöld was not 'bucking up' the situation very much, while the Secretary himself expressed the fear that Hammarskjöld was 'going to produce another Munich'.[42]

On the British side, this fear mingled with a belief that Hammarskjöld might also be trying to drive a wedge between the British and Americans over Lebanon, by fostering the impression that the British were pushing the US on, in order to create a showdown with Nasser and to vindicate the Suez operation. In a meeting with the Secretary General on 19 June, during a stopover before his departure for the Middle East, Selwyn Lloyd had sought to persuade him that: 'there was no truth in any ideas current in some American quarters that we were longing to go into Lebanon with the US to prove how right we had been over Suez and how wrong the US.'[43] Indeed, Selwyn Lloyd himself does appear to have been well aware of the potential dangers of intervention in the Lebanon, if this were merely to prop up the regime of Chamoun. In view of the UN role, Britain could not offer Chamoun a blank cheque in respect of military intervention. This would now have to be 'negotiated through the Security Council'.[44]

However, despite Lloyd's assurances, reports were soon received from Jordan that Dag Hammarskjöld was repeating the opinion that Britain was behind the pressure for military action in the Lebanon.[45] Brian Urquart too notes that Hammarskjöld found 'a disturbing feeling among diplomats in Beirut that the British were eager to become involved in the Lebanese situation, and also to have the US involved'.[46] Lloyd felt it necessary to write to him in the strongest terms, since the British could not afford to have their cooperation with the US threatened by the implication that they were somehow trying to manipulate the Administration into vindicating their stance against Nasser.[47]

In fact, what Secretary Dulles believed to be at issue in the Lebanon was something much broader than just the West's attitude towards Nasser's influence in the Levant. During a meeting with Allen Dulles, Donald Quarles, the Deputy Secretary of Defence, and Assistant Secretary of State William Rountree on 22 June, he stressed that although the governments of Iraq and Jordan might be swept away whether or not the US responded to a call for intervention in the Lebanon, 'the real difference lay in the peripheral countries', such as the Northern Tier states, Sudan and Libya, whose confidence would be undermined if the US did not demonstrate its resolve to act when called upon. More than this, on an even broader scale, 'what was at stake here was the whole periphery of the Soviet Union. . . . Our failure to respond would destroy the confidence in us of all the countries on the Soviet periphery throughout the Middle and Far East.'[48] Thus the US's behaviour over Lebanon would be a test of her cold war credibility worldwide. As Eisenhower himself later acknowledged, 'behind everything was our deep-seated conviction that the Communists were principally responsible for the trouble . . .'.[49]

In these circumstances, Dulles resolved that pressure must be exerted on Secretary General Hammarskjöld to ensure that the United Nations took a firm stand over what he perceived to be ultimately Soviet-inspired attempts to destabilize the region. On 24 June he told Harold Caccia that the Lebanon must be treated as 'a test case for the United Nations. . . . If the UN were powerless in this situation, there was a grave question as to its future. It would also raise the question as to whether the free world should not try to get closer together in order to protect its interests.'[50] Foster Dulles's rather hawkish attitude on the UN role was mirrored by Harold Macmillan, who thought it would be a good thing for Selwyn Lloyd to tell Dulles he was greatly struck by the fact that they were thinking along the same lines: 'namely that we should make the Lebanon situation a real test of the value of the UN and either make that organisation work or prove that it was useless.'[51]

Dag Hammarskjöld seems to have been well aware of the need to tread carefully over the Lebanese problem. His main objective was to isolate it from outside influence, whether from the UAR, or from the Western powers.[52] From Nasser, he sought assurances that the UAR would call a halt to military assistance to the Lebanese rebels. Indeed, one report from Amman which greatly surprised the British suggested that Hammarskjöld even 'had it in mind to seek the imposition of sanctions upon the UAR and to declare them the aggressors' if Nasser did not cooperate in his attempts to prevent cross-border infiltration.[53]

However, the indications as to the content of the UN Observers' report suggested that they would not substantiate Chamoun's claims. On 26 June Lodge told Dulles that Hammarskjöld felt 'the situation can perhaps best be summed up by the statement of Gallo Plaza that "the world is being taken for a ride." '[54] The observers had found little or no indication of the substantial intervention alleged by Chamoun, and believed that Chamoun himself had engineered much of the tension for his own political purposes. This was much the sort of finding that the British and Americans had feared would result from what they regarded as the observers' inadequate efforts. Indeed, the initial observers' report published two days later confirmed many of the worst fears of the British. It noted that it had not been possible to establish where arms found in Lebanon had been acquired, nor whether 'any of the armed men observed had infiltrated from outside'.[55] On his copy of the document, Macmillan annotated the words 'this is very poor stuff'.[56]

Nevertheless, it is important to note that despite the general sense of dissatisfaction on both sides of the Atlantic with the UN role in the Lebanon, the possibility of the use of Anglo-American forces was now receding. The tension in Lebanon was eased by Chamoun's unequivocal announcement that he would not now be seeking to stand for a second term as President. On the military side, the forces of both countries, which had been in position since the middle of May ready to carry out Plan 'Blue Bat', had already begun to scale down their state of readiness in view of the assessment that Anglo-American intervention was becoming less probable due to the involvement of the UN. Even if there should be a call for such assistance, it would probably have to be negotiated through the Security Council in the first instance, which would provide a short breathing space in which to bring the necessary forces back to the peak state of readiness.[57]

However, while both the British and the Americans now believed that any solution to the Lebanese problem would have to come through the UN, in a meeting with Hammarskjöld on 7 July, Secretary Dulles stressed that, although he regarded armed intervention as 'a very undesirable outcome', he stuck to his views about the disastrous consequences should America ignore an appeal for help from the pro-Western Government of Lebanon.[58] Since the touchstone of US credibility in the cold war was the ability to back her rhetoric with action when circumstances demanded it, the US, on Dulles's reasoning, would have to intervene if requested in the Lebanon or see her other positions around the world crumble in the face of the Communist threat.

It was this posture that was to dictate the swift decision by the Administration to respond to Chamoun's appeal for US troops immediately after the Iraqi Revolution. The sending in of forces really had very little to do with the demands of the Lebanese situation itself, a fact that was to be mirrored by the lack of any significant military action during their stay in the country. What it was intended to do was to give a signal to the Soviet Union that the US was prepared to support friendly governments throughout the Middle East and indeed around the world, by force if necessary. In fact, the crisis in Lebanon fitted in with Eisenhower and Dulles's belief that the Soviets would attempt some form of subversion of a pro-Western regime in the Middle East during the course of 1958. The equivocal attitude which the two had adopted towards Nasser from the formation of the UAR onwards hardened noticeably during the course of the crisis in Lebanon, which seemed to them to provide evidence that Nasser might after all be sold to the Soviets.

To the British, developments fell in with their steadfast belief that Nasser was the enemy of the West, intent on building his own empire at their expense in the Middle East. Although the good offices of UN Secretary General Dag Hammarskjöld, and the internal dynamics of the Lebanese situation, were serving to diminish tensions in the region by the middle of July, the Iraqi Revolution was soon to turn the Middle Eastern world upside down again.

11 The Iraqi Revolution

The coup d'etat in Iraq early on the morning of 14 July 1958, which swept away the Hashemite Royal Family and replaced it with a cadre of officers led by Brigadier Abdel Karim Qassem, seems to have struck both the British and American Governments as a bolt from the blue.[1] In fact, closer attention to the internal situation in the country might have revealed that the atmosphere in the capital was unusually tense even by Iraqi standards in the weeks immediately preceding the coup attempt. For instance, a visit by King Feisal to a degree-giving ceremony at the University of Baghdad early in July met with a particularly sullen response, with one observer sympathetic to the government arguing that it was reminiscent of the period immediately preceding Rashid Ali's insurrection in 1941.[2]

The origins of the July coup were bound up with the development of an Iraqi Free Officers movement which paralleled that in Egypt, and which can be traced back to the return of certain officers from the Palestine War in 1949.[3] Disillusioned with the conduct of politics in the Arab world, these men were greatly impressed by the example of the Egyptian Revolution of 1952. Meeting spontaneously and in small groups, the movement continued, if in a somewhat disorganized manner, over the years that followed. The isolation of Iraq in the Arab world as a result of its membership of the Baghdad Pact, the Cairo Radio attacks on the monarchy and government as stooges of British imperialism, and finally the Suez crisis, all served to reinforce the convictions of the officers that something akin to the Egyptian Revolution was needed if Iraq was to return to the mainstream of Arab politics.

The leader of the coup, Brigadier Qassem, was a close protégé of Nuri's. Because the Prime Minister held him in close affection, even when he was presented with direct evidence of his disloyalty he refused to dismiss him or move him to some post distant from Baghdad. Thus, at the critical moment, his brigade was stationed close to the capital, while potential rivals for the leadership of the movement were serving in the far north or south of the country, or holding staff appointments without troops at their disposal.[4] The issue of Qassem's own personal convictions and the nature of the Iraqi Revolution will be examined below in the context of a discussion of developments in post-revolutionary Iraq. However, what is significant for the present is the impact of the coup on British and American strategy, and the perceptions of policy-makers in the two countries as to its ramifications.

Clearly, from the British point of view, the removal of the Hashemite regime in Iraq struck at the very basis of the regional strategy which had been pursued since the formation of the Baghdad Pact. Although the initial indications were uncertain as to whether the entire Royal Family had been massacred, and whether Nuri had died with them, the first reaction of Harold Macmillan in particular was bellicose and extravagant. It was presumed as a matter of course that Nasser was behind the coup, and that it was all part of his plan to subvert the entire region, denying Britain access to the oil supplies vital to her national survival.[5] In these circumstances, Macmillan felt, half-measures would not be enough. What would be required was a broad operation sweeping throughout the area to rectify the position in favour of the West. The lesson of Suez had been that Britain did not have the resources to undertake such an operation herself. The thrust of Macmillan's efforts since then had been to bring Britain and America much closer together, not for some abstract and sentimental goal of showing the specialness of their relations, but to meet the hard-headed reality that Britain needed US power and support, both military and diplomatic, to achieve her aims in the Middle East. In the short term, these aims boiled down to the defeat of Nasser.

As soon as news arrived on the morning of 14 July of the events in Iraq, President Chamoun of Lebanon called in the British and American Ambassadors. First, he upbraided them for the inactivity of their governments in the face of the palpable threat from Nasser and the Communists, which he claimed they had ignored. Then he called in the promises of assistance which they had made to him should Lebanon be threatened with subversion from without.[6] Of course, as British Chargé d'Affaires Scott and American Ambassador McClintock both pointed out, it was quite possible that Chamoun was simply seizing on the events in Iraq as 'his last card to play to bring about friendly military intervention in Lebanon'.[7] However, to a US Administration primed for Soviet attempts to undermine pro-Western governments in the region, the Iraqi Revolution had delivered a profound shock. All contingency planning had been based on the assumption that Lebanon and Jordan were much more unstable than Iraq, and much more likely to be the target of subversion. With the regime in Iraq gone, the remaining pro-Western governments in Lebanon and Jordan looked particularly vulnerable.

What was needed, therefore, was some demonstration of American resolve to protect the friends of the West, however dubious the basis of their requests for assistance might be. The cold war game with the Soviets dictated that the Administration should live much more in the realm of potential, as opposed to real or proven, threats. At a meeting with the CIA and the military, Secretary Dulles argued that American intervention in Lebanon would be very important symbolically. If the US did not respond, then three developments would result. Firstly, Nasser would take over the whole area. Secondly, the US would lose influence not only in the Arab states of the Middle East, but in the region generally. Finally, and most importantly, 'the dependability of United States commitments for assistance in the event of need would be brought into question throughout the world.'[8]

The Americans, like the British, initially believed that Nasser had helped to organize the plot in Iraq. Unlike their counterparts across the Atlantic, however, they did not regard him as the principal threat in the region. Although the Iraqi coup was taken in its initial stages as evidence that the worst fears about Nasser's relationship with the Soviets had proven to be true, it was the Soviets themselves who were regarded as the main sponsors of instability in the Middle East. While it now seemed that the hopes that had been raised as to Nasser's independence of mind by his disagreements with the Russians over Syria were unfounded, he himself, according to Eisenhower, was 'so small a figure, and of so little power, that he is a puppet, even though he probably doesn't think so'.[9] He was of importance only in so far as he was acting as a front for Soviet plans to undermine the interests of the West in the region.

In reality it seems that despite the initial convictions of the British and American Governments that Nasser was implicated in the Iraqi coup, the Free Officers who had organized the insurrection had not made contact with the UAR. Nasser's knowledge does not seem to have extended beyond the existence of the movement itself, with which he had some earlier contacts through friends in Baghdad. He certainly does not seem to have been consulted about the specific plans for a takeover on 14 July.[10] Still, it was not until several days after the revolution, and after the British and American Governments had made their respective decisions to intervene in Lebanon and Jordan, that the suggestion started to be made that the new rulers of the country might be 'more Iraqi nationalist than Nasserite'.[11]

The US decision to intervene in the Lebanon at Chamoun's request seems to have been taken by Eisenhower almost immediately on 14 July, and with little internal debate in the US Administration.[12] Eisenhower told a crisis meeting of his advisers convened at 10.50am that it was clear in his mind that 'we must act, or get out of the Middle East entirely. . . . To lose this area by inaction would be far worse that the loss of China . . .'[13] He noted later that this was 'one meeting in which my mind was practically made up regarding the general line of action we should take, even before we met'.[14] The 'trend toward chaos' in the region had to be halted, and the President believed this could only be done by high profile US military action. Having decided that the US must send forces to Lebanon, the next question to be answered was whether the existing plan for intervention alongside the British, 'Blue Bat', should be implemented. Of course, the specific circumstance that the plan envisaged was a deterioration in the internal situation in Lebanon leading to a request for military assistance from Britain and America by the Lebanese Government.[15] Despite Chamoun's insistence to the contrary, the reports cited above from the two countries' representatives within Lebanon indicated that there had in fact been no change in the position in Lebanon. Eisenhower either disregarded the reports, or convinced himself that since the coup in Iraq had occurred without warning, the same thing might happen in the Lebanon. Either way, it was important for US credibility to respond quickly.

Although the circumstances surrounding the operation were different from those which had been envisaged, they did not invalidate its logistical underpinning. The plan stated: 'US forces will be committed initially, followed by British forces which will conduct operations as directed.' Two possible operations were contemplated. The first involved a US Marine amphibious assault to secure the Beirut area, followed by the deployment of British land forces. The second would be the air-dropping of a US airborne battle group from Europe into the Beirut area, followed again by the deployment of British land forces. As was noted in the previous chapter, Admiral Holloway, the overall commander of the operation, felt that the US was likely to favour the amphibious assault because it would involve fewer political complications. In either case, the British troops, although not the first into Beirut, would play an equally important role in securing the capital.

At the meeting in which US intervention was agreed, however, President Eisenhower argued that the best course of action would be for the US to put forces ashore immediately, 'with the United Kingdom holding its forces ready for Iraq or Jordan'.[16] This justification for unilateral US action in the Lebanon, which was to be repeated to the British, is the starting point for the myth, fostered by both Eisenhower and Macmillan, and repeated by certain subsequent commentators, of a joint Anglo-American operation in Lebanon and Jordan.[17]

What were Eisenhower's motives in acting unilaterally in the Lebanon? Certainly, he may have believed that British forces might be needed to carry out operations elsewhere. However, as will be seen, the very great reluctance of the Administration to acquiesce in the British intervention in Jordan, and the suspicions voiced of British motives, tend to suggest otherwise. Even if it is argued that he may have envisaged British intervention, but at a rather later date than that sought by Prime Minister Macmillan, the question still must be answered as to why he wanted the first and highest profile action to be undertaken by America. One subsidiary explanation may have been fear of reminding the Arabs of the Suez operation undertaken by the British two years earlier. Indeed, in the planning for 'Blue Bat', Dulles had emphasized that the commander of the Anglo-American forces 'must be an American, because of resentment felt toward Britain throughout the Middle East'.[18] Henry Cabot Lodge had also urged that: 'if intervention in Lebanon by US troops becomes unavoidable it would be very much better for US troops to go in alone. The world sees us in an entirely different light than it sees the UK and France. If we go in alone the contrast with Suez would be brought out.'[19]

However, the main reason at this stage for the US acting unilaterally appears to have been bound up with the point which Eisenhower sought to make through the operation. This was to show the Soviet Union that the US would act to protect its friends around the world, and more specifically, that it had the military might available and the political will to defend the Middle East which both Eisenhower and Dulles now saw as the Soviets' principal target for subversion. As Dulles told a meeting of Congressional leaders, 'if we move quickly and decisively the Soviet Union – which is undoubtedly behind the whole operation – may feel that Nasser has gone too far too fast and may call on him to pull back.'[20]

Certainly, the British were immediately suspicious that the US intention might be to deal with the Lebanon, and then to back away from retrieving the position in Iraq and Jordan.[21] Initially, therefore, it was the Cabinet's conclusion that:

> it might be wiser to offer at least a token British contingent for the operation in the Lebanon and to make it clear to the US Government that, even if they regarded such a contingent as unnecessary, we should expect them to regard the whole enterprise of restoring political stability in the Middle East, with the possible exception of Kuwait, as a joint task which they should share with us.

Macmillan passed on his conviction to Eisenhower that what was required was a wide-ranging Anglo-American operation throughout the region, in a crucial phone conversation following the first Cabinet meeting on the evening of 14 July.[22] If the Americans had nurtured any suspicions about British intentions in the Middle East lingering from Suez, or from Macmillan's bellicose language during the Syrian crisis of the previous autumn, this conversation undoubtedly fuelled them.

In response to Eisenhower's suggestion that he might want to hold British troops in reserve for action elsewhere, 'depending on developments in the Lebanon', Macmillan argued: 'the point is this. If you do this thing in the Lebanon, it is really only part of a much larger operation, because we shall be driven to take the thing as a whole. I want to feel that we both regard it as a whole. It looks like a showdown.' Eisenhower's terse response to this was: 'so far as we are concerned we cannot undertake anything beyond Lebanon. The situation elsewhere is going to be much more complicated.'[23] Although Macmillan pressed him, Eisenhower would not make a commitment to any operations beyond Lebanon, arguing that this went 'far far beyond' anything which he had the power to do constitutionally. In passing, Macmillan also referred to a request which had been received from King Hussein of Jordan, who, under the terms of the Arab Union, could now technically claim authority over Iraq as well. King Hussein had apparently asked for an early indication of the willingness of the British and American Governments to support him militarily should he feel it necessary to call on them. Again Eisenhower was non-committal.

Although the upshot of the conversation was that Macmillan agreed to unilateral US action in Lebanon, he gained no guarantee of American support for further operations in the region. While Eisenhower accepted that by intervening in the Lebanon he was 'opening a Pandora's Box', he refused to assent to any of Macmillan's grander plans until it became clear exactly what might emerge.[24]

Macmillan persuaded the reconvened Cabinet that 'the balance of advantage lay in accepting the US offer to release us from contributing to the Lebanon operation, provided that the US Government did not regard this as absolving them from cooperating actively with us in restoring the situation in Iraq and Jordan'.[25] British efforts were now to be focused particularly on Jordan, with the Cabinet concluding that 'from every point of view . . . it would be advantageous if King Hussein would issue without delay his formal appeal to the US and ourselves'. This conclusion was the beginning of what amounted, over the next 48 hours, to an unseemly scramble on the part of the British Government to get forces into Jordan somehow, anyhow. The reasons for this were much bound up with the questions both of making a point to Nasser about continuing British determination to thwart his intrigues, and of bolstering British prestige in the region. If Britain were seen to be sidelined, with the US taking the only effective military action, then her remaining positions in the Middle East, particularly in the Persian Gulf, might be further undermined.

Immediately after the Cabinet meeting, therefore, Macmillan cabled the President and Dulles, arguing that both countries should agree immediately to Hussein's request for an assurance of military assistance should he require it.[26] More than this, however, he asserted that 'we ought, in my opinion, to urge the King to make his request at once, since if our military support is to be effective and have a real impact upon the whole situation in the Middle East, it will have to be given promptly.' The urgency with which Macmillan viewed the question of getting British forces into the region, and the degree of pressure which the British Government sought to exert on King Hussein, were re-emphasized at a meeting between Macmillan, Defence Minister Duncan Sandys and the Chiefs of Staff. Here it was agreed that:

> provided . . . the reply from President Eisenhower satisfactorily meets the main political objective that any British action in Jordan should be part of a joint Anglo-American plan for the whole Middle East area, King Hussein should be given the assurance for which he has asked, but he should be urged to ask for military assistance at once. . . . The Jordanian Government should also be advised of the terms in which their request for military assistance should be expressed.[27]

To be sure, there were sound military reasons for getting forces into a potential trouble spot before the airfield, for instance, fell into rebel hands. However, arguments of this nature do not obscure the fact that Macmillan was anxious to get troops into Jordan as part of a broader Anglo-American enterprise to thwart Nasser's designs. Macmillan wanted to send forces to the area, and secure American cooperation in this greater goal before the opportunity passed.

The Americans, however, were extremely sceptical, both as to the need for sending forces to Jordan immediately, and as to British motives for urging their dispatch. Dulles's initial response to the messages to him from Macmillan, conveyed by Lord Hood, was that he could not commit the US to any action in Jordan. Moreover, he wondered whether in fact, Anglo-American military intervention in support of the King might actually weaken his position by alienating his remaining support in the country.[28] Discussing the situation with Eisenhower, Dulles noted that what the British seemed to be asking for was 'a blank check'. Both he and the President agreed that they could not be given it. Moreover, Hussein should not be pressurized into calling for assistance immediately.[29] The American attitude frustrated the British, with the Cabinet noting that 'the initial response of the US Government to our proposal for immediate action in Jordan was disappointing'.[30]

However, the British kept up the pressure on Dulles and Eisenhower. In a cable to Hood, briefing him on the line to take with Dulles, Selwyn Lloyd argued that:

> the situation in Iraq may not be irretrievable. If a Western force could be firmly established in Jordan before disorder starts there it would serve the double purpose of stiffening the King's resolve and forming a bridgehead for such possible future action as may be necessary in Iraq. If we had Western forces in both Lebanon and Jordan we should have some cards in our hands in working towards a restoration of the Western position in the Arab world.[31]

However, this line of argument seems only to have aroused Dulles's suspicions of British motives. Did the British in fact want to indulge in their familiar ruse of getting the US to pull their chestnuts out of the fire for them? Were they trying to drag the US into a broad operation to counter Nasser's influence of the kind which they had engaged in only two years earlier over Suez? Dulles made it plain to Hood that he could not involve America in any intervention in Jordan until he 'could see more clearly what it was intended to achieve'. 'Did we [the British] hope that Hussein with our support would be able to re-establish the situation in Iraq? Or rouse the tribes in Syria?'[32] At this stage, Secretary Dulles and his State Department colleagues all agreed that 'the question of Jordanian and British motives were both too unclear to permit any conclusions by us'.[33] Eisenhower too noted that 'the United Kingdom wants to get us to commit ourselves now to clearing up the whole mid-East situation, and this gives . . . [me] a good deal of concern'.[34]

With American troops landing alone in Beirut, however, the possibility of British exclusion from operations now appeared a very real one. At this point, however, news came to light of a projected plot against King Hussein intended to take place on the morning of 17 July. The coincidence was all too convenient for British purposes. Uriel Dann argues that Hussein had in fact been presented with evidence about an intended coup against him by the US diplomatic mission in Amman two weeks before the Iraqi Revolution.[35] Its central figure was Lieutenant Colonel Mahmud Rusan, who had apparently received the support of Syria for his intrigues. There was, however, no proven link between Rusan's plans, of which the Syrians were aware, and the coup in Iraq, which seems to have taken them as much by surprise as anyone else.

The events in Iraq had a profound impact on King Hussein. Hearing of the murder of his cousin, Feisal, he immediately assumed the leadership of the Arab Union, and seemed intent on some action to reimpose Hashemite rule on Iraq. The possibility that Jordanian forces might be needed, either to intervene in Iraq or to defend the borders of the country, explains his perception of the need to call on the British and American Governments to give guarantees of assistance in holding the capital should it be required. What seems to have convinced the King to call in the British forces on the evening of 16 July, however, was information presented to him that the Rusan plot was scheduled to take place the following day.

In discussing the situation in Jordan with Eisenhower on 16 July, Dulles noted that 'this intelligence came from the British who gave a digest of it to Hussein'.[36] Although there was confirmation of the British information from a 'reliable source' in Israel,[37] the convenience of the timing of the plot for British purposes, and Dulles's suggestion that it was the British themselves who had made this discovery, is at least a little suspicious. Certainly, this seems to have been the opinion of the US Chargé d'Affaires in Amman, Thomas Wright. When he asked Jordanian Prime Minister Samir Rifai whether there was other evidence beyond that supplied by the US, presumably from the

Israeli channel, about the impending coup, he was interrupted by the British Chargé, Mason. Mason told him that he: 'had given [the] King information from what HMG considered [a] "most reliable source" indicating UAR agents had penetrated not only [the West] bank refugee camps but also [a] considerable portion [of] East Jordan, that they had responsive groups within [the] security forces including [the] Army who in all probability would not "fire on their brothers" once mob action began.'[38] Thus, although the analysis presented by Uriel Dann confirms that there probably was some form of plot in the offing, it seems that intelligence information supplied by the British was decisive in persuading the King to act. British purposes were well served by the discovery of the imminence of the coup.

In the light of all the evidence presented about the pressure exerted by the British Government to get forces into the region alongside the US, and the dealings over Jordan from the news of the Iraqi Revolution until the decision to intervene at Hussein's request on the evening of 16 July, Macmillan's statements to the House of Commons on the subject appear disingenuous in the extreme. Reporting on the events of the previous evening to the House on 17 July, Macmillan argued that two telegrams he had received from Amman the evening before had been the first he had heard of the Jordanian appeal for assistance.[39] Of course, he was technically correct that this was the point at which the Jordanians made their formal request for military intervention. However, Macmillan himself had spent the previous two days trying to persuade the Americans and the Jordanians that this request should be made and accepted.

Moreover, he reversed the flow of intelligence about the projected plot against King Hussein, asserting that 'this was the information which the Jordanian Government communicated to us last night and of which we had independent corroboration from various sources'. In view of Prime Minister Macmillan's enthusiasm for British participation in military operations in the region, his claim that this was 'the most difficult decision that I personally ever remember having to take, or being asked to take, or being associated with' must be taken with rather more than the proverbial pinch of salt.

From the beginning, the Americans were at best unenthusiastic about the British intervention in Jordan. Macmillan told the Cabinet that 'Dulles had expressed the view that the situation might develop less quickly than we feared, and he hoped that we might feel able to defer action until there had been time for further Anglo-American consultation . . .'.[40] The Secretary noted that he and Eisenhower 'both had some reservations . . . as to the need of the operation and its desirability. . . . However . . . the decision seemed such a close one that I had not felt like trying to impose that view'.[41] With the British pressing so hard, Dulles evidently believed that it would cause the US more difficulties than it was worth in terms of strained relations with her ally if he should actually oppose the operation as he had done over Suez two years earlier. Apart from anything else, the US was going to need Britain's support in the United Nations over her own intervention in Lebanon. He agreed, therefore, to provide diplomatic assistance to the British, together with logistical aid for their operations in Jordan. However, he did not commit himself on the question of the involvement of US forces.

In truth, the Americans were right to regard the British intervention in Jordan as precarious. Just how precarious was revealed by the immediate objections of the Israelis to the overflights of British planes carrying in the paratroops to Amman. The only feasible method of landing and supplying the British forces was from Cyprus through Israeli airspace. However, through an extraordinary oversight, indicative of the haste with which the Government was acting in a bid to get troops into the area, the Israelis were not asked permission for the first flights. Consequently, they actually fired on some of the planes. Although, with American assistance, the Israelis were pressured into letting the flights through, they continued to cause difficulties over the transit of supplies. As noted by Charles Rundall, British Ambassador in Tel Aviv, Prime Minister Ben Gurion seemed to have decided that this was 'the psychological moment to extract his long term price'. This was likely to be 'integration into the Western defence system, a tacit guarantee of Israel's present frontiers and the supply of armaments she needs'.[42]

The only factor which was to save the British from their potentially exposed position with a lightly armed force at the end of a long and uncertain supply line, was the fact that the projected insurrection, for whatever reason, was never to materialize. The British operation in Jordan and the American intervention in Lebanon are perfect examples of the adage that history favours the victors, even when, in fact, they had little or nothing to vanquish.

With forces already in Amman, the British now focused on the goal of securing an American contingent, however small, to stand beside their troops. The reasoning behind this was, no doubt, that with their own men committed, the Americans would be under a direct obligation to provide much more extensive assistance should major unrest break out in the country. Despite the importunities of Prime Minister Macmillan and Foreign Secretary Lloyd, however, the American refusal to become involved in Jordan was adamant. Justifying the British intervention in Jordan to President Eisenhower, Macmillan was already beginning to scale down his grand schemes for taking the opportunity to rectify the situation throughout the region, which had not been well received in Washington. Now, he argued that having 'started on this difficult road I do not see how we can withdraw until we have somehow restored stability and strength in at least some areas of the Middle East'.[43]

Indeed, some initial indications as to the Americans' intentions were positive, with Lloyd concluding from his talks in Washington that: 'the best feature of the day has been my impression that both Foster and the President regard the Lebanon and Jordan as combined Anglo-American operations.'[44] However, when Lloyd argued that the best way to add substance to this sentiment was for a US contingent to join the British in Jordan, Eisenhower's response was telling. He asserted that: 'the fact that our forces were now engaged on two countries so closely adjacent was in itself proof that we were acting together.'[45] This set the scene for the US Administration's response to repeated requests from Lloyd and Macmillan for American forces to be sent to Jordan. This, as Hood noted, was 'wholly negative'.[46]

The reasons for the Americans' refusal were expounded by Dulles at a meeting with the President, and representatives of the CIA, State Department and military, on 23 July. Dulles argued that:

we must regard Arab nationalism as a flood tide which is running strongly. We cannot successfully oppose it, but we can put sand bags around positions we must protect – the first group being Israel and Lebanon and the second being the oil positions around the Persian Gulf. The Soviets are seeking to incite the floods, and we cannot compete with them because they play to the Arab desire to 'drive Israel into the sea' and throw out the West.[47]

According to this reasoning, Jordan, which Dulles viewed as an unviable state, was not a position which could be defended in the long term. There was therefore little point in exposing US troops to the dangers involved in what Dulles viewed as an ultimately pointless intervention. He later described the British as 'foolishly exposed in Jordan',[48] and during the meeting itself recalled that 'we had not wanted the British to go in'. All in all, although, as Eisenhower suggested, the operations might appear to be linked by their proximity and by the diplomatic support the two countries offered each other at the United Nations, the US Administration wanted to steer clear of direct involvement in what it regarded as the ill-founded British action in Jordan.

It is clear that Prime Minister Macmillan had begun to scale down his grand plans for Anglo-American operations throughout the region as soon as British forces reached Jordan. This did not mean any reassessment of the steadfast British belief that Nasser was at the root of the Middle East's problems, and that he must be defeated at all costs. Rather what took place was some revaluation of the state of affairs in Iraq. The first British reaction, like that of the Americans, had been that Nasser had been involved in the organization of the coup, with the Americans seeing him as the puppet of the Soviet Union. News coming out of Baghdad, however, indicated that, as Macmillan cabled Lloyd, there was 'quite a chance . . . from the character of the men and some of their first statements that they may turn out to be more Iraqi nationalist than Nasserite'.[49]

In fact, as will be seen in the discussion of events in post-revolutionary Iraq, Brigadier Qassem, who emerged as the new leader of the country, was anything but a Nasserite. He may more properly be classified as 'an Iraqi patriot' than as 'a pan-Arab nationalist'.[50] Growing up under British tutelage, Qassem had developed an aversion to foreign domination in any form. Thus, although he had a great deal of sympathy for the goals of Arab nationalism in so far as they involved the rejection of Western influence, and was ready to establish close relations with the UAR, 'he would never have agreed to surrender Iraq's sovereign rights, as did Syria in her hasty union with Egypt'.[51] The first months after the revolution in Iraq were to be marked by a struggle for power between Qassem and other leaders of the coup, such as Colonel Aref, who sought much closer relations with Nasser.

At a special Cabinet committee meeting on 22 July, convened to discuss future Middle East policy, it was agreed that the military support of countries in the area, along the lines of the action taken in Jordan, was not a long-term solution to the problem of maintaining stability and access to the oil supplies of the region. In some form or other, Britain would have to come to terms with the growth of Arab nationalism. However:

> Arab nationalism should not necessarily be looked upon as an indivisible movement. History had shown that Damascus and Baghdad and Cairo provided different focal points for the growth of national feeling. In the long-term, it might be possible to exploit the natural differences of outlook between the Iraqis and the Egyptians. There was much to be said for establishing good relations with the new Iraqi Government and building it up as a counterpart to the power of the UAR. In brief, coming to terms with the growth of Arab nationalism did not necessarily mean the establishment of a friendly relationship with Colonel Nasser.[52]

In hindsight, the speed with which the British Government was to move in trying to establish close relations with Qassem does indeed appear extraordinary. However, as will be seen, since the priority of the British remained the countering of Nasser's influence, as soon as it became clear that Qassem was not to be a tool of the Egyptian leader the British were keen to encourage his independence of spirit, even though this was to involve him in a flirtation with the Iraqi Communist Party. This attitude was to cause conflict with the US Administration, which still had its eyes focused on the primary goal of preventing the Soviets profiting from the situation.

In addition to the substantial direct investment in the oil industry of Iraq held by the British-owned Iraqi Petroleum Company, one very important explanation for the British attitude towards the new Iraqi regime was the position of Kuwait. Iraq maintained a long-standing claim to the territory of the emirate dating back to the First World War, and resented the cavalier fashion in which the boundaries of the two states had been fixed during the carve-up of the region. More recently, even during the negotiations for the formation of the Arab Union, and despite the pleas of Prime Minister Nuri, the British Government had refused to sweeten the pill of union for Iraq by allowing Kuwait to be brought within the federation. Indeed, during the June talks in Washington, Macmillan had expressed his surprise at the degree of pressure exerted by Nuri to secure Kuwaiti accession to the Arab Union.[53] On this issue, Macmillan would not give ground.

Kuwait was particularly significant to the British economy at this stage, both because it was the largest oil producer in the region and because it was the source of oil which could be paid for in sterling. As early as the morning of 15 July, Dulles was explaining the British desire to conduct operations to retrieve the situation in Iraq in terms of their 'tremendous investment in oil there and in nearby Kuwait'.[54]

During the discussions between Lloyd and Dulles in Washington it had been agreed, according to Dulles, 'to take a strong line on holding the Persian Gulf'.[55] Lloyd had told Dulles that British reinforcements were en route to the Gulf, and a decision would be taken within the next two or three days as to whether these 'should occupy Kuwait against [the] wishes [of the] Ruling Family'.[56] Although Lloyd was inclined not to take such action, and made this recommendation to Macmillan, the example of the Iraqi coup which had broken without warning meant that the British had to be ready to move swiftly and decisively in Kuwait. Dulles indicated a similar US willingness to take whatever measures were necessary to hold on to the Dharan airbase, and to defend Saudi Arabia. The two agreed to make the Persian Gulf the subject of a new Working Group between the two countries.[57] US intelligence reports on

23 July indicated that the British were 'redeploying forces on a worldwide scale to strengthen [the] Persian Gulf area'. The US itself also took action to protect the Gulf, with President Eisenhower ordering the transfer there of a Marine regimental combat team from Okinawa.[58] However, the direct approach of defending the Gulf by moving forces there could only be a short-term solution, due to the financial demands it imposed. Far more desirable in the longer term was the establishment of sound relations with the new regime in Baghdad.

Thus, the first week after the Iraqi Revolution had witnessed extensive action by both the British and American Governments in the Middle East. Due to the initial lack of information as to the nature of the coup, both countries reacted by fearing the worst. For the Americans, this meant that the coup was part of the broader Soviet design to destabilize the whole region, making use of the forces of Arab nationalism. A point had to be made to the Soviets and to Nasser, the man who was now seen once again as their 'puppet', about American resolve to defend friendly nations in the area. Hence the rapid dispatch of troops to Lebanon.

For the British, the Iraqi coup was part of Nasser's systematic attempt to undermine their position in the region by sweeping away their key Baghdad Pact ally. Harold Macmillan sought at first to enlist American assistance in a broad operation to counter Nasser's designs, and then had to settle for a limited and exposed British intervention in Jordan, and a redeployment of forces to try to protect the Persian Gulf. Although some support was provided by the Americans, particularly in the latter area, and in the form of logistical aid for the operation in Jordan, this fell far short of what Macmillan might have hoped for. In particular, despite the plans laid for joint intervention in the Levant, the Americans insisted on keeping the two operations essentially separate. The British were to be left to fend for themselves in Jordan, despite pleas for US ground forces, a situation which amply demonstrated the limitations on the restored post-Suez 'special relationship' between the two countries.[59]

12 The Course and Conclusion of British and American Intervention

Paradoxically, almost as soon as their forces were established in Lebanon and Jordan, the principal preoccupation of both the American and British Governments was how to secure their withdrawal. The reason for this was not difficult to comprehend. The Iraqi Revolution, far from being part of a grand plot to destabilize the region, turned out to be an isolated, indigenous affair. Therefore, there was little for the troops to do in Lebanon and Jordan, and, particularly in the case of the Americans in Lebanon, there was no evidence of an imminent threat to the stability of the country. The irony of the American intervention was that the US Administration was to disengage on the basis of a political settlement, which was almost exactly what Nasser had suggested during his secret contacts with the US Government in early June.

The tone for the American operation had been set by the decision to storm in over the main pleasure beaches of Beirut, rather than over equally suitable but rather less populated sands to the north. As the diplomat Charles Thayer notes, 'the watching bathers were duly impressed'.[1] The landing was also hampered at the last minute by the attempts of Ambassador McClintock to intercept the first wave of marines by sending out a launch to meet them. General Chehab had apparently persuaded him that he would be unable to maintain internal order if the US forces landed. However, the marines swept ashore, unmoved by the pleas of the ambassador. The despatch of Deputy Under Secretary of State Robert Murphy to Beirut by Eisenhower was evidence both of a lack of confidence in McClintock,[2] and of a desire to set about immediately the task of seeking a political solution in Lebanon. In this context, the continuing presence of the United Nations Observer

Force in the country seemed to offer the most promising avenue of approach. If the UN could be persuaded to oversee any political settlement in the country, then this would smooth the process of American withdrawal, and do so, moreover, without loss of face.

As early as the morning of 15 July, Henry Cabot Lodge had contacted Secretary General Dag Hammarskjöld asserting that the US Government intended to base its actions on Article 51 of the United Nations Charter. Hammarskjöld's initial reaction was that the American intervention would interfere in the actions of the United Nations Observer Group in Lebanon (UNOGIL), and that a new decision would be required from the Security Council on its role. The observers themselves regarded the US operation as a major setback to what they had been trying to achieve, especially since a political solution seemed in sight, based on the election of General Chehab to the Presidency.[3] President Eisenhower was keen to emphasize to the Security Council through Lodge that the American action had been taken not to supplant the United Nations, but only to guard against any potential destabilization of the country resulting from the events in Iraq. The US was 'obviously anxious that UNOGIL survive but also that it be enlarged in order to provide a justification for a US withdrawal'.[4]

Acting on his own initiative after the Soviet veto had blocked the passing of a Japanese Resolution intended to facilitate a UN role in covering the US withdrawal from Lebanon, Hammarskjöld set to work on a substantial enlargement of the Observer Group. The idea was that the larger group should have a calming effect on the internal situation in Lebanon, thereby creating the conditions for the US departure. However, by far the most significant development in this respect was the election of General Chehab as President on 31 July. Although this did not result in any immediate scaling down of the US presence, which actually reached its numerical peak on 8 August, the basis of an indigenous Lebanese settlement was now in place. Whatever the claims of Eisenhower regarding the good offices of Murphy, who had been in contact with all of the main Lebanese factions, this had resulted largely from the willingness of the Lebanese themselves to solve their political problems.[5]

The British Government was anxious that the UN should

take on some role in Jordan to parallel that which it was already playing in the Lebanon. On 17 July, the Jordanian Government had asked for an urgent meeting of the Security Council to consider UAR interference in its internal affairs. Hammarskjöld remained suspicious that the British would attempt to persuade the US not to withdraw quickly from the Lebanon, a suspicion that seems to have been fostered by his own talks with Selwyn Lloyd in Washington.[6] Indeed, Hammarskjöld's impressions are confirmed by Macmillan's advice to Lloyd that: 'the essential thing is that the US should not be jostled or persuaded out of the Lebanon as we were out of Suez.'[7] The root of British fears seems to have been that the Americans would take advantage of any political settlement in Lebanon, and of the expanded UN role, to withdraw, leaving Britain isolated in Jordan. This fear became even more pressing after the election of Chehab as President. Lloyd cabled the Washington Embassy pointing out that should the US decide to withdraw at an early date, 'all the heat would be turned on us in Jordan and we should have to make a rapid decision about our future policy there'. This danger was all the more real since 'the link between the Lebanon and Jordan has never been absolutely established'.[8]

In addition to their uncertainty as to American aims in Lebanon, the British were to become increasingly exasperated over the US Administration's attitude to Jordan. Having taken the rash decision to intervene in that country, Macmillan was all too well aware that the British position depended on both the logistical support of the Americans, involving their intercession with the Israelis, and the Americans' financial assistance to the Jordanian Government. However, as might be expected from the opinions expressed by Dulles as to the likely course of the flood-tide of Arab nationalism, the Americans were pessimistic about the long-term prospects for stability in the country under the existing government. During discussions in Washington in early August, Assistant Secretary Rountree had told Lord Hood that 'no form of United Nations presence in Jordan would be adequate to maintain King Hussein in power without the presence of our troops . . .' In these circumstances, he 'wondered whether our objective should not be to look for some means of bringing about a "peaceful change" in

Jordan through UN action, with the object of minimizing the effect on our interests and prestige of the removal of King Hussein'.[9]

In private, the Foreign Office seems to have shared the American view, although Selwyn Lloyd was to characterize the attitude of the US authorities as 'unduly pessimistic and far from helpful'.[10] A memorandum on the subject argued: 'it is doubtful whether Jordan has any long term future as an independent country. . . . If it were not for the presence of British troops and the prospect of a UN meeting, Nasser would probably unseat King Hussein tomorrow.'[11] However, British objectives in the short term should be to preserve Jordan in some form for as long as possible, and to ensure that the UN was physically engaged in the country to cover the withdrawal of British troops. During discussion of the paper, Harold Macmillan pointed out that if the UAR were to attempt to attack or subvert Jordan in these circumstances then 'the attack would be directed against a ward of the UN'.[12]

In communications with the Americans, however, the British had to adopt a different line. Clearly, they could not afford to seem pessimistic as to the future of the country when they were engaged in attempts to gain US financial support for the regime, together with backing for their efforts to secure some form of UN role there. One genuinely optimistic voice on the British side, however, seems to have been that of the ambassador in Amman, Charles Johnston, who challenged the conclusion of the US Chargé d'Affaires that King Hussein could only count on the allegiance of 10–20 per cent of the population.[13] His exasperation with his American colleague's defeatism is summed up by the conclusion that: 'we and the Jordanians are . . . faced with a situation in which our holding operation may be brought to an end not by Nasser but by the US Government.'[14] As Johnston was later to remark, there was a stark difference in outlook between the two embassies in Amman, with the British believing that Jordan would survive the emergency and the Americans certain that it would not.[15]

The battle over the future of Jordan was fought over two issues, both of which the British Government believed to be vital indicators of the confidence of the US Administration in the survival of the Hussein regime. The first was that of finance, and the American refusal to supply budgetary aid more than one month in advance. As Ambassador Johnston pointed out, whether or not it was intentional, this gave the impression that the US Administration had so little confidence in the Jordanian regime that it believed the life expectancy of the government could be measured in weeks. Johnston argued passionately that the Americans had a 'double standard in judging governments in the Arab world', and that 'some of Mr Dulles' advisers must be indifferent to the triumph of our joint opponents in this area, unless indeed they would actually like to see it happen'.[16] This fell in with his earlier assertion: 'Mr Rountree perhaps imagines that the alternative to King Hussein could be a nice cosy pro-American and anti-British republic. If he does, he could not be more mistaken.'[17] The pressure from Johnston on his American colleagues, however, seems to have produced results. He was soon reporting that the US Chargé d'Affaires had recommended to the State Department that American budgetary support should be made available on a quarterly basis, a compromise solution which satisfied the British and the Jordanian Government.[18]

The other issue was that of the equipping of two additional Bedouin brigades to help to maintain internal order in the kingdom. From the outset, the Americans were opposed to this measure, arguing that it would only be of advantage 'if we desired to maintain Jordan as [a] Free World fortress in [the] Middle East. However, we do not believe it would be in US interests to attempt to do this and in fact we would be happy if some way could be found for us to disengage ourselves from our responsibilities in Jordan with minimum political disadvantage.'[19] Despite constant British pressure on the issue, the Americans refused to provide the necessary arms and finance for the brigades. In view of the sensitivity of the Israelis, the Americans were particularly concerned, as Lord Hood reported to Selwyn Lloyd, that what the Jordanians were in fact seeking was an addition to their offensive military capability.[20] Despite the intervention of Lloyd himself, the Americans would not budge on the matter.[21]

In any event, the precarious British position in Jordan had by this stage been substantially eased by action within the UN. Due largely to the course of developments in Iraq, President

Nasser proved to be rather more pliable over Jordan than might have been expected. With Iraqi Prime Minister Qassem beginning to emerge as a potential rival to him in the Arab world he did not want to become embroiled in a struggle with the Western powers over the future of Jordan, which seemed to be a lesser issue. The process of compromise began on 18 August with a Norwegian sponsored resolution that took note of British and American declarations regarding withdrawal. It reaffirmed that: 'all member nations should refrain from threats, direct or indirect, aimed at impairing the freedom, independence or integrity of any State, or of fomenting civil strife and subverting the will of the people of any State.' The resolution called on all countries to put this into effect with regard to the Middle East, and requested the Secretary General, in consultation with the governments concerned, to uphold the principles of the Charter in relation to Lebanon and Jordan.

However, agreement on the resolution could not be reached and, at the suggestion of the UAR representative, Mahmoud Fawzi, it was agreed that the Arab states should meet separately to try to produce a satisfactory formula. The resolution which resulted from their deliberations contained much of the Norwegian plan, but added a reference to the obligation stated in the pact of the Arab League that the Arab states should strengthen the ties linking them. It also referred to the need for measures by the Secretary General in Lebanon and Jordan that would facilitate the early withdrawal of foreign troops. This Arab resolution was unanimously adopted by the UN Assembly on 21 August, with Foster Dulles hailing it as a new opportunity, and Selwyn Lloyd as a constructive first step.[22] The resolution, which Hammarskjöld described as 'one of the strongest' ever adopted by the UN, gave him new responsibilities in Jordan which he discharged by developing the idea of a 'representative office' in Amman, intended to promote good relations with neighbouring Arab states and facilitate the departure of British troops. This, together with the general easing of tensions in the region, allowed the British Government to move towards the evacuation of its forces on a similar timetable to that adopted by the US Administration in Lebanon. The last American forces left Beirut on 25 October, the British leaving Jordan by 2 November.

In hindsight, both operations have been characterized as extraordinarily successful in view of the fact that little or no internal disorder erupted in the countries concerned, and the troops departed without incident.[23] Moreover, a smooth transition took place in the government of Lebanon, and King Hussein's regime in Jordan emerged unscathed despite the prophecies of its imminent demise. Furthermore, the coincidence of the arrival and departure of British and American forces, and the diplomatic cooperation of the two countries, has tended to foster the image of a smoothly concerted, even pre-planned, Anglo-American operation. The realities, as the preceding analysis has shown, are rather different.

The Americans intervened in Lebanon with little regard for the dynamics of the situation there, and largely in order to make a credibility-building point to the Soviets about their resolve to defend their friends in the Middle East and, indeed, worldwide. In common with the British, they believed that the Iraqi Revolution was only the beginning of a much broader plot to destabilize the region. However, for the US Administration, this plot was ultimately orchestrated by the Soviet Union, and President Nasser was merely their willing puppet. In the first week of the crisis all the hopes that Nasser might re-emerge as a potential rival to the Soviets in the region because of his differences with them over Syria were thrown into shade. It was, as will be seen, only as a result of developments in post-revolutionary Iraq that the Administration was to return to, and build on, its earlier pragmatic approach to Nasser.

Having made its point by intervening in Lebanon, the US Administration was left with the problem of what role to play in the country. It was helped out of its dilemma by the fact that a compromise solution, embodied in the election of General Chehab to the Presidency, and already proposed by Nasser, was at hand. From the point of view of Lebanese internal politics, therefore, the American intervention appears, for all of its bluster, to have been largely an irrelevance. Donald Cameron Watt has argued that: 'American intervention in 1958 ... was mismanaged and misconceived in its operation, and wound up by removing from power those who had called the United States to their aid.'[24]

In Jordan, the British operation had been from the outset

rash, and motivated by dubious considerations. The British too believed the Iraqi Revolution was the beginning of a regionwide plot. However, they concentrated on Nasser, their *bête noir*, as the driving force behind it. They felt particularly endangered both because the overthrow of the regime in Baghdad cut the ground from under their strategy of promoting Iraq and the Baghdad Pact, and because the revolution seemed directly to threaten their oil interests in Iraq and, more importantly, in Kuwait and the Persian Gulf. Because of their exclusion from their planned role in the operation in Lebanon, and the Americans' subsequent reluctance to support intervention elsewhere, the British action in Jordan, intended originally to prime the pump for broader Anglo-American operations in the region, ended up as an independent and exposed gambit. For all their recently reinforced distrust of Nasser, the Americans were not prepared to join in a wider operation to extirpate his influence from the region. As the desperate tone of British requests for US ground forces in Jordan and the Americans' equally adamant refusal reveals, the two operations may more properly be characterized as coincidental and contemporaneous than combined and concerted.

It is difficult to avoid the conclusion that despite all the fair words spoken since Suez, and the new institutional arrangements for Anglo-American cooperation, when called upon in practice, the familiar limitations and suspicions which governed the relationship of the two powers in the region remained and dictated that they act separately.

13 Post-Revolutionary Iraq and the Reassessment of American and British Strategy

The developments which, more than anything else, conditioned the reassessment of British and American strategy in the Middle East in the last months of 1958 took place in post-revolutionary Iraq. Ideologically, the officers who had led the coup were a heterogeneous collection of men, ranging from those with sympathy for the Communists, through Iraqi nationalists, to pan-Arab nationalists. The direction which Iraq was to take, therefore, was very much to be determined by who won the struggle for power between these men, and on which allies he chose to rely to achieve his victory.

The principal rivals for the leadership of Iraq after the revolution were the two men who had taken the most prominent role in organizing and executing the coup, Abdel Karim Qassem and Abd al-Salim Muhammad Aref. Qassem, although he had some sympathy for the ideas of Nasser, was decidedly reluctant to achieve these broader pan-Arab goals at the cost of sacrificing Iraqi sovereignty. Aref, on the other hand, was an unabashed admirer of Nasser, whose devotion 'had more than a touch of hero worship'.[1] Qassem's attempt to resist the embrace of the United Arab Republic was made all the more difficult in the first weeks after the revolution by the wave of popular sentiment in favour of 'Unity Now' which swept the country. Indeed, the initial acts of the new Government indicated a gravitation into the orbit of Nasser. Its first measure in the field of foreign affairs was the recognition of the UAR, followed closely by the signature, by an Iraqi ministerial delegation headed by Aref, of a UAR–Iraqi Mutual Aid Pact in Damascus on 19 July. Various other gestures of cooperation between the two countries ensued, including the extradition by

Iraq of certain political opponents of Nasser and even the arrival at Habbaniya of a UAR air force detachment.

The point at which Qassem's differences with Aref emerged decisively was the end of the first week of August.[2] This was the time of the first of the major 'Unity Now' demonstrations. Since Aref had spent the first three weeks after the revolution publicizing his role as its hero, and expressing his strong support for 'Unity Now', Qassem began to suspect Aref of disloyalty. On 26 August, Aref was welcomed in Basra with shouts of 'Long Live Aref – the Nasser of Iraq', and on 10 September he became involved in a public argument with Communist hecklers, chanting for 'Federation', which had become the established slogan of the opponents of 'Unity'. On 30 September, his fate was sealed when Baghdad Radio announced a reorganization of the Cabinet, with Aref posted as ambassador to the German Federal Republic. Aref was very reluctant to leave the country, and in early November attempted to return, whereupon he was arrested, put on trial, convicted, and imprisoned.

This simple chronology of the decline of Aref's fortunes and the corresponding rise of Qassem's omits any reference to the political allies that the two employed in their struggle for power. 'In the immediate aftermath of the revolution, the Communist Party and its sympathizers were undoubtedly the largest political force in Iraq. . . .'.[3] Although the actual number of its members was small, probably only around three thousand at the time of the coup, the individuals concerned were devoted to their cause, and well-organized across the country.[4] Because Qassem had neither a regional nor a family network at his disposal, unlike Aref at the time or Saddam Hussein in later years, it was useful to him to move at least some way towards accommodating the Communists.

Because of developments in Syria, where the Baath's pressure for union with Egypt had been largely intended to control Communist influence, pan-Arab nationalists had become the principal enemies of the Communists. The Iraqi Communist Party, therefore, was of particular importance to Qassem as a counterweight to the Baathist and Nasserist elements tapped by Aref. Equally, because of the Communists' superior organization, they were more valuable allies. Of course, one effect of Qassem's toleration, and even encouragement, of the Communists was the accusation that he was in fact a fellow traveller himself. Although with hindsight the marked decline in Communist influence from the middle of 1959 onwards shows that Qassem was merely using the Communists in a game in which personal power was the prize, at the time this was not so clear, either to those inside or outside Iraq.

It was the spectre of the defeat of Aref, and the consolidation of control in the hands of Qassem as 'Sole Leader', as he came to be known from October onwards, that provoked significantly different responses from the British and American Governments. It laid bare the underlying tensions in their approach to the problems of the region, which this study has traced from the formation of the Baghdad Pact onwards.

The first strategic question that confronted both countries in the wake of the revolution, however, was what future policy to adopt towards the Baghdad Pact. As might have been expected from the Americans' repeatedly expressed reservations about the organization, they were not disposed to answer the pleas of its indigenous members to join and fill the void which was expected to be left by Iraqi defection. Although voices were raised within the US Administration as before, in favour of the pact, it was concluded that what was needed was 'an entirely new pact, with a new name, as the Baghdad Pact does not lend itself to adherence by us even if the Iraqis should denounce it'.[5]

Indeed, Secretary Dulles himself went so far as to attribute the revolution to Iraq's involvement with Britain in the pact. At a Cabinet meeting on 18 July, he had 'recalled that the United States had not favoured Iraqi membership in the Pact, hence the United States had not joined in it. He believed that the strain placed upon the Iraqi Government by membership in the Pact may have considerably contributed to that government's downfall.'[6] He made this sentiment even more explicit when he argued at an NSC meeting on 24 July that: 'the Iraqi Government fell because Iraq was in an unnatural association with Turkey and the United Kingdom in the Baghdad Pact.'[7]

Still, the fall of the monarchy did at least make possible closer US relations with the organization. At the pact council meeting in London in late July, Dulles pledged the US to enter into bilateral agreements with the member nations to ensure their security and defence.[8] He still stopped short of agreeing to full US membership of the organization, however. The promised bilateral agreements were eventually signed with the governments of Turkey, Iran and Pakistan in Ankara on 5 March 1959.[9]

From the British perspective, the fall of the Hashemite regime had cut the ground from under its regional strategy based on Iraq. As will be seen, this was to necessitate some rethinking of the purpose of British involvement in the Middle East, leading to a concentration of effort more directly on the protection of the economically vital oil-supplying Gulf states. It was also likely to involve some reassessment of military strategy in the region, but as the Joint Planning Staff pointed out in a telling comment, 'the UK from the start has viewed the military affairs and organization of the Pact rather as a framework for its political aims than as a serious military undertaking.'[10] It was taken for granted that the new Iraqi regime would want to have no further dealings with the organization. However, although Iraq did withdraw in March 1959, it is interesting to note that Qassem himself was not as hostile to the pact as might have been expected, due to the favourable impression made on him by a visit to Turkey as part of a military mission during 1955.[11] This may at least in part explain the government's hesitation in announcing its withdrawal.

Apart from the issue of the Baghdad Pact, developments in Iraq began to have an impact on the approach adopted by the two countries towards 'Arab nationalism' even before it became clear that Qassem was not a wholehearted admirer of Nasser. The British were the first to see the potential of Qassem as a rival pole to Nasser in the Middle East, largely because their interest was the greater in finding rivals to the Egyptian leader. The guiding tenet of British policy still remained that Nasser was the threat to be countered, and any and every means should be employed to prevent him making gains.

The development of opinion on the American side, however, was rather more complicated. Secretary of State Dulles seems initially to have set himself against any thought of compromise with Nasser in the wake of the Iraqi Revolution. His attitude appears to have stemmed from a belief which lingered longer with him than with anyone else, that the Soviets had been behind the coup, and that Nasser had been their willing adjutant. Perhaps also, Dulles's stance was a reaction to the feeling that the US had somehow been deceived into dealing with Nasser over Syria and the Lebanon while the Iraqi plot was being hatched. Whatever his motivations, Dulles at first resisted the drive from within his own Department to improve relations with Nasser. He argued that he did not see how the US could compete successfully with the USSR for the favour of Nasser. Nor did he believe that Nasser would give up his ambitions in return for US aid. These ambitions Dulles characterized as 'insatiable', going so far as to compare Nasser to Hitler.[12]

However, despite this, he did not believe that the US 'should engage on frontal opposition to everything Nasser tries to do'. Rather, referring again to his metaphor of the 'overflowing stream' of Arab nationalism, Dulles argued that America should merely 'try to keep it in bounds . . . until events deflate the great Nasser hero myth'. One of the best methods of holding Nasser in check would in fact be to work on the attitude of the Soviet Union. 'If the Soviet Union feels that Nasser's ambitions might lead to general war, it will pause and exert a restraining influence on Nasser.'

Thus, at this stage, in the immediate aftermath of the Iraqi Revolution, Dulles's attitude towards Nasser was every bit as hostile as that of his British counterparts. However, as has been seen in the context of, for instance, the Syrian crisis of August 1957, Dulles had expressed this sort of view of Nasser before, but this had not stopped the US Administration from dealing with him on a pragmatic basis when the circumstances had subsequently demanded it. National Security Council discussions over the next six months were to witness a gradual softening of the US position, with even Dulles diluting his opposition as it became clear that the US might have an interest in working with Nasser to stem the Communist tide in Iraq.

The deciding factor, as always, was the Soviet threat. A revised version of NSC5801/1 on US policy toward the Near East, discussed by the NSC at its meeting on 21 August, defined its two 'bedrock' objectives as the denial of the area to the Soviet Union, and access to its oil supplies. Of these, and other secondary objectives, the paper concluded: 'from the standpoint of our global interests, denial of the area to Soviet domination stands out above all others.'[13] However, reporting on the deliberations of the NSC Planning Board which had produced the paper, Gordon Gray, Special Assistant for National Security Affairs, noted that: 'the principal split occurred in the Board's discussion of the US attitude toward pan-Arab nationalism and toward Nasser.' Some members of the Board evidently felt that the Administration could afford to move towards a rather more positive effort to 'work with' rather than merely to 'accept' Nasser.[14]

This sentiment gathered weight under the impact of news from Iraq. On 18 September, General Cabell told the NSC that 'Cairo and Nasser were manifesting great concern over factional struggles among the leaders in the new regime in Iraq',[15] although the following week he cautioned that despite this, 'there was still obvious military cooperation between Egypt and Iraq'.[16] Nevertheless, the news in early October that the Iraqis had concluded a trade agreement with Moscow, and had begun to implement their recent arms agreement with the Soviets, seems to have caused some consternation in Washington.

The next draft revision of NSC5801/1 presented to the Council on 16 October reflected the changes in the climate of the region being brought on by developments in Iraq. Secretary Dulles argued that the majority proposals presented by the Planning Board went further than he himself was prepared to go, 'especially with respect to accepting Nasser not only as the head of the United Arab Republic, but as the leader of the whole Arab world'.[17] However, he was prepared to accept the conclusion of the Board that the Administration should:

> be alert to any possibilities which may occur for broader understanding or consultation between the United States and the UAR. Explore particularly the extent to which greater United States cooperation with the UAR might serve to limit UAR contacts with the Soviet Bloc and Soviet influence in the area and might also reduce UAR dependence upon Soviet trade and military assistance.

In fact, this language was to form the basis for the agreed final version of NSC5820/1, adopted on 4 November.[18]

In Iraq itself, Qassem's problems had not ceased with the disposal of Aref. Early in December, a planned coup organized by the former nationalist leader, Rashid Ali, whom Qassem himself had invited back to the country, was exposed. It was this development that brought to the fore the differences between Britain and America over policy in Iraq, which mirrored the divergence in their regional strategy. Despite denials at the time, and in subsequent commentaries,[19] evidence has emerged that the British Ambassador went so far as to tip Qassem off about the coup attempt which was in the making against him. This fell in with the British policy, adopted very soon after the revolution, of supporting the Qassem regime as that most likely to steer a middle course between the rival claims of the Communists and Nasserists. An independent Iraq of this nature was very much in the British interest in view of the fact that the principal British strategic goal was to ensure the defence of the Persian Gulf oil reserves. In this connection, either a Communist or a Nasserite regime in Baghdad would, to the British way of thinking, constitute a threat.

However, the Americans, who were much more concerned by the dangers of a pro-Soviet takeover in Baghdad, and less worried by an extension of Nasser's influence which might, indeed, be a good thing if it served to block a Communist coup, were far from pleased about the British action. They themselves had been in possession of the information about the projected coup, and had elected not to pass it on to Qassem.[20] A memorandum to Selwyn Lloyd from Sir Roger Stevens, Head of the Foreign Office's Eastern Department, noted that:

> the Secretary of State will recall that in connexion with the warning about a Nasserite coup given by Sir Michael Wright to General Qassem last week-end, the State Department at desk level went so far as to express doubts about the policy that the preservation of Qassem was in the Western interest. It seems possible that the State Department official concerned [Rockwell] was irked by our independent action and that his objections were directed primarily towards positive efforts to preserve Qassem against Nasser rather than based on any belief that an alternative government would be better (which seems hard to believe).[21]

Selwyn Lloyd responded by writing to Lord Hood in Washington stressing that:

> It seems to us that our basic interest is to ensure that Iraq remains independent both of the United Arab Republic and of Communism. While it is true that Qassem has had to lean heavily on the Iraqi Communist Party for support in the action taken against United Arab Republic elements, his Government, backed by moderate elements and with a considerable hold on the Army still seems to present the only hope of a moderate government dedicated to the principle of preserving Iraq's independence. If he were to go down there is every prospect that he would be succeeded by an extremist regime. Whichever form this takes it would be a bad exchange from our point of view.[22]

Although Hood reassured Lloyd that the State Department did not view Qassem's position as hopeless, he noted that they were concerned about the longer term implications of his reliance on the Communists. Hood concluded that:

> There is not any serious divergence either of assessment or policy *at present*. There is, however, a danger that the Americans will conclude before we have reached the same conclusion, that there is no longer any possibility that Qassim will maintain his independence of the Communists. At that point, the Americans would regard the success of pro-Nasser forces as preferable.[23]

The potential division between the two countries came into the open as a result of a tour made by Assistant Secretary of State William Rountree to various Middle Eastern capitals, including Baghdad and Cairo, in the middle of December. His trip to Baghdad on 15 December was marked by demonstrations and press attacks organized by the Communists. One historian has portrayed the visit as an illustration of the extent to which Qassem wanted to pursue an independent line from the Iraqi Communist Party (ICP), emphasized by the positive official communiqué that he issued about his meeting with Rountree, and the photograph of the two in friendly conversation published in the press the following day.[24] However, it was the Communist-inspired demonstrations which appear to have made more of an impression on the US Administration.

The atmosphere in Baghdad seems to have contrasted sharply with that in Cairo, where Rountree apparently found President Nasser in cooperative mood. On a stopover in London during his return from the region, Rountree told Roger Stevens, Head of the Foreign Office's Eastern Department, that he had 'sensed again strongly the Egyptian concern over Communist developments in Iraq'.[25] He felt that 'a distinct community of interest was appearing because of the fear of Communism'. Rountree reported that Nasser had expressed 'astonishment about the UK action in regard to the plot in Iraq', with Stevens noting that the Assistant Secretary 'did not disguise his own surprise'. Macmillan's minuted comment on Stevens's report was dismissive, however. 'Mr Rountree seems easily alarmed', he wrote. Philip de Zulueta, his Foreign Affairs Private Secretary, argued that: 'this is rather what we had expected and shows again that there is a real danger of another disagreement between us and the US about policy in the Middle East.' Unless the Administration was prepared to back the 'middle of the road' strategy favoured by Britain, 'we may well have to choose between Nasser and Communism in the short term; but either would be bad for us in the long term.'

It is perhaps fortunate in this respect that British officials were not privy to the discussion held between Rountree, Eisenhower, Vice President Richard Nixon and Under Secretary of State Christian Herter on Rountree's return to Washington.[26] Here Rountree stressed: 'Nasser is showing real concern over Communist penetration of the Middle East.' Moreover, he reported that 'Nasser desires to work with us on Iraq. He is much concerned over Communist influence with Qasim'. Rountree concluded that the US should 'work with Nasser on the Iraq situation'. The President's view was that: 'Nasser could oppose Communists better than can the US in the three-cornered struggle of the Middle East. He . . . felt that possibly something could be worked out if Nasser would agree that we would ignore the Israeli problem.' This was easier said than done, however. As Dulles observed at an NSC meeting a month later, 'there was an organized campaign from Israel in this country whose object was to check any rapprochement between Nasser and the US. Apparently supporters of this campaign would rather see Iraq taken over by Communists than controlled by Nasser.'[27]

Thus, while the British still could not yet bring themselves to deal with Nasser, the US Administration was once again beginning to consider the possibility that he could fulfil that role for which historically they had tried to prepare him, that of the indigenous, anti-Communist warrior of the Middle East. The wheel in this sense was coming full circle. The reassessment of the American position was facilitated by Dulles's bad health and eventual resignation from office in April 1959. President Eisenhower, as has been noted, was ambivalent about Nasser. On the one hand, earlier that year, during the period of secret negotiations with Nasser over the Lebanese crisis, he had spoken of regretting his decision to back King Saud in the Middle East power struggle. He confided to his diary that 'no matter what you think of Nasser, at least he is a leader'.[28] On the other hand, however, he described choosing between backing Nasser and Qassem in Iraq as being 'a case of whether we decided to support a baby-faced Dillinger or an Al Capone'.[29] Perhaps Nasser's cherubic looks better suited him for the role of 'baby-faced Dillinger'.

Parallel discussions in London, however, addressed the question of whether Britain might not actually be better placed to secure American cooperation in the region if the Communists were to gain the upper hand in Iraq. A meeting of senior ministers at 10 Downing Street noted that:

> the question arises as to whether a Communist controlled Iraq would be more inimical to our interests than a Nasserite controlled Iraq, the point being that against a Communist controlled Iraq American help could be rallied, and perhaps the whole Arab nationalist movement turned into a patriotic anti-Communist feeling. On the other hand, Nasserism and Arab Nationalism may well threaten our interests in Kuwait...[30]

The defence of the Gulf, which had always been important to the British, had now become a priority due to the overthrow of the friendly regime in Baghdad. Even without the difficulties caused by Iraqi claims to Kuwait, the possibility of a hostile government in Iraq meant that this was a much more pressing problem than it had been in the past. Following discussions with Dulles in late July,[31] Macmillan had managed to secure a commitment from the Secretary of State to 'step up joint military planning for possible contingencies in the area'.[32] The intention was to build on the established contacts between Admiral Holloway's planning staff and the British Chiefs of Staff in London, which had helped to produce 'Blue Bat', to discuss problems in the Gulf, and also other potential trouble spots such as Libya, Sudan and Jordan.

However, although the planning group quickly produced an outline paper, and agreed that the 'US and UK could act in [the] Gulf militarily either separately or simultaneously without undue interference with each other',[33] this was as far as the process went for the time being. In all subsequent communications, the Americans went out of their way to emphasize that 'US military planning and operations with the UK should be on the basis of coordination as distinguished from combined or joint plans and operations'.[34]

The preferred British strategy for the defence of Kuwait at the beginning of 1959 remained to support Qassem, and even to engage in the 'unobtrusive supply of arms [to Iraq], so long as he maintained a policy of independence'.[35] The Americans were certainly not willing to go so far as to sell Qassem weapons, although they were prepared to acquiesce, somewhat reluctantly, if the British chose to do so.[36] However, the British went some way towards accommodating the American point of view by admitting that: 'the more serious long term threat to the West would be the emergence of a Communist-controlled regime and the lesser evil would be an increase in Nasser's influence.' Still, as Philip de Zulueta emphasized, of the three alternatives of an independent Iraq, a Communist Iraq, and a pro-Nasserite Iraq, the first was by far the most to be preferred. The choice between the two other alternatives would remain difficult because 'as Nasser is fundamentally unreliable from our point of view, a Nasserite victory in Iraq might also in time lead to communist domination since the Russians might then switch back to full support of Nasser'.[37]

At a series of informal meetings at the presidential retreat of Camp David in late March, the differing Anglo-American perspectives on the Iraqi situation were aired. Foreign Secretary Lloyd argued that Nasser had enormously increased Qassem's difficulties. For the British, 'Nasser was a completely uncertain quantity. It was good that he was now anti-communist but . . . he must work his way. Dining with the devil called for a long spoon.' Eisenhower's line was that 'he was . . . more suspicious than the British of Kassim [Qassem] who from the day he had murdered the King and Nuri Said had appeared to be a bad actor'. Nevertheless, both parties agreed that in the short term Qassem should continue to be supported, although Macmillan conceded that 'there might be a slight difference in emphasis' in their approaches. This would best be resolved by the setting up of a working group to consider contingencies that might arise in Iraq, Iran and Kuwait.[38]

In Washington, the course of events in Iraq during 1959 continued to cause great concern, particularly the effects of the Mosul revolt in March, which was one of the high water marks of Communist over Nasserite influence. A paper written by Special Assistant for National Security Affairs Gray on 1 April noted that: 'recent reports from the Ambassador and other sources paint a picture of rather complete gloom in that the trend seems to be towards a Communist government without any arresting factors in sight.'[39] Gray expressed great frustration about affairs in Iraq. 'We sit and watch unfolding events which seem to point inevitably to Soviet domination of Iraq, acknowledging, I am afraid, an inability to do anything about it. It is almost like watching a movie whose end we will not like but which we are committed to see.'[40] Certainly, Gray was not alone in his deepening concern about Iraq. Following further discussion of the Iraqi problem in the National Security Council on 2 April,[41] the President asked Gray to set up a special Interdepartmental Group to monitor events in Iraq on a regular basis.[42] This was to be a high-level team, including the heads of the JCS, Defense, the CIA and the US Information Agency, meeting under Acting Secretary of State Herter's chairmanship.[43]

Even before the group's first meeting, however, the State Department had prepared an assessment of events in Iraq for consideration by the National Security Council which stressed the need to keep Nasser attacking Communism. Due to the United States' lack of 'assets', presumably for the purpose of mounting covert operations in Iraq, and its unwillingness to contemplate direct military intervention, the paper concluded that support for Nasser represented the best means available for limiting Communist advances in Iraq.[44]

At the subsequent NSC meeting on 17 April which considered the State Department paper, the belief that the British were so concerned about the possibility of Nasser gaining the upper hand in Iraq that they were complacent about the much more serious Communist threat was expressed again. Certainly, this was Vice President Nixon's view, and Defense Secretary McElroy 'felt it was outrageous that our British and French allies were treating developments in Iraq so casually when these were the very nations who would suffer first and the most acutely if Middle Eastern oil were lost to Western Europe and the Free World'.[45]

Although the State Department took a more measured view of British actions, developments in post-revolutionary Iraq nevertheless highlighted the differences over Nasser between the two countries which lay at the root of the tensions of the late 1950s. As Stuart Rockwell had emphasized to Selwyn Lloyd, in response to the latter's assertion that Nasser's attacks on Qassem might actually be driving him to rely on the Communists, 'the risk of pushing Qasim further towards Communism was a serious one, but it was worth taking in order to keep Nasser attacking Communism. It would be disastrous if, as a result of an initiative from our side, Nasser switched away from his anti-Communist line.'[46] Nasser, the anti-Communist warrior, was most certainly being rehabilitated in Washington.

The NSC meeting on 17 April also endorsed the idea of the establishment of the Interdepartmental Group to monitor events in Iraq. Vice President Nixon was particularly concerned that the group should not spend its time haggling about nuances of language, but should come up with concrete suggestions as to what else the US could do to stop Iraq turning Communist.[47] The group proceeded to meet regularly, and set up a working party to discuss what response the US might make to various contingencies in Iraq.[48] This apparatus was in addition to the parallel US–UK Working Group discussed above which was considering British and American plans for military intervention in Iraq.[49] However, although the Interdepartmental Group continued to function during the rest of 1959, the receding influence of the Communists over Qassem from midsummer onwards meant that it never developed into the kind of crisis management team which was originally envisaged. Apart from a brief resurgence of concern during the following January, there is little evidence that the Interdepartmental Group's reports merited consideration at the highest level during 1960.[50]

In passing, however, it should be noted that the events of the pivotal crisis month of March 1959, which had prompted the establishment of the Interdepartmental Group, had included Iraq's formal withdrawal from the Baghdad Pact which had been created by the accession of Britain to the Turco-Iraqi Pact a mere four years earlier. During that period, the entire complexion of the Middle East had changed, and Britain had withdrawn from a regionwide attempt to maintain political influence over the oil supplying and transporting states through the Baghdad Pact, to the defence of her strategic heartland in the Persian Gulf. Indeed, it was the primary importance of the defence of this heartland that was slowly to bring about a significant shift in British policy during the second half of 1959.

According to American accounts, disillusion with Qassem at the lower levels of the British Government had set in early in the year, even though those at the top remained 'relatively complacent' about his intentions for some time afterwards.[51] If Qassem could not be relied upon to remain friendly towards Britain, he could pose a threat to British interests in Kuwait. In these circumstances, those at the top of the British Government might have to swallow their pride and consider improving relations with Nasser to help facilitate the protection of Kuwait.

The first evidence of this change of approach comes in a memorandum of 25 May 1959 from Selwyn Lloyd to Harold Macmillan.[52] In it Lloyd argued that 'it seems as though Colonel Nasser and his colleagues are prepared to think again about their future relationship with this country. Although I still fundamentally distrust him, I think it is wholly to our advantage to procure a detente in our relations . . .'. One argument for such a detente was that it might reflect itself in a greater

willingness on the part of the Egyptian Government to consider outstanding British compensation claims in respect of the
nationalization of the Suez Canal. In addition, however, Lloyd
argued that: 'we now feel that it is extremely important to
oppose Communism in the Middle East in a manner likely to
be effective, that is by encouraging the non-Communist elements in Iraq, and doing nothing to oppose a detente between
the Arab states.' This was a diluted version of the view already
adopted in Washington, at which both Lloyd and Macmillan
had earlier demurred.

Even now, certain of Macmillan's advisers had doubts about
the approach. Philip De Zulueta bracketed Lloyd's comments
regarding the best means of opposing Communism in the
Middle East, indicating that he remained to be convinced as
to their efficacy.[53] Macmillan himself, however, seems to have
felt the time was right to change tack. He approved Lloyd's
suggestion, but minuted that the approach to Nasser should
be 'simple and short, not complicated ideas'.

One does not have to delve too deeply to fathom the motives behind the shift in British strategy which began around
this time. In discussions with US officials in Washington at the
end of August, Sir Roger Stevens admitted that 'everything
turned on Kuwait; nothing else was of really vital importance,
and indeed our other positions in the Gulf and even Aden
itself were maintained ultimately in order to secure Kuwait'.[54]
As doubts increased about Qassem's intentions so did fears for
the future of Kuwait. The ramifications for British strategy in
the region were considerable. If Qassem could not be trusted,
then opening a channel of communications to Nasser, the
former *bête noir* of the British Government, made strategic sense.
In addition, if the threat to Kuwait was becoming more palpable, then a renewed drive to secure coordinated planning
with the US Administration for contingencies involving Iraq
and Kuwait would be prudent. Sure enough, Macmillan now
put his weight behind a new, personal approach to Eisenhower
over contingency planning.

On 14 May Macmillan wrote to the President arguing that
the time had come to turn the earlier general studies of the
Gulf into joint plans.[55] His aim, as he later expressed it to the
Cabinet Defence Committee, was 'to lead the US authorities

by stages to be prepared to participate in joint operations in the Middle East, particularly in Kuwait and Iraq'.[56] Although the initiative breathed more life into the planning process, the Americans continued to insist on coordinated as opposed to combined or joint planning. Even the persuasive skills of the Chief of the Defence Staff, Mountbatten, could not progress matters much further in Washington.[57] In September 1959 he reported to the Cabinet Defence Committee that agreement had been reached only to exchange national plans, which might then be revised in the light of the intentions of the other party, and the facilities which each might make available to the other.[58] This fell well short of the goal of combined planning.

Just as the advance of the Communists in Iraq during April and May 1959 had given impetus to the British Government's moves to open channels to Nasser and enhance Anglo-American planning, so a series of political setbacks for the party from June onwards gradually reduced the sense of urgency behind these initiatives. For instance, on 13 June, Sir Humphrey Trevelyan, the British Ambassador in Baghdad, reported that 'there are growing indications of divergence between Qasim and the Communist party'.[59] Later in the month he reported Baghdad to be full of rumours of the arrest of Communists.[60] Soon after this he was referring to 'a marked change in the internal situation in Iraq', with the tide having turned against the Communists.[61] Looking back over the events of the year in his annual report, Trevelyan judged that this was the period when the Communists had overplayed their hand, particularly through their persecution of nationalists and infiltration of the army. Their loss of influence with Qassem was hastened by their part in instigating the disturbances in Kirkuk during July.[62] Although, following the Baathist attempt on Qassem's life in October, there was a temporary resurgence in Communist influence, this never again reached the levels achieved during April and May 1959.

The ebbing of the Communist tide in Iraq, together with a period of relative calm in most Arab countries, was in fact to render 1960 the quietest year for a decade in respect of British and American policies in the Middle East. On the US side, with the Eisenhower years drawing to their close, no new intiatives were apparent in the Middle East. The moribund

Administration's attention was only briefly drawn back to the region by the tensions caused as a result of the assassination of Jordanian Prime Minister Hazza al-Majali in August 1960, and the discovery of the beginnings of the Israeli nuclear programme during September.

On the British side, the attempt to improve relations with Nasser was maintained, although matters proceeded at little more than snail's pace. While Chargés d'Affaires were exchanged on 1 December 1959, it was not until 26 January 1961 that Harold Beeley, the new British Ambassador, presented his credentials in Cairo. In the meantime, although Macmillan had met Nasser twice at the United Nations in New York during late September and early October 1960, relations between the two governments had been subject to periodic bouts of recrimination which had held up the exchange of ambassadors. These reflected the continuing depth of suspicion between the two sides, and their differences over issues such as the Congo crisis. Still, in view of Macmillan's own earlier comments about Nasser, the tone of their discussions when they met at the UN seems remarkably businesslike and friendly. The Prime Minister professed himself to be 'very glad' to have met the Egyptian President, and stressed his desire to improve relations between the two countries.[63] In an era of new strategic realities in the Middle East, there was perhaps little point in clinging steadfastly to the animosities of previous years.

Indeed, if one casts an eye backwards over the evolution of British strategy in the region during the previous decade, one can begin to see what a watershed the Iraqi Revolution of July 1958 was. As the implications for British interests of having a new, unreliable revolutionary regime in Baghdad emerged, so the government was forced to confront the shibboleths of its Middle East policy. If the priority was to protect Kuwait, as a review of Middle East policy at the end of 1958 had confirmed,[64] the Iraqi threat seemed likely to be the most immediate. In these circumstances, blank opposition to any initiative taken by Nasser might not be the best method of defending British interests. While on the part of the British Government, this admission required something of an 'agonizing reappraisal', for the US Administration the process of revaluation was not so difficult. Nasser merely seemed to be returning to the role of regional rival to Communism which it had always been hoped he would fill.

The Iraqi Revolution had also set a pattern for Anglo-American intervention in the Middle East which was soon to be repeated in the Kuwaiti crisis of 1961. This essentially involved independent action by both powers in areas where each believed itself to have a special interest. Drawing on the lesson of Suez, however, such action would first be cleared with the other Atlantic ally, and appropriate diplomatic and logistical assistance would be sought. Britain's special interests in the region were now concentrated in the Gulf and in particular on the oil reserves and sterling balances held by Kuwait. Its strategy would be framed to protect these assets. The US Administration would continue to focus on the broader interest of preventing Communist advances in any part of the Middle East. The role of the British Government in this new era of Anglo-American relations in the Middle East might, therefore, best be characterized as subsidiary rather than subservient to that of the US.

14 Conclusions

Viewed from one angle, the differences between Britain and America over strategy in the Middle East were small. If one accepts that the three dynamic factors in the region from the perspective of the Western powers were the increasing economic importance of Persian Gulf oil, the attempts of the Soviet Union to gain a political foothold in the area, and the desire of radical Arab nationalists to extirpate Western influence, then one can point to a broad unity of purpose between the governments of the two countries. Both agreed that access to oil supplies must be secured; both agreed that the Soviet Union was a threat to unhindered access; and both agreed that where Arab nationalists allied themselves with the Soviets in a bid to eject the Western powers from the area, they must be opposed.

However, this broader unity concealed a number of tactical fissures, which, under the pressure of the crises which erupted in the region during the period, were to broaden into genuine strategic rifts between the two powers. The first and foremost of these tactical fissures concerned the Egyptian leader, Colonel Nasser.

Of the three 'interests' outlined above, the American priority was to prevent Soviet penetration of the region. All other factors, including secure access to oil supplies were ultimately subservient to this goal.[1] The British were aware of this American priority, and of the impact it had on the relations of the two countries in the Middle East. A paper agreed in October 1959 on 'The Future of Anglo-American Relations' by the Working Group on US/UK Cooperation, noted that:

> there are . . . potential differences between us over the Middle East due primarily to differences of circumstance. Most important of these is that American interest is overwhelmingly absorbed in the Communist threat and that the Americans tend to regard everything else as of subordinate importance, whereas two other problems figure largely and assume coordinate importance in our thinking: radical

208

nationalism, and the security of our oil supplies which is threatened both by Communist penetration and by radical nationalism. This difference is reflected in our attitudes towards Nasser, and towards the new Iraq as it was towards the old.[2]

Earlier drafts of the same paper had been even more explicit on the subject of the divergence in approach to Nasser. The Group argued that:

the American attitude to Nasser has always varied with the degree of his attachment to Moscow. If Nasser's quarrel with the Russians becomes irreconcilable and the Americans convince themselves that he is basically anti-Russian, they will not necessarily be restrained by respect for our oil and communications interests from supporting his ambitions for a Middle East empire.[3]

It is difficult to avoid the conclusion that the exclusion of the Soviets from the region was, for various reasons of global cold war strategy, simply an end in itself for the US Administration, while for the British it was a means towards the end of securing oil supplies. In view of this, the US attitude towards Nasser was pragmatic. Where he could be shown to be opposing the Soviets, credence might be given to the notion that America should deal with him. Where he appeared to be supporting Soviet designs, he should be opposed. The British attitude, on the other hand, from March 1956 onwards, was implacably anti-Nasserite. This was the root of the differences between the two that emerged most overtly over Suez, and more covertly over Syria, the United Arab Republic, Jordan and Iraq.

That this was the issue over which the two countries would divide was far from clear at the beginning of the period covered by this study, however. The Anglo-Egyptian agreement of July 1954, and the British belief that Egypt would have to play a pivotal role in any system of regional defence, meant that the government was lukewarm about the concept of the 'Northern Tier' promoted by the Americans. Evelyn Shuckburgh emphasized to his US counterparts that the British Government did not believe that any system of regional defence would be viable if the Egyptians were implacably opposed to it.

The US Administration, on the other hand, had been working towards the 'Northern Tier' as the best means of bolstering the resolve of the states bordering the Soviet Union in the north. Although Secretary of State Dulles was later to claim that the US had not favoured Iraqi accession to the organization, because of the complications in Arab politics which resulted, at the time of the negotiations between Iraq and Turkey no such sentiments were voiced. The Americans went so far as to upbraid the British for their lack of enthusiasm for the pact.

However, the positions of the two governments were to shift significantly during the early months of 1955. The British, having secured the prize of the Anglo-Iraqi Special Agreement, began to see the pact as a vehicle for the maintenance of their political influence throughout the region. If the Anglophile regime in Baghdad could be promoted as the leader of the Arab world, then Britain would be able to secure her access to the oil reserves of the region by political means. In these circumstances, the British Government became rather less concerned about Egyptian fears over the pact, hoping that these might be allayed as time went on.

The US Administration, on the other hand, seeing the potential destabilization of the area which might result from any contest between Iraq and Egypt over the pact, and fearful of the opportunities which might thus be presented to the Soviet Union, became far more reticent about the organization. Concerns over the Saudi attitude played a part in this, but one of the main motivations was the belief that Nasser might drag the whole region into conflict by exploiting the Israeli issue to isolate Iraq in the Arab world. American efforts during 1955 and early 1956, therefore, were devoted to an attempt to promote some form of negotiation between Israel and Egypt as the first step along the road to a broader Middle Eastern peace.

'Project Alpha', as it became known, was coordinated with the British who also had a vested interest in stability in the area, and who still believed at this stage that it might be possible to reach an understanding with Nasser in spite of his objections to the Baghdad Pact. Not only did the peace efforts survive the Egyptian 'Czech' arms deal of September, they even received a new impetus, with Dulles believing that the US could still manage to make the agreement an isolated instance of Russian infiltration into the region if it pressed forward with negotiations with Nasser. The British too, although increasingly wary of Nasser, played along with the American strategy, which revolved around the promotion of an offer to finance the construction of the Aswan Dam.

However, the failure of Robert Anderson, the President's special envoy, to make any progress with Alpha led the US Administration to abandon for the present its attempts to woo Nasser into the Western camp. All the same, the US split with Nasser was not decisive, and although it was conceded that Nasser was not likely to cooperate in American efforts to exclude the Soviets from the area in the short term, the Administration did not rule out the possibility that Egypt, even under Nasser, might pursue a more favourable policy in the longer term.

The British Government, on the other hand, identified Nasser as its enemy from March 1956 onwards. Instrumental in forming this belief were the events in Jordan during the winter of 1955–6. First the British attempt to secure Jordanian accession to the Baghdad Pact was stymied by Egyptian propaganda attacks, backed by Saudi money. Then, King Hussein dismissed General Glubb, the British commander of the Arab Legion. Although it was later admitted that the King had acted for his own reasons, and had not been Nasser's puppet, the sentiment nevertheless remained that Nasser was somehow plotting behind the scenes to undermine the whole British position in the Middle East.

The withdrawal of the Aswan Dam offer, and the nationalization of the Suez Canal which it precipitated created a crisis which, from the British perspective, involved an issue which was vital to national survival. It held out the prospect of a hostile leader controlling the principal oil supply route to Western Europe, and conjured up images of the economic jugular vein of the nation in the grip of man who was likened to Mussolini or Hitler.

To the Americans, the Canal issue was further evidence that Nasser was trying to outbid the Western powers for control of the region. However, it was not a crisis where Soviet influence was sufficiently manifest to necessitate high profile military action by the US. From the outset, whatever impression the

British may have gained, President Eisenhower and Secretary of State Dulles felt that the nationalization of the Canal was not the issue on which to confront Nasser. Dulles's diplomacy during the crisis was intended merely to spin matters out to a point where British and French tempers had cooled sufficiently to enable them to negotiate some form of international control for the Canal.

The British purpose was entirely different. Anthony Eden only seized on Dulles's proposals for a Suez Canal Users' Association because they were sufficiently confused and ambiguous to serve as a means of involving the US in military action alongside Britain. The government had, from the beginning, felt that the only solution to the problem that would be acceptable to them was one which would humiliate Nasser. Since he was unlikely to accept humiliation through negotiations, the British had decided that the Canal issue was one which would require the use of force. The pretext which was eventually adopted for military action, however, involving collusion in an Israeli attack on Egypt, followed by an Anglo-French occupation of the Canal zone, was one which seemed calculated to arouse American anger. Although the extent of US opposition was conditioned by Eisenhower's own codes of international propriety, the British Government could hardly have expected the US to remain silent and inactive in the face of such flagrant breaches of international law.

Anglo-American relations in the wake of Suez, as a result of the economic and political pressures exerted by the Administration to secure British withdrawal, were reduced to a postwar low. However, while it must be acknowledged that the succession of Harold Macmillan to the premiership paved the way for the improvement in relations between the two countries, publicly illustrated by the camaraderie of the Bermuda talks of March 1957, this should not be allowed to distract us from the fundamental continuity in British strategy in the Middle East. Macmillan was every bit as vehement in his opposition to Nasser as had been Eden. There is no need to look for indications of political opportunism in his conduct in this regard before and after Suez, since his views on Nasser do not seem to have changed. During his time as Foreign Secretary, he had been one of the principal proponents of pushing forward with the development of the Baghdad Pact through the Templer mission to Jordan, irrespective of Nasser's objections. Then, during the Suez crisis itself, he had been the foremost of the 'hawks' advocating a military solution to the problem.

The lesson Macmillan learnt from Suez was that Britain could not pursue her goals in the region in the face of US opposition. From the point of view of Middle Eastern policy, therefore, he set about renewing the alliance not for sentimental or historical reasons, but as a result of the practical calculation that Britain needed at least US acquiescence, and preferably US assistance, to combat Nasser's influence. This, of course, confirms Donald Cameron Watt's general conclusion that 'the underlying basis of the Anglo-American relationship has always been interest and not, in the first place, emotion'.[4]

From the American perspective, however, Suez showed that it was important for the US to develop the means of independent action in the area. Already, in the wake of the abandonment of detente with Nasser in March 1956, Eisenhower and Dulles had considered the promotion of King Saud as his rival for influence in the Arab world. They now determined to pursue this policy more vigorously, effectively in competition with the British approach of continuing to build on Iraq and the Baghdad Pact. It was not surprising in this respect, therefore, that the Administration refused all requests to join the pact, and instead developed the Eisenhower Doctrine as its own instrument for independent political action.

In hindsight, of course, the Doctrine seems to have been a signal failure. This was largely because by effectively classifying any threat to a pro-Western government in the region as Communist-inspired, it allowed the Administration no scope to work with the Arab nationalist movement. Although Dulles spoke of sandbagging around positions which must be protected from the fast flowing stream of nationalism, the US might have been better placed seeking to divert the less destructive currents, rather than building unreliable earthworks.

More than this, however, the Doctrine was to prove unworkable in practice because it was very difficult to isolate and identify a Communist threat. Thus, although it was to be used as a justification for the limited response of the US to the crises in Jordan and Syria during 1957, when it came to the crucial test in Lebanon in 1958, the Administration could not find the means to invoke it. US action was legitimized instead by referring to the terms of Article 51 of the United Nations Charter.

It therefore appears that the paradox of post-Suez Anglo-American relations in the Middle East was that, on the one hand, a framework was established for much closer cooperation between the two countries, while on the other they remained in strategic competition. Thus, although the US Administration had provided itself with a means for independent action in the region through the Eisenhower Doctrine, during the latter part of the year a close working relationship developed with the British over the Syrian situation.

This was not, of course, a wholly new departure in Anglo-American relations, as the earlier phase of planning for operations in Syria preceding the Suez crisis had shown. However, what it did show was that where the interests of the two countries coincided, as they did over Syria, they were capable of very close cooperation. Put simply, the Syrian crisis seemed to embody both of the principal threats with which the two governments were concerned; Communism and Nasserism. Where these two pernicious forces seemed to be working together, then the British and Americans found it in their interests to cooperate closely to defeat them.

Coming on top of the convergence of purpose over Syria, the Sputnik launch in October 1957 convinced the Americans that the Soviets were an even more powerful threat to the 'Free World' than had been imagined, and that in view of this resources should be combined more effectively with all of the United States' allies throughout the world to combat them. Since the British were still, at this stage, by far the most important of America's individual allies, it was decided to begin by setting up new consultative structures with them in order to discuss the countering of the Soviet threat worldwide. However, although Macmillan's purpose was to secure a formal two-country relationship, Dulles and Eisenhower had other ideas. The Working Groups set up with Britain were intended to be only the start of a process which was meant to 'spill over' into all of the United States' alliances.

Indeed, the true test of what Harold Macmillan was fond of referring to as 'interdependence' was to be provided by events in the Middle East in 1958. Although a process of joint planning for Anglo-American military operations in the Levant had been set in train in the wake of Macmillan's October 1957 meeting with Eisenhower, the immediate results were disappointing. The perennial American concern with security, and the fear that it might be discovered that the US was preparing for possible intervention in the region alongside the British who had so recently been discredited over Suez, meant that the plans developed were short on logistical detail.

Moreover, the divergence of British and American views over Syria in the wake of the formation of the United Arab Republic with Egypt removed the unifying threat which the two had confronted the previous summer. After some initial contradictory signals from Dulles, the US Administration settled down to waiting to see if there was any potential for broadening the division between Egypt and the Soviet Union which had arisen because of Nasser's intervention in Syria. Although Dulles for one remained suspicious of Nasser's intentions because of his willingness to deal with the Soviets in the past, this phase of US policy shows the fundamentally pragmatic view that the Administration had of Nasser.

Eisenhower and Dulles also waited on events in the region in the conviction that the Soviets would sooner or later show their hand. When the expected crisis, occasioned by President Chamoun's unconstitutional and divisive attempt to secure a second term of office, broke out in Lebanon, both men believed that the Communists were somehow orchestrating the trouble. The situation was sufficiently serious for the Americans to agree to a resumption of contingency planning with the British for potential military intervention in Lebanon. The result was the development of 'Blue Bat', a detailed Anglo-American plan for combined operations in Lebanon which would involve the landing of roughly equal numbers of troops from each country in the event of a crisis. Although the effort to deal with Nasser was not immediately abandoned, with secret approaches being made to him during early June to try to evolve a solution to the crisis, the evidence of infiltration into Lebanon from Syria convinced Eisenhower and Dulles that Nasser was implicated in the supposed Soviet schemes.

The Iraqi Revolution reinforced this sentiment and appeared, in its first days, to portend some regionwide conspiracy, backed by the Soviets, and implemented by Nasser, to undermine Western interests and subvert friendly regimes. Again, as over Syria the previous year, a crisis seemed to have arisen which combined the two threats which principally concerned Britain and America. Despite the detailed plans for combined intervention in Lebanon, Eisenhower requested that Macmillan should hold British troops in reserve, supposedly for potential operations in Iraq and Jordan. However, as soon as Macmillan began to press for immediate intervention in Jordan, both Eisenhower and Dulles were reluctant to give US approval. Their motivations remain difficult to fathom, but were probably compounded of a fear as to the British purpose in intervening, and a belief that Jordan was, in any case, not one of the positions which could be protected from the flood tide of Arab nationalism. The myth of a joint operation, carefully fostered subsequently by both Macmillan and Eisenhower themselves, is exploded by the evidence of the Americans' reluctance to back the British move, and their subsequent refusal to send in even token ground forces to support the precarious British position. The two operations emerge as parallel and contemporaneous, but independent and exclusive.

The American action in Lebanon was intended to make a point directly to the Soviet Union that the US was prepared to defend not only its friends in the Middle East, but also those all around the world, by force of arms if necessary. It demonstrated to Nasser as well that, if he chose to act as what Eisenhower termed the 'puppet' of the Soviets, then the US would move to counter his influence.

For the British, the Iraqi Revolution, and their subsequent intervention in Jordan, elucidated some of the uncomfortable new realities of the Middle East. Firstly, and most importantly, the revolution swept away the Anglophile regime in Baghdad which had been the principal prop of Britain's regional policy. According to Harold Beeley, 'the event which more than any other symbolised the end of an era was the death at the hands of the Baghdad mob . . . of Nuri Said, the adroit and far-sighted leader for whom association with Britain had been axiomatic throughout his long career.'[5] Although the Suez crisis might have undermined Britain's prestige in the Middle East, it had not affected her fundamental strategy for maintaining political influence. It was the Iraqi Revolution that marked the decisive watershed in this respect.

Not only did the revolution appear to invalidate Britain's broader policy, it also threatened her position in the Persian Gulf. Since this was the core of the British interest in the region, the political changes in Iraq pointed to the need to concentrate much more directly on the protection of the Gulf. Although attempts were made to involve the Americans in joint planning for its defence, these foundered in the face of the obdurate resistance of the American military to indulge in anything which might be construed as combined planning with the British. This resistance pointed towards another of the uncomfortable realities of the new Anglo-American relationship in the Middle East. While the machinery for Anglo-American cooperation put in place since Suez was an impressive achievement in theory, the practical results when put to the test in the crisis of July 1958 were decidedly disappointing. A detailed combined plan for operations with the Americans in Lebanon had been shelved, and even the gaining of US acquiescence in, and logistical support for, the British action in Jordan had been a close-run thing. Macmillan had been plagued by fears throughout the operation that the Americans would settle matters in the Lebanon leaving Britain isolated in Jordan. This could hardly be construed as a promising example of 'interdependence' in action.

Developments in post-revolutionary Iraq were to highlight the differences between the two countries over strategy in the region which had caused much of the friction during the second half of the 1950s. Concerned as to the implications of a hostile regime in Baghdad for their clients in the Persian Gulf, the British moved with almost indecent haste to befriend the new ruler of Iraq, Brigadier Qassem. Their overtures were made in the light of the belief that he might well prove to be more of an Iraqi nationalist than a Nasserite, and might thus pursue a policy independent of the United Arab Republic. The great British fear was that Nasser, their principal enemy in the region, might gain control of Iraq and thus be in a position to threaten the Gulf.

Unfortunately, from the British perspective, although Qassem showed himself willing to maintain a policy independent of Nasser, he was forced to rely to some extent on the assistance of the Iraqi Communist Party. Of course, the British acknowledged that any direct takeover in Iraq by the Soviets would be a bad thing, However, they seem to have regarded this as a much more remote threat than the imminent danger of a revolution fostered by forces loyal to Colonel Nasser. It was this sentiment which lay behind what both Nasser and the Americans regarded as the astonishing British decision to tip Qassem off about Rashid Ali's projected coup attempt in late November 1958.

At the same time, however, the Iraqi Revolution had forced the British Government to review its whole position in the Middle East with a view to developing a new strategy to protect its interests. The primary concern was to secure the oil supplies and investments of Kuwait, for these were the key to the whole British position in the Gulf. As Communist influence in Iraq reached its high water mark during the middle of 1959, therefore, the government had to contemplate a shift in strategy which would have been unthinkable six months earlier. Since Nasser was Qassem's rival for influence in the region, it now made strategic sense to open diplomatic channels of communication to him. However, the approach was to be cautious, with Foreign Secretary Lloyd still professing a fundamental distrust of Nasser. The possibility of an Arab nationalist threat to British interests in the Gulf remained a concern alongside that of the more direct Iraqi threat.

American policy with regard to post-revolutionary Iraq was, on the other hand, far less complicated, and was dictated, as it had been throughout the period, by the primacy of the Soviet threat. The Administration's willingness to deal pragmatically with Nasser in situations where he too appeared to be concerned to stem Communist advances, showed through in Qassem's Iraq. Because Nasser and his supporters were in the opposite camp to the Iraqi Communists, they became potential allies of the US. Since the Americans were far from confident about Qassem's desire to maintain an independent line, Nasser was rehabilitated somewhat as the anti-Communist warrior.

Thus, reducing the equation to its simplest form, tensions

between Britain and America in the Middle East during the period from March 1956 onwards were the result of the Americans' view that the Soviet threat was paramount, and the British view that the threat from Nasser was paramount. However, it was in the creation of the Baghdad Pact that the origins of this division lay. The pact was the poisoned chalice which the British Government could not resist accepting. It seemed perfectly fashioned as the vessel for maintaining British political influence in the region, and hence of protecting access to the oil supplies seen as vital to national survival. However, in the refusal of the Americans to join the pact, and the strategic division which resulted between the two powers, together with the implacable opposition of Nasser, lay the seeds of the collapse of the British position.

Paradoxically, looking back to the beginning of the period, before the creation of the Baghdad Pact, it had been the British who had been the more concerned to work with Nasser. Indeed, in September 1959, William Morris, First Secretary at the British Embassy in Washington, wrote to the Foreign Office's Eastern Department noting that:

> During Sir Roger Stevens' visit I mentioned to him a Minute of a conversation between Evelyn Shuckburgh and Evan Wilson of the US Embassy in London at the Foreign Office in, I think, January 1955, a copy of which I used to keep at the bottom of my tray here in Washington.
>
> Shuckburgh . . . appended to this record a comment that there was . . . a difference between us and the Americans. . . . The Americans were so keen to get on with the Northern Tier project that they were prepared to discount Nasser's reactions. We, however, having just got our agreement with Nasser, were anxious not to throw away the gains we saw in it and were more concerned than the Americans with the dangers of dividing the Arab world.[6]

On the bottom of his telegram, Morris annotated the words 'ironical in retrospect'.

15 Postscript: The Kuwaiti Crisis and the Break-up of the United Arab Republic

After the comparative tranquillity of 1960, the Middle East returned to a more familiar pattern of turbulence in 1961. The year was marked by two particularly significant crises, occasioned by the declaration of Kuwait's independence from Britain in June, and the break-up of the United Arab Republic of Egypt and Syria in late September. In view of all that has been said about the importance of Kuwait for British interests in the region it is not surprising that it was the Kuwaiti crisis which loomed largest in British policy during 1961. Here it was to be Britain that played the leading role of the Western powers, and the US that stayed on the sidelines, offering in the main logistical and diplomatic support.

Concerns over the intentions of Qassem's regime in Iraq, which had been more muted during 1960, began to re-emerge early in the new year. This was not the result of any new Iraqi initiative, but rather a product of the pressure applied by the Ruler of Kuwait for a modification of the 1899 Agreement by which Britain had established her 'protection' over the emirate. Since this pressure could not be indefinitely resisted, it concentrated the minds of ministers on the question of Kuwait's future relationship with her powerful northern neighbour.

Negotiations over the independence of the emirate progressed during the early months of 1961 alongside consideration in London of the contingency of an Iraqi attack on Kuwait. The thrust of military advice, however, was very much that if action had to be taken to defend Kuwait, it would be very much better from every point of view if this could be pre-emptive, a so-called 'fire brigade operation'. The forces required to defend Kuwait given notice of four days or more of an Iraqi attack would be far fewer than those required to dislodge Iraq if an occupation had already taken place. In the latter case it would be very probable that the objective could only be achieved with substantial American assistance, which could not be taken for granted.[1]

However, since the possibility remained that sufficient warning of an Iraqi attack might not be available, the contingency of evicting an established Iraqi force still had to be considered. To this end, moves were again made to see if the US could not be persuaded to engage in joint planning. As Richard Beaumont of the Foreign Office's Eastern Department observed, even the small measure of coordinated planning agreed to by the previous Administration in 1959 did not seem to have produced practical results on the ground.[2] The US Admiral and his staff based in Bahrain had not engaged in any planning activities with their British counterparts. Foreign Office Permanent Under-Secretary Sir Frederick Hoyer Millar described it as 'really rather ludicrous that there should be an American Admiral stationed in Bahrain alongside a British Admiral (and a British Brigadier) both of them apparently working in water-tight compartments and not having much idea of what the other is doing'.[3] Although another approach to the Americans by Foreign Secretary Home was suggested, little hope was held out that the situation could be changed. Thus, in contrast to the position in Lebanon in 1958, no detailed contingency plans existed in the summer of 1961 for Anglo-American intervention in Kuwait.

Another problem for the British Government in considering the contingency of any pre-emptive intervention in Kuwait was the attitude of the Ruler himself. British representatives were far from happy with the course of political development in the country, but had to temper their criticisms so as not to risk offending the Ruler and other senior members of the al-Sabah family. The reaction of the ruling family to the substantial immigration which had accompanied the growth of the oil industry in the 1940s and 1950s had been to seek to entrench the privileges and power of those born Kuwaitis. This trend gathered pace during the period 1959–61. The Kuwaiti Nationality Law promulgated in December 1959 made it almost impossible for an Arab foreigner, let alone a non-Arab,

to acquire Kuwaiti citizenship. This was followed during 1960
by further laws securing the privileges of Kuwaiti nationality.
For instance, only a Kuwaiti could practice law, open a phar-
macy, receive a state pension, or be director of a government
department. According to the British Political Agent in Kuwait,
John Richmond, this made clear the determination of born
Kuwaitis 'to remain a privileged minority in a growing community in which their numbers and to which their contribution grow less and less'.[4]

The difficulty this posed the British Government was clear
to Richmond. 'Because of their interest in the stability of the
area there must always be a strong temptation for Her Majesty's
Government to welcome and support conservative movements
of opinion in the Middle East; and because the preservation of
the independence of Kuwait is such an important British interest, there is added inducement . . . for us to flatter Kuwaiti self-
esteem and to applaud their determination to "go it alone".'
Richmond argued that, on the contrary, it would be more in
Britain's long-term interests 'to do what we can to modify these
Kuwaiti attitudes'.[5] The irony is, of course, that three decades
later a further Western military intervention was to take place
in defence of a Kuwait where the domestic political environ-
ment was substantially unchanged.

An additional problem presented to the British Government
by the domestic situation in Kuwait at the beginning of the
1960s was the sensitivity of the Ruler over the issue of joint
military contingency planning. Here again, the position in 1961
provides a precedent for that in 1990. The Ruler did not want
to be seen to be too dependent on Western support for fear
of attracting criticism in the Arab world. He had first agreed
to joint military planning with British forces in May 1959 during the high tide of Communist influence in Iraq. Thencefor-
ward, discussions of 'Operation Vantage', the British plan for
protection of the emirate in the event of an Iraqi attack, were
carried forward in cooperation with the Commander-in-Chief
of the Kuwaiti army, Sheikh Abdullah Mubarak. Richmond
believed that the Ruler had 'little idea of how far joint military
planning has progressed, and that he might be alarmed if he
knew'. He wanted 'the security resulting from military plans
without risking the odium of making them'.[6]

Anecdotal evidence supported Richmond's contention that the Ruler himself was remote from the practicalities of Kuwaiti defence policy. At a military parade in honour of the visit of King Saud, Sheikh Abdullah Mubarak put on display all the hardware owned by the Kuwaiti armed forces, together with British equipment stockpiled (or pre-positioned) there against the contingency of an Iraqi attack. The Ruler wore a uniformly glum expression as the equipment was paraded by.[7]

Thus, the British Government faced a number of serious problems in considering the contingency of an operation to forestall Iraqi designs on Kuwait. No American forces could be relied upon to support those of Britain, and the leaders of the emirate itself seemed likely to be very squeamish about accepting British assistance. Add to that the warning time needed of Iraqi intentions, and the narrow power base of the al-Sabah regime, and the whole operation seemed likely to be fraught with perils and pitfalls. If Britain could not successfully pre-empt an Iraqi attack, and had instead to evict an established Iraqi force, her military and, no doubt, diplomatic resources seemed likely to be stretched to breaking point. Indeed, Sir George Middleton, the Political Resident in the Persian Gulf, argued that unilateral British intervention, even of the limited pre-emptive type envisaged by 'Vantage', was no longer politically or militarily practical.[8]

Whatever the perils from the point of view of British interests, the government had little choice but to accede to the Ruler's wishes in respect of future status of the emirate. An exchange of notes on 19 June abrogated the 1899 agreement under which Kuwait had been afforded British 'protection'. However, the proviso was added that: 'nothing in these conclusions shall affect the readiness of Her Majesty's Government to assist the Government of Kuwait if the latter request such assistance.'[9] The announcement of the new agreement provoked a furious response from the Iraqi leader Qassem. Radio Baghdad broadcast its condemnation and asserted that Kuwait was part of Iraq. It was unclear initially to Sir Humphrey Trevelyan in Baghdad whether the Iraqi response was mere posturing, or the prelude to military action.[10] However, he was soon suggesting that Qassem's outrage may have been fuelled by the fact that the Anglo-Kuwaiti Agreement had scotched an

existing plan to invade Kuwait under cover of the 14 July cele-
brations in Iraq.[11]

The problem for the British Government in all of this was
that in order to defend Kuwait effectively and economically it
needed at least four days' notice of an Iraqi attack so that
forces could be deployed pre-emptively. Unfortunately,
Trevelyan acknowledged, 'if there is movement of troops from
the area south of Baghdad, we shall not see it and Basra's
communications will probably be blocked.' He could therefore not guarantee that the embassy could give much warning
of any attack.[12] Furthermore, according to the Military Attaché
in Baghdad, the most likely form of any Iraqi attack on Kuwait
was 'a quick dash from Basra with one brigade group plus
tanks, artillery and air support, of which no advance warning
could be given'.[13]

The initial American response to Qassem's posturing was
to seek to play the tensions down. Sir Harold Caccia reported
that: 'the State Department are clearly anxious to keep out of
the matter as far as possible.'[14] On 28 June Foreign Secretary
Home cabled Secretary of State Rusk promising to keep the
Administration informed of any British moves in relation to
Kuwait, and expressing the hope that Britain and the US could
'act with the closest cooperation'.[15] In fact, the State Department's 'hands off' approach to the Kuwaiti question at this
stage was in keeping with the new Kennedy Administration's
initial handling of Middle Eastern questions. While President
Kennedy himself had evinced some interest in the problems
of the region as a senator, speaking out for instance on the
question of the French role in Algeria, and criticizing the
Eisenhower Doctrine, the Middle East did not seem to occupy
a high place in his initial order of foreign policy priorities.

Indeed he was evidently somewhat annoyed by the results
of the one initiative in the area recommended by his advisers,
a letter to Arab leaders concerning his hopes for good relations with them.[16] 'I want a report from the State Department
. . . on whose idea it was for me to send the letters to the
Middle Eastern Arab leaders', he minuted. 'The reaction has
been so sour I would like to know whose idea it was, what they
hoped to accomplish, and what they think we have now accomplished.'[17] Although the Administration was later to become

more closely involved in the region, particularly in respect of the Yemeni Civil War and the Johnson Plan for the Palestinian refugees, at this stage it was happy to leave the Kuwaiti problem in British hands.

Alarmed by the rumours of Iraqi troop movements, and the probable lack of warning of any impending attack, Foreign Secretary Home moved on 29 June to ask the Ruler of Kuwait to make a formal request for British assistance under the terms of the Exchange of Notes.[18] US Secretary of State Rusk was immediately informed of the British approach.[19] Home expressed the hope that the US would give Britain full political support, which would be 'absolutely essential' to the success of any operation.

The lack of any immediate response from the Ruler to the initial British approach led Home to despatch another telegram to Kuwait early on the morning of 30 June.[20] In it he urged the British Agent Richmond to secure the assent of the Ruler to British counter-measures 'as soon as practicable'. Richmond was instructed to caution him that any Iraqi force assembled near the border could 'drive right through to Kuwait town in a matter of hours if sufficient British forces were not already in position in Kuwait territory'. The intention was evidently to frighten the Ruler into overcoming whatever qualms he may have about the reaction in the Arab world to any request on his part for help from Britain. It reaped dividends in the form of an immediate request for British military assistance.[21] This kind of manoeuvring is reminiscent of that which preceded the Jordanian request for similar assistance on 16 July 1958. Again, the question remains open as to how palpable the threat the British Government acted to thwart really was.

If this question in the Kuwaiti case is perhaps unanswerable what certainly can be assessed is British Government *perceptions* of the Iraqi threat. How convinced were the British ministers who took the decision to intervene in Kuwait in a succession of meetings of the Cabinet Defence Committee on 29 and 30 June and 1 July that Iraq intended to invade the emirate? One handicap in answering this question is the absence from the released records of the minutes of a crucial meeting on the afternoon of 29 June. The meeting preceded Home's initial despatch concerning the need for a request from the Ruler for

British assistance. References to it in the minutes of a further meeting of the Defence Committee on the evening of 29 June, together with a memorandum from de Zulueta to Macmillan, indicate that the considerations involved in any British military intervention were first aired at this point.[22] If the minutes themselves are unavailable, de Zulueta's contribution at least indicates that a range of political and economic factors, relating to the effect of any intervention on Britain's position in the Gulf, were probably considered alongside the intelligence concerning Iraqi intentions. 'If we let Kuwait go without a fight', de Zulueta cautioned, 'the other oil Sheikdoms (which are getting richer) will not rely on us any longer.'

The next crucial meeting took place on the afternoon of 30 June.[23] Its purpose was to decide on the scale of British intervention in response to the Ruler's request. Coincidentally, the minutes of the meeting record that:

> in the course of discussion on what limited British forces might be moved urgently into Kuwait to forestall this threat ... further information was received which indicated that the movement of tanks from Baghdad to Basra had probably begun, and that certain Iraqi naval preparations were in hand. In these circumstances it was agreed that operations VANTAGE, involving the full deployment of forces required to counter a full-scale Iraqi attack on Kuwait, should commence forthwith. . .[24]

This was another case of serendipity with echoes of, although not perhaps quite on the scale of, the discovery of the plot against King Hussein of Jordan on 16 July 1958. If action was to be taken to protect Kuwait, it would be far more convenient from the military point of view if this conformed to the plan of operations envisaged under 'Vantage'.

The version of events passed to the US Embassy by George Hiller, head of the Foreign Office's Western Department, was that:

> [the] decision to send troops was based on [a] military appreciation [of the] situation following [the] realization [that] Intelligence had lost track [of a] squadron of Iraqi tanks and that Iraqi forces currently present in [the] Basra

area plus tanks would be sufficient [to] invade Kuwait in [the] absence [of] any British strength on [the] ground.[25]

Interestingly, a retrospective assessment of the operation produced by the US London Embassy in early September noted that: 'the Foreign Office and undoubtedly other members in the Government were reluctant actually to put troops on the ground because of the adverse political results which might flow from such an action.'[26] While stressing that the Ruler had requested British intervention, the document argued that: 'he was undoubtedly supported in British Cabinet deliberations by the British military and some in the Government reflecting the views of the City where the feeling existed that Britain should, at all costs, take no chances with the oil supply represented by Kuwait.' The assessment concluded that 'the British move into Kuwait was taken on the basis of intelligence which at the moment seemed valid. There is still some question, however, whether Iraqi forces actually moved toward Kuwait . . .'.

Having taken the decision to intervene in Kuwait, the British Government was soon confronted by a problem which had further echoes of the July 1958 crisis: the question of overflying rights. The Turkish Government, which had initially agreed to British overflights of its territory, temporarily withdrew its consent. The Sudanese Government also demurred.[27] Although the use of alternative forces and routes was considered, by the time the Defence Committee met again, the Turkish Government had changed its mind and agreed to the overflights. At this meeting it was also noted that 'there was no further information to show that more Iraqi forces were assembling at Basra in preparation for an attack on Kuwait'. However, 'the Iraqi forces already assembled, together with General Kasim's threats, fully justified the entry of British forces into Kuwait in answer to the Ruler's request.'[28]

The initial reaction of the US Administration to the British move was supportive. The NSC had agreed on 29 June to give full political and logistical assistance should British intervention prove necessary.[29] On 1 July, after the British decision to implement 'Vantage' had been taken, Secretary of State Rusk went further and offered the assistance of a small US naval force, the 'Solent Amity', should it be required.[30] Although as matters transpired this US offer did not have to be taken up, it was at least a welcome sign of backing for British operations in Kuwait.

However, as her troop build-up continued over the course of the ensuing week, Britain was forced to defend her actions in the United Nations against accusations that she had fabricated the Iraqi threat. By 5 July, the State Department and the US Delegation at the UN were expressing concern about 'the lack of fresh evidence of aggressive Iraqi preparations against Kuwait or the reinforcement of their forces in Basra'.[31] The US Embassy in Baghdad had earlier reported that it still had 'no direct evidence that Iraqi armor has been moved south from [the] Baghdad area'.[32] Although the Administration continued its public support of the British action, disquiet was expressed in private about the size of the British build-up. A memorandum from Phillips Talbot of the State Department's Near Eastern section to Secretary Rusk argued that: 'the British have placed more force in and off Kuwait than was justified by the magnitude or even the seriousness of the Iraqi threat.'[33] Rusk's response was to arrange for discussions to take place with British Embassy officials on the political implications of the Kuwaiti operation. Early the following month, Rusk was again to raise the question of the magnitude of the original Iraqi threat with Home, who responded that 'there was no doubt whatever that if we had not acted promptly, then the Iraqis would have seized Kuwait'.[34]

British press reaction to the intervention was also less than wholeheartedly supportive. Several papers including the *Financial Times*, the *Observer*, and the *Guardian* questioned whether propping up sheikhs was really the best way for Britain to protect her interests.[35] In Kuwait itself opinion was divided as to the need for so substantial a British operation. As Political Agent Richmond noted, 'over 40 years and a fortune of a million rupees ensures support for our intervention. . . . The majority however are by no means so grateful to us.'[36]

A further difficulty which soon began to concern the government was how it would be able to withdraw its forces from Kuwait without a recurrence of the Iraqi threat. One alternative was the introduction of UN peacekeepers, and another the creation of an Arab force. In the event, it was to be Arab action, as in the case of the Jordan operation, which was to pave the way for the departure of British troops. Qassem's threats against Kuwait had largely isolated him in the Arab world. His existing rivalry with Nasser, together with the fears of Saudi Arabia about Iraqi expansionism, meant that there was a powerful axis in the Arab world ready to oppose his designs on the emirate. This was reflected first in the decision to grant Kuwait membership of the Arab League, and then in the negotiations which led to the establishment of an Arab Deterrent Force (ADF) to protect the emirate.

Although the British Government was very diffident about the possible presence of any substantial UAR contingent in the ADF, the willingness of the Arab League to take over from British forces the burden of the defence of Kuwait was a welcome solution to what had initially appeared to be a thorny problem.[37] The question remained, however, as to whether Britain should be prepared to maintain her military forces in the area at a level which would enable her to carry out possible future operations in defence of Kuwait. Here the answer from both the Ministry of Power and the Foreign Office was unequivocally positive. The Foreign Office supported a proposal to spend £600 000 building new facilities for British forces in Bahrain to enable any future deployment in Kuwait to take place within 36 hours of warning being received. It was pointed out that: 'the value of Kuwaiti independence to the United Kingdom balance of payments is probably enormous, quite apart from our general interest in maintaining stability in the area and keeping Communist penetration at bay.' A figure of at least £100 million per annum was put on the value of Kuwaiti oil and investments to the UK economy.[38]

Interestingly, though, there were dissenting voices within the government. Perhaps not surprisingly, the Treasury opposed the level of spending required. However, the Cabinet Secretary, Sir Norman Brook, also argued against maintaining the British commitment to Kuwait. He asserted that: 'in Kuwait we are still pursuing our traditional policy of extracting oil concessions from an autocratic Ruler in return for military protection. I doubt whether this policy is realistic in the circumstances of today.' It was becoming increasingly difficult to maintain the necessary level of military spending, and increasingly perilous to rely on the survival of the regimes themselves. Britain's policy, Brook argued, was really a short-term one: 'to get the oil out of each of these territories for as long as the inhabitants remain fairly primitive'.[39]

However, although compromises were struck which took account of the reluctance of the Treasury to commit resources, the central political commitment to defend Kuwait remained for the time being. Brook's views were out of line with those of Macmillan himself, and powerful figures in the Cabinet such as Home and Butler.

At the end of September, during the course of the process of reduction of British forces in Kuwait, and their replacement by the ADF, news broke of an army coup in Syria. After three and a half years of high-handed rule from Cairo, Nasser had managed to alienate almost all sections of Syrian society. Although Nasser himself tried to present the coup as being inspired by the reactionary landed and business classes, the truth seems to be that there was a much broader base of support in Syria for secession from the United Arab Republic. The break-up of the UAR was a significant set-back for Nasser, and marked what in hindsight seems to have been the beginning of the turning of the tide against his brand of Arab nationalism.

On the one hand, in view of its continuing mistrust of the Egyptian leader, the British Government could not fail to take some satisfaction from the blow to his pride occasioned by the collapse of the UAR. However, while three years earlier the collapse of the UAR might have raised a cheer to shake Whitehall to its rafters, by the autumn of 1961 the British Government had other more pressing matters on its mind. In the regional context, the most immediate issue was what effect the Syrian secession might have on the British position in Kuwait. The process of troop withdrawal was well advanced by this point, with the last forces expected leave the emirate by the middle of October. However, Foreign Secretary Home's view was that it was unlikely that Qassem would seize the opportunity to attack Kuwait. In Syria itself he predicted instability, and likely gains for the Communists. As to recognition of the new regime, he believed that Britain should hold back to avoid needlessly antagonizing Nasser.[40]

The other pressing issue which occupied both the British

and American Governments was the need to restrain King Hussein of Jordan. Although there had been a slight improvement in relations between the King and Nasser during the course of 1960 and 1961, the news from Syria led Hussein to put the Jordanian army on alert. It seems probable that he was guarding against any attempt by Nasser to restore the union by force.[41] He also moved immediately to recognize the new regime in Damascus, leading Nasser to break off diplomatic relations with Jordan. Both the British and American Ambassadors were instructed by their governments to counsel caution on the King.[42]

In more general terms, both governments seem to have agreed that Syria's secession from the UAR was likely to increase instability in the region. The immediate reaction of the State Department was that the coup was not in the United States' best interests, and that it might indeed welcome the restoration of the union provided this took place without bloodshed.[43] Both Britain and America moved only cautiously towards recognition of the new Syrian regime. Nasser himself seems quickly to have abandoned the idea of restoring the union, and although he did not welcome the eventual Anglo-American recognition of the Damascus Government, he acquiesced in it when it came.

It is arguable, then, that the turbulent summer of 1961 had gone some way towards clarifying the new British role in the Middle East. The period after the Iraqi Revolution had seen a reorientation of Britain's strategy towards a more exclusive concentration on the defence of her interests in the Gulf. Although efforts had been made to secure American cooperation, their lack of success meant that the British Government had to plan to rely on its own resources in defending Kuwait. Britain had little option but to acquiesce in the Ruler's pressure for the granting of Kuwaiti independence. The nature, immediacy and extent of the Iraqi threat to this independence remains difficult to judge. Certainly, the lack of subsequent confirmation of the intelligence reports on which the government acted on 30 June clouds the operation with a degree of suspicion. On the other hand, the need for a four-day advance warning of Iraqi intentions in order to implement 'Vantage' meant that the government had to act even on the possibility of an attack.

The Kuwaiti operation confirmed that Britain continued to be prepared to use force to protect her interests in the Middle East. However, in the post-Iraqi Revolution years these interests were concentrated in the Gulf. Nevertheless, the myth that Britain continued to manipulate the politics of the whole region lived on well after the reality. Sir Humphrey Trevelyan, noted in June 1960 that the puzzling belief was held in many quarters in Iraq that the British had in fact organized the Iraqi Revolution. 'Realising that Nuri was no longer any use to us, we selected Qasim as our new instrument of policy.'[44] The following October, when he relinquished his post as ambassador, Trevelyan reported with amusement the small talk of the Iraqi drivers and policemen outside the farewell dinner party thrown for him by Qassem. They were puzzled as to why Qassem should throw a party for a man whom he had publicly accused of plotting against Iraq. 'Everyone knows that Qasim is a man of the British', argued one driver. With a shrug of the shoulders a policemen agreed: 'without the British Qasim is nothing.'[45] As Trevelyan had earlier reminded the Iraqi leader, these sentiments were illustrative of a well-known Arabic saying: 'if there are two fish fighting in the sea, the British are behind it.'[46]

Notes

Notes to Chapter One

1 Louis, W. R., *The British Empire in the Middle East* (Oxford, 1984), p. 588.

2 Cooper, C. L., *The Lion's Last Roar: Suez, 1956* (New York, 1978).

3 Dooley, H. J., 'Great Britain's "Last Battle" in the Middle East: Notes on Cabinet Planning during the Suez Crisis of 1956', *International History Review* xi/3 August 1989, pp. 486–517.

4 For revisionism on Suez see for example Barnes, J., 'From Eden to Macmillan', in eds Hennessy, P. and Seldon, A., *Ruling Performance* (Oxford, 1987).

5 Lamb, R., *The Failure of the Eden Government* (London, 1987), p. 242; Neff, D., *Warriors at Suez* (New York, 1981), pp. 182–3; Rhodes James, R., *Anthony Eden* (London, 1986), p. 366.

6 Watt, D. C., *Succeeding John Bull* (Cambridge, 1984), pp. 13–20.

7 Caccia–FO, 11/2/57, PRO FO371/126684. Caccia refers to the President's 'remoteness', and 'boy scout views about colonialism, the UN, and the effectiveness of phrases as acts of policy'. Adams, S., *Firsthand Report* (New York, 1961), p. 44, argued that 'Eisenhower gave Dulles a free hand and wide responsibility in shaping the administration's foreign policy.' Only one perceptive contemporary commentator seems to have dissented from this view, Lubell, S., *Revolt of the Moderates* (New York, 1956).

8 Greenstein, F. E., *The Hidden-Hand Presidency: Eisenhower as Leader* (New York, 1982); Divine, R. A., *Eisenhower and the Cold War* (Oxford, 1981); Ambrose, S. E., *Eisenhower the President* (London, 1984), all follow the revisionist line.

9 Crabb, C. V. and Mulcahy, K. V., *Presidents and Foreign Policy Making: From FDR to Reagan* (London, 1986), p. 157.

10 Ambrose, *Eisenhower the President*, p. 19.

11 Meeting with the President, 17/11/56, Eisenhower Papers: Box 4, John Foster Dulles, White House Memoranda Series.

12 Conference with the President, 20/11/56, ibid.

13 Memorandum dictated by the President, 28/3/56, Eisenhower Papers: Box 13, Ann Whitman File, DDE Diary Series.

14 Magazine Clippings, *Saturday Review of Literature*, undated, John Foster Dulles Papers, Box 480, Seeley G. Mudd Library, Princeton.

15 Magazine Clippings, *Life*, 19/8/57, John Foster Dulles Papers, Box 481, Seeley G. Mudd Library, Princeton.

16 Winthrop Aldrich, interviewed 15/7/64, John Foster Dulles Papers, Oral History, Seeley G. Mudd Library, Princeton.

17 Gerson, L. L., *John Foster Dulles* (New York, 1967), pp. 44–5.

18   Comments to foreign service personnel, 21/4/56, John Foster Dulles Papers, Box 106, Seeley G. Mudd Library, Princeton.
19   Eisenhower–Eden, 3/9/56, PRO PREM11/1100.
20   Morris–Hadow, 27/2/57, PRO FO371/127741.
21   Caccia–Lloyd, 20/3/58, PRO PREM11/2403.
22   Adamthwaite, A., 'The Foreign Office and Policy-Making', from ed. Young, J., *The Foreign Policy of Churchill's Peacetime Administration* (Leicester, 1988), pp. 8–9.
23   This sort of criticism is typical of the work of, among others, David Carlton. See Carlton, D., *Britain and the Suez Crisis* (Oxford, 1988), p. 46.
24   Horne, A., *Macmillan, 1891–1956* (London, 1988), and *Macmillan, 1957–1986* (London, 1989).
25   Thorpe, D. R., *Selwyn Lloyd* (London, 1989), p. 439.
26   Lloyd–Macmillan, 25/5/59, PRO PREM11/3266.
27   Memorandum by Bevin, 25/8/49, PRO CAB129/36.
28   Shwadran, B., *The Middle East, Oil, and the Great Powers* (New York, 1973), p. 532.
29   Edmonds, R., *Setting the Mould: the United States and Britain, 1945–50* (Oxford, 1986), p. 116; and 'Middle East Oil', 30/4/56, PRO FO371/121273.
30   Roberts, D., 'The Consequences of the Exclusive Treaties: a British View', from Pridham, B. R., *The Arab Gulf and the West* (London, 1985), p. 10.
31   Shwadran, *The Middle East, Oil, and the Great Powers*, p. 532.
32   Stoff, M. B., *Oil, War, and American Security* (London, 1980), p. 209.
33   Ovendale, R., *The English Speaking Alliance: Britain, the United States, the Dominions and the Cold War, 1945–51* (London, 1985), p. 280.
34   Monroe, E., *Britain's Moment in the Middle East* (London, 1963) p. 79.
35   Shuckburgh, E., *Descent to Suez* (London, 1986), p. 311.
36   Cohen, M. J., *Palestine: Retreat from the Mandate* (London, 1978), p. 191.
37   Stoff, *Oil, War, and American Security*, p. 40.
38   Ibid., p. 59.
39   Long, D. E., *The United States and Saudi Arabia: Ambivalent Allies* (Boulder, Colorado, 1985) p. 103.
40   Ibid., p. 6.
41   Conversation between Eisenhower, Eden, Dulles and Lloyd, 30/1/56, PRO PREM11/1334.
42   Louis, *The British Empire in the Middle East*, p. 386.
43   Ovendale, *The English Speaking Alliance*, p. 274.
44   Louis, *The British Empire in the Middle East*, p. 561.
45   Safran, N., *Israel: the Embattled Ally* (London, 1978), p. 338.
46   Ibid., p. 348. The 'Doctors' Plot' of January 1953 involved the linking of four Jewish physicians with the CIA in an attempt to assassinate top Soviet leaders. It perfectly illustrated Stalin's anti-Semitic paranoia.
47   Press cutting, 'Statement on Jews Confronts Dulles', 8/6/53, John Foster Dulles Papers, Box 73, Seeley G. Mudd Library, Princeton. Dulles was supposed to have told the Lebanese premier that US policy in the

Middle East was not Zionist-dictated and that the Jews had voted against him in the 1949 New York senatorial race which he lost.

48   Ambrose, *Eisenhower the President*, p. 387.

49   Safran, *Israel: the Embattled Ally*, p. 334.

50   Melanson, R. A., 'The Foundations of Eisenhower's Foreign Policy', in eds Melanson, R. A. and Mayers, D., *Reevaluating Eisenhower: American Foreign Policy in the 1950s* (Chicago, 1987), p. 43.

51   Ambrose, S. E. and Immerman, R. H., *Ike's Spies* (New York, 1981), p. 199.

52   Copeland, M., *The Game of Nations* (London, 1969), pp. 63.

53   Ibid., p. 78.

54   Keith Kyle goes so far as to argue that 'initial expectations in London about the new regime were conditionally favourable.' Kyle, K., *Suez* (London, 1991), p. 42.

55   Neff, *Warriors at Suez*, p. 68.

56   Vatikiotis, P. J., *Nasser and his Generation* (London, 1978), pp. 230–1.

57   Fawzi, M., *Suez 1956: An Egyptian Perspective* (London, 1986), p. 14.

58   Amery, J., 'The Suez Group: A Retrospective on Suez' in Troen, I. T. and Shemesh, M., *The Suez–Sinai Crisis 1956: Retrospective and Reappraisal* (London, 1990), p. 116.

59   Ibid.

60   Vatikiotis, P. J., *Egypt since the Revolution* (London, 1968), p. 118.

61   Reynolds, D., 'A "Special Relationship"? America, Britain and the International Order since the Second World War', *International Affairs*, Vol. 62, Winter 1985/6, p. 6.

62   Edmonds, *Setting the Mould*, p. 12.

63   Reynolds, D. and Dimbleby, D., *An Ocean Apart* (London, 1988), pp. 78–84.

64   Hogan, M. J., *The Marshall Plan: America, Britain, and the Reconstruction of Western Europe, 1947–52* (Cambridge, 1987), pp. 440–1.

65   Neustadt, R. E., *Alliance Politics* (London, 1970), p. 76.

66   Lucas, W. S., 'The path to Suez: Britain and the Struggle for the Middle East, 1953–56', in Deighton, A., *Britain and the First Cold War* (London, 1990), p. 269.

67   Telephone Call, Dulles–Eisenhower, 15/7/58, Eisenhower Papers: Box 34, Ann Whitman File, DDE Diary Series.

68   Neustadt, *Alliance Politics*, p. 71.

Notes to Chapter Two

1   Gordon, J., *Nasser's Blessed Movement: Egypt's Free Officers and the July Revolution* (Oxford, 1992), p. 17.

2   Ibid., pp. 17–18.

3   Yapp, M. E., *The Near East Since the First World War* (London, 1991), pp. 218–19.

4   Hopwood, D., *Egypt: Politics and Society 1945–1981* (London, 1982), p. 17.

5   Yapp, *The Near East since the First World War*, p. 81.

6   Ibid., p. 82.
7   Marr, P., *The Modern History of Iraq* (London, 1985) pp. 131–2.
8   For example, 'The Outlook for Jordan', 10/3/59, *FRUS*, 1958–60, Vol. XI, p. 687: 'we have little confidence in Hussein's ability over the long run to hold his throne in the face of the political forces at work in Jordan and throughout the area.'
9   For example, 'Settlement for Jordan', 6/8/58, PRO PREM11/2381: 'it is doubtful whether Jordan has any long term future as an independent country . . .'.
10   Vatikiotis, P. J., *Politics and the Military in Jordan* (London, 1967), p. 7.
11   Lenczowski, G., *The Middle East in World Affairs*, 4th edn (London, 1980), p. 473.
12   Vatikiotis, *Politics and the Military in Jordan*, p. 5.
13   Wilson, M. C., *King Abdullah, Britain and the Making of Jordan* (Cambridge, 1987); Shlaim, A., *Collusion Across the Jordan. King Abdullah, the Zionist Movement and the Partition of Palestine* (Oxford, 1988), and *The Politics of Partition: King Abdullah, the Zionists and Palestine, 1921–51* (Oxford, 1990); Bar-Joseph, U., *The Best of Enemies: Israel and Transjordan in the War of 1948*, (London, 1987).
14   Cobban, H., *The Making of Modern Lebanon* (London, 1985), p. 70.
15   Maksoud, C., 'Lebanon and Arab Nationalism', in Binder, L., *Politics in Lebanon* (New York, 1966), p. 239.
16   Hourani, A., 'Lebanon: the development of a political society', ibid., p. 28.
17   Salem, E. A., 'Lebanon's political maze: the search for peace in a turbulent land', *Middle East Journal*, Autumn 1979, p. 450.
18   Morris, B., *Israel's Border Wars, 1949–56* (Oxford, 1993).
19   For treatment of this topic see Morris, B., *The Birth of the Palestinian Refugee Problem, 1947–1949* (Cambridge, 1987), and *1948 and After: Israel and the Palestinians* (Oxford, 1994).
20   For the debate on this topic see for example Rabinovich, I., *The Road Not Taken: Early Arab-Israeli Negotiations* (New York, 1991); Shlaim, A., *The Politics of Partition* (Oxford, 1990).

Notes to Chapter Three

1   'Middle East Oil', 30/4/56, PRO FO371/121273.
2   Hahn, P. L., *The United States, Great Britain and Egypt, 1945–56*, (London, 1993), p. 53.
3   Jalal, A., 'Towards the Baghdad Pact: South Asia and Middle East defence in the Cold War, 1947–55', *International History Review*, xi/3, August 1989, pp. 409–33.
4   Ibid., p. 418.
5   Ibid., p. 419.
6   Ibid., p. 424.
7   Ibid., p. 425.
8   Memorandum, 'Important Points of Trip', undated, John Foster Dulles

Papers, Box 73, Seeley G. Mudd Library, Princeton. 'Pakistan [is] aware of [the] Soviet danger and has excellent troop material. Pakistan desires US military assistance without awaiting formal defense concepts. If this is given [the] army unquestionably would be effective and on our side.' (p. 6).

9   Memorandum, 'Conclusions on Trip', undated, p. 1, John Foster Dulles Papers, Box 73, Seeley G. Mudd Library, Princeton.

10   Jalal, 'Towards the Baghdad Pact', pp. 431–3.

11   Reid, B. H., 'The Northern Tier and the Baghdad Pact', in Young, J. W., (ed.), *The Foreign Policy of Churchill's Peacetime Administration* (Leicester, 1988), pp. 159–79.

12   Kyle, *Suez*, p. 56.

13   This interpretation is also followed by Frederick W. Axelgard ('US Support for the British Position in Pre-Revolutionary Iraq' in Fernea, R. A. and Louis, W. R., *The Iraqi Revolution of 1958: The Old Social Classes Revisited*, London, 1991). 'The United States and Britain exchanged roles with respect to the Baghdad Pact, with London becoming the active advocate of its virtues and Washington (ignoring its paternal responsibility for the alliance) showing only reluctance and diffidence.' (p. 87).

14   Louis, W. R., 'The Tragedy of the Anglo-Egyptian Settlement of 1954', in Louis, W. R. and Owen R., (eds) *Suez 1956* (Oxford, 1989), p. 48.

15   FO–Cairo, 15/1/55: 'I realize that there can be no complete Middle East defence arrangements without Egyptian participation . . .'. PRO FO371/115484.

16   Penrose, E and E. F., *Iraq: International Relations and National Development* (London, 1978), p. 120.

17   Reid, 'The Northern Tier and the Baghdad Pact', p. 176.

18   Seale, P., *The Struggle for Syria*, 2nd edn (London, 1986), p. 189; Axelgard, 'US Support for the British Position in Pre-Revolutionary Iraq', p. 87.

19   Thacher, N. G., 'Reflections on US Foreign Policy towards Iraq in the 1950s' in Fernea, R. A. and Louis, W. R., *The Iraqi Revolution of 1958: The Old Social Classes Revisited* (London, 1991), p. 67. Thacher argues that Nuri saw the pact as a way of replacing 'the increasingly burdensome tie with the British' with a new American alliance.

20   Shuckburgh's minute, dated 11/1/55, forms part of a dossier of documents assembled by Hadow of the Levant Department under the heading 'The Baghdad Pact: Changes in the US Attitude', dated 24/1/56, PRO FO371/121282.

21   Ibid., memo of a meeting between Shuckburgh and State Department officials, dated 28/1/55.

22   Telephone Conversation, Eisenhower–Dulles, 7/4/56, Eisenhower Papers: Box 15, Ann Whitman File, DDE Diary Series.

23   Memorandum of a conversation between Assistant Secretary Allen and the Shah of Iran, US State Department 780.5/3–2255. Additionally, the telegrams quoted above assembled by Hadow illustrate the US's initial enthusiasm for the Pact.

24   State–Karachi, US State Department 780.5/3–755.
25   A similar line of argument is followed in Devereux, D. R., *The For-mulation of British Defence Policy towards the Middle East* (London, 1990), p. 167; and Axelgard, 'US Support for the British Position in Pre-Revolutionary Iraq', p. 87.
26   Meeting with Malik, 9/2/55, Eisenhower Papers: Box 1, John Foster Dulles, General Correspondence.
27   Eden–Churchill, 21/2/55, PRO FO371/115492. David R. Devereux (*The Formulation of British Defence Policy towards the Middle East*) argues that 'the meeting with Nasser removed any remaining desire on Eden's part to cooperate with Egypt on defence.' (p. 165).
28   Stevenson–Shuckburgh, 28/3/55, PRO FO371/115504.
29   Ibid., Shuckburgh–Stevenson, 28/4/55.
30   Beeley–Shuckburgh 24/3/55, Annex E, PRO FO371/121282.
31   Ibid., Eden–Beeley, 31/3/55, Annex F; Kyle, *Suez*, p. 56.
32   'The Turko-Iraqi Pact', Memo by Brewis, 28/3/55, PRO FO371/115505.
33   Ibid., annotated comments.
34   Oren, M. B., *Origins of the Second Arab–Israel War* (London, 1992), p. 60.
35   Memo by Arthur, 31/3/55, PRO FO371/115505.
36   Memo by Brewis, 4/4/55, PRO FO371/115507.
37   State–Ankara, US State Department 780.5/5–2155; State–Karachi 780.5/5–2655; and State–Baghdad, Beirut, etc, 780.5/7–1555.
38   Lucas, N., *The Modern History of Israel* (London, 1974), p. 375.
39   Green, S., *Taking Sides: America's Relations with a Militant Israel 1948–67* (London, 1984), p. 95.
40   Meyer, G. E., *Egypt and the United States: The Formative Years* (London, 1980), p. 115; Kyle, *Suez*, p. 65; Hahn, *The United States, Great Britain and Egypt, 1945–56*, p. 189. Freiberger, S. Z., *Dawn Over Suez: The Rise of American Power in the Middle East, 1953–57* (Chicago, 1992), takes a subtly different view. 'The Gaza raid only added urgency to Nasser's search for allies and weapons sources.' (p. 102).
41   Meyer, *Egypt and the United States: the Formative Years*, p. 115.
42   Seale, *The Struggle for Syria*, p. 213.
43   Ibid., p. 224.
44   Kyle, *Suez*, p. 70.
45   The State Department took a 'dim view' of the suggestion from Harry Kern of *Newsweek* magazine that, as a gesture of goodwill, President Eisenhower should offer Nasser the use of his own plane to fly to the conference! (John Foster Dulles Papers, Box 96, Kern–Dulles, 28/3/55).
46   Ginat, R., *The Soviet Union and Egypt, 1945–55* (London, 1993), p. 192.
47   Burns, W. J., *Economic Aid and American Policy toward Egypt (1955–81)*, (New York, 1985), p. 26; Hahn, *The United States, Great Britain and Egypt, 1945–56*, p. 190.
48   Ginat, *The Soviet Union and Egypt, 1945–55*, pp. 205–22, argues a dif-ferent case. He asserts that there were two separate arms deals, one of which was concluded before the Gaza Raid in early 1955, and the

other in September 1955. These deals were part of a gradual Soviet–Egyptian rapprochement which cannot be assigned directly to the impact of the Gaza raid. Further, he argues that Nasser's public explanations of the 'Czech' deal in terms of the strings attached by the West to the supply of arms were spurious. They were merely justifications for a course dictated in any case by Nasser's policy of neutralism. However, Ginat's case does not seem wholly convincing. The September deal was by far the more significant, and its origins cannot be disconnected in Soviet and Egyptian policy from the Baghdad Pact and the Gaza Raid.

49   News Conference, 4/10/55, John Foster Dulles Papers, Box 95, Seeley G. Mudd Library, Princeton.
50   Burns, *Economic Aid and American Policy toward Egypt (1955–81)*, p. 38.
51   Ibid.
52   NSC 260th meeting, 7/10/55, Eisenhower Papers: Box 7, Ann Whitman File, NSC Series.
53   Ambrose, S. E. and Immerman R. H., *Ike's Spies* (New York, 1981), p. 200.
54   Gorst, A. and Lucas, W. S., 'The other collusion: Operation Straggle and Anglo-American intervention in Syria, 1955–6', *Intelligence and National Security*, 4/3, July 1989, pp. 576–95; p. 593, p. 581.
55   Ibid., p. 584.
56   Library of Congress, Loy W. Henderson Papers, Box 9, Iran – Background, covering letter, Hannah–Henderson, 19/6/74, 'A case of "relevant diplomacy" – Iran'; Box 6, Subject File, 1918–78, Baghdad Pact, 1956–7, covering letter, Decker–Henderson, 11/11/74, Hannah's letter to *Foreign Affairs*, April 1974.
57   Cabinet Conclusions, 20/10/55: 'We should adopt a policy of moderation in our dealings with Egypt and we should endeavour to persuade the Americans to do the same.' PRO CAB128/29. Steven Freiberger, however takes a rather different line on Alpha. From the end of March 1955 he argues that 'the priorities of the two allies were poles apart' in respect of Project Alpha. (*Dawn Over Suez: The Rise of American Power in the Middle East*, p. 116.)
58   Shamir, S., 'The collapse of Project Alpha', in Louis and Owen, *Suez 1956*, p. 81.
59   Burns, *Economic Aid and American Policy toward Egypt (1955–81)*, p. 62.
60   Kyle, *Suez*, p. 71.
61   Macmillan, H., *Tides of Fortune* (London, 1969) p. 652.
62   Touval, S., *The Peace Brokers: Mediators in the Arab–Israeli Conflict, 1948–79* (Princeton, 1982), pp. 122–3; Kyle, *Suez*, pp. 81–2.
63   Kyle, *Suez*, p. 84. The intelligence referred to was the so-called 'Lucky Break' information supplied by someone close to the Egyptian leader. However, although it was given a great deal of credence in London, the Americans were less convinced of its validity.
64   Devereux, *The Formulation of British Defence Policy towards the Middle East* (p. 167) argues that the pact 'brought out the profound differences' between the British and American approaches to the region.

Notes to Chapter Four

1 Lucas, W. S., 'The path to Suez: Britain and the struggle for the Middle East, 1953–56', in Deighton, A. (ed.) *Britain and the First Cold War* (London, 1990), pp. 261–2.

2 Macmillan, *Tides of Fortune,* p. 656.

3 Dann, U., *King Hussein and the Challenge of Arab Radicalism* (Oxford, 1989), p. 26.

4 Quoted in Satloff, R. B., *From Abdullah to Hussein: Jordan in Transition* (Oxford, 1994), p. 114.

5 Aldrich–State, US State Department 780.5/10–2755.

6 State–Ankara, US State Department 780.5/11–255.

7 Eisenhower Papers: Box 5, Ann Whitman File, Dulles–Herter Series, 3/11/55.

8 Macmillan–FO, 28/10/55, PRO PREM11/1033.

9 Copeland, *The Game of Nations,* p. 136.

10 Dann, *King Hussein and the Challenge of Arab Radicalism,* p. 177.

11 Memorandum of a conversation between Dulles and Macmillan, 28/10/55, *FRUS,* 1955–57, XIV.

12 Meetings between Macmillan and Dulles on 26/9/55 (*FRUS,* 1955–57, XIV p. 517), and 26/10/55 (ibid., p. 653).

13 Minutes of a Cabinet meeting, 20/10/55, PRO CAB128/29.

14 Dann, *King Hussein and the Challenge of Arab Radicalism,* p. 26. Selwyn Lloyd recollected that it was Macmillan who was responsible for the Templer mission: Eden was not its initiator. (Interview with Selwyn Lloyd by Kennett Love, 28/2/66, Seeley G. Mudd Library, Love Papers, Box 5.)

15 Dann, *King Hussein and the Challenge of Arab Radicalism,* p. 27.

16 Lucas, W. S., 'The path to Suez: Britain and the struggle for the Middle East, 1953–56' in Deighton, *Britain and the First Cold War,* p. 266; Meeting between Macmillan and Dulles in Geneva, 9/11/55, *FRUS,* 1955–57, XIV, p. 722.

17 Dulles–Macmillan, 5/12/55, *FRUS,* 1955–57, XIV, p. 821. Scott Lucas indicates that: 'the US, originally indicated it would not oppose Jordan's accession but reversed its position when Nasser suggested that Cairo might consider secret talks on a settlement with Israel, provided other Arab states did not join the Baghdad Pact.' (Lucas, W. S., 'Neustadt revisited: a new look at Suez and the Anglo-American "alliance"' in Gorst, A., Johnman, L. and Lucas, W. S. (eds) *Post-War Britain, 1945– 64: Themes and Perspectives* (London, 1989), p. 186.) In his more recent work, Scott Lucas refers to Macmillan's telegram of 28/10/55, reporting Dulles's supposed support for Jordanian accession, but does not explore its possible implications for Macmillan's and Dulles's strategy in the Middle East (Lucas, W. S., *Divided We Stand: Britain, the US and the Suez Crisis,* London, 1991, p. 68).

18 Abidi, A. H. H., *Jordan: a Political Study 1948–57* (New York, 1965), p. 132.

19 Templer was particularly critical of Prime Minister Mufti's role in the

negotiations over the pact. He described him as behaving with 'spineless pusillanimity'. (Report by General Templer on his visit to Jordan, 16/12/55, PRO FO371/115658.)

20 Interestingly, much of the agitation was directed against US targets as the British rather circumspectly deployed the Arab Legion to protect their own interests in the country. (Beirut–State, US State Department 785.00/1–556.)

21 Eisenhower's diary comment, Kyle, *Suez*, p. 91.

22 Dann, *King Hussein and the Challenge of Arab Radicalism*, p. 30.

23 Thorpe, D. R., *Selwyn Lloyd* (London, 1989), pp. 191–2.

24 Shuckburgh–FO, 14/1/56, PRO FO115/4548.

25 Prime Minister's visit to Washington, 30/1/56, PRO PREM11/1334. In fact, Shuckburgh (*Descent to Suez*, p. 327) argues that Eden was going even further in his opposition to Nasser at this stage, in private. He apparently compared Nasser to Mussolini and said that 'his object was to be Caesar from the Gulf to the Atlantic, and to kick us out of it all'.

26 Ambrose, S. E., *Eisenhower the President* (London, 1984), p. 316.

27 Discussion between Dulles and Makins, 5/1/56, FRUS, 1955–57, XV, p. 9.

28 Kyle, *Suez*, p. 96. In later years Anderson was to be convicted of tax evasion and imprisoned.

29 Burns, *Economic Aid and American Policy toward Egypt*, p. 60.

30 Ibid., p. 61.

31 State–Baghdad, US State Department 780.5/1–3056.

32 Anderson–Dulles, 19/1/56, and Dulles–Anderson, 19/1/56, *FRUS*, XV, pp. 28–37.

33 Touval, *The Peace Brokers*, pp. 131–3.

34 Dann, *King Hussein and the Challenge of Arab Radicalism*, p. 31.

35 Some substance was added to the belief in Nasser's involvement by the anti-Glubb propaganda which had been broadcast over the 'Voice of the Arabs' radio station. (Satloff, *From Abdullah to Hussein: Jordan in Transition*, p. 138.)

36 Vatikiotis, *Politics and the Military in Jordan*, pp. 115–16.

37 Shuckburgh, *Descent to Suez*, p. 340.

38 Duke–FO, 2/3/56, PRO FO371/121540.

39 Dann, *King Hussein and the Challenge of Arab Radicalism*, p. 32. Heikal, M., *Nasser: the Cairo Documents* (London, 1972), p. 85, also argues that Nasser was surprised by Glubb's dismissal, even believing it to have been orchestrated by the British themselves as a sign of good faith.

40 Eden–Eisenhower, 5/3/56, PRO PREM11/1895.

41 Shuckburgh, *Descent to Suez*, p. 346.

42 Duke–FO, 4/3/56, PRO FO371/121541.

43 Shuckburgh, *Descent to Suez*, p. 343, PRO CAB128/30 part 2, 5/3/56.

44 Lucas, 'The path to Suez' in Deighton, *Britain and the First Cold War*, pp. 267–8.

45 Gorst and Lucas, 'The other collusion: Operation Straggle and Anglo-American intervention in Syria, 1955–56', p. 585.

46 Ambrose, *Eisenhower the President*, p. 317.

47   Petersen, T. T., 'Anglo-American Rivalry in the Middle East: The Struggle for the Buraimi Oasis, 1952–57', *The International History Review*, XIV, 1, February 1992, p. 85. Petersen sees the reoccupation of the oasis as a turning point for Britain, underlining British willingness to use force to protect her interests in the region. However, he seems to exaggerate the significance of the issue for both British strategy and Anglo-American relations.

48   In passing, on a slightly lighter note, it may be noted that Buraimi, which was little more than a handful of oases in the middle of a great expanse of desert, came to occupy such a position of prominence in US perceptions of international politics during this era, that an American travel company, no doubt hoping to profit from the notoriety of the 'Buraimi dispute', actually wrote to the British Embassy in Washington asking for a current list of the best hotels there for visitors! (Hawley, D., *The Trucial States* (London, 1970), p. 186.)

49   Prime Minister's Visit to Washington, 30/1/56, PRO PREM11/1334.

50   Aldrich–State, US State Department 780.5/3–656.

51   Dulles (in Karachi)–Hoover, US State Department 780.5/3–656.

52   Memorandum by Murphy, US State Department 611.80/12–356.

53   Memorandum for the President: Near Eastern Policies, 28/3/56, Eisenhower Papers: Box 5, Ann Whitman File, Dulles–Herter Series.

54   Conference with the President, 28/3/56, Eisenhower Papers: Box 13, Ann Whitman File, DDE Diary Series.

55   Memorandum by the President, 28/3/56, Eisenhower Papers: Box 13, Ann Whitman File, DDE Diary Series.

56   Gorst and Lucas, 'The other collusion: Operation Straggle and Anglo-American intervention in Syria, 1955–56', p. 585.

57   Telephone Call, Eisenhower–Dulles, 7/4/56, Eisenhower Papers: Box 15, Ann Whitman File, DDE Diary Series.

58   Quoted in Warner, G., 'The United States and the Suez Crisis', *International Affairs*, 67, 2, 1991, p. 304.

59   Memorandum for the Chairman, 'The Baghdad Pact', 21/3/56, US Joint Chiefs of Staff, Records of the Chairman, Radford, 092.2: 'I have attached hereto a draft Chairman's Memorandum . . . which will clearly put the Joint Chiefs of Staff on record in favor of US adherence to the Baghdad Pact from the military point of view.'

60   'UK aims in the Middle East', memo by Brook, 14/4/56, PRO PREM11/1457.

61   Comments to foreign service personnel, 21/4/56, John Foster Dulles Papers, Box 106, Seeley G. Mudd Library, Princeton.

62   Lucas, *Divided we Stand: Britain, the US and the Suez Crisis*, pp. 116–34.

63   Ibid.

Notes to Chapter Five

1   Kyle, *Suez*, p. 121; Dooley, H. J., 'Great Britain's "Last Battle" in the Middle East: Notes on Cabinet Planning during the Suez Crisis of

1956', *International History Review* xi/3 August 1989, pp. 486–517; pp. 490–1.

2   Minutes of a meeting between Eden, Lloyd, Eisenhower and Dulles in Washington, 30/1/56, PRO PREM11/1334.

3   Gorst and Lucas, 'The other collusion: Operation Straggle and Anglo-American intervention in Syria, 1955–56', p. 584.

4   Ibid., p. 593.

5   Dooley, 'Great Britain's "Last Battle" in the Middle East: Notes on Cabinet Planning during the Suez Crisis', pp. 514–15; Lucas, *Divided We Stand*, pp. 325–6.

6   Burns, *Economic Aid and American Policy toward Egypt*, p. 76.

7   Dooley, 'Great Britain's "Last Battle" in the Middle East: Notes on Cabinet Planning during the Suez Crisis', p. 493.

8   Caccia–Lloyd, 23/11/56, PRO FO371/121274.

9   Burns, *Economic Aid and American Policy toward Egypt*, p. 98.

10 Dooley, 'Great Britain's "Last Battle" in the Middle East: Notes on Cabinet Planning during the Suez Crisis', p. 493.

11 Burns, *Economic Aid and American Policy toward Egypt*, p. 87.

12 Ibid., p. 86; Keith Kyle argues that, in addition to the desire to teach Nasser a lesson, Dulles had come to believe that it would not be in the United States' interests to maintain too close a hold over the Egyptian economy, for fear of drawing down the criticism of the people for any necessary austerity measures (Kyle, *Suez*, p. 126).

13 Copeland, *The Game of Nations*, p. 151.

14 Hillal Dessouki, A. E., 'Nasser and the Struggle for Independence', in (eds) Louis and Owen, *Suez 1956*, pp. 37–8.

15 Handwritten notes by Eden, 27/7/56, PRO PREM11/1098.

16 Cabinet Conclusions, 27/7/56, PRO CAB128/30.

17 Egypt Committee, 1st meeting, 27/7/56, PRO CAB134/1217.

18 Kyle, *Suez*, p. 173.

19 Eisenhower–Eden, 31/7/56, and covering note by Dulles, 1/8/56, PRO PREM11/1098.

20 Eden–Eisenhower, 5/8/56, PRO PREM11/1098.

21 Dooley, 'Great Britain's "Last Battle" in the Middle East: Notes on Cabinet Planning during the Suez Crisis', p. 499. The Egypt Committee had been informed on 10 August that the first possible date for a military operation was 15 September.

22 Kyle, *Suez*, pp. 194–5.

23 In a paper written in February 1957, Guy Millard of the Foreign Office described this as 'one of the decisive points of the crisis'. (Memorandum on relations between the United Kingdom, the United States and France in the months following Egyptian nationalization of the Suez Canal Company in 1956, officially dated August 1957, PRO FO800/728.)

24 Eisenhower–Eden, 3/9/56, PRO PREM11/1100.

25 Murphy, R., *Diplomat amongst Warriors* (New York, 1964), p. 386.

26 Memorandum by Lloyd, 'Suez Canal', Egypt Committee, 26th meeting, 18/8/56, PRO CAB134/1217.

27 Kyle, K., 'Britain and the Crisis', in Louis and Owen, *Suez 1956*, p. 122.

28 Horne, *Macmillan, 1894–1956*, p. 425.

29 Note of a private conversation with Eisenhower, 25/9/56, PRO PREM11/1102.

30 Note of a private conversation with Dulles, 25/9/56, ibid.

31 Egypt Committee, 2nd meeting, 28/7/56, PRO CAB134/1216.

32 Record of a meeting held at 11 Downing Street, 3/8/56, PRO CAB134/1217.

33 Carlton, D., *Britain and the Suez Crisis* (Oxford, 1988), p. 31.

34 Ibid., p. 46.

35 Horne, A., *Macmillan 1894–1956* (London, 1988), p. 422.

36 Ibid., p. 423.

37 Dulles–Dillon, 4/10/56, Eisenhower Papers: Box 6, Ann Whitman File, Dulles–Herter Series: 'I know the British and French want us to "stand with them". But we do not know where they stand nor are we consulted.'

38 Quoted in Kyle, *Suez*, p. 272.

39 Nutting, A., *No End of a lesson: The Story of Suez*, (London, 1967), pp. 76–9; Lloyd, S., *Suez 1956: A Personal Account* (London, 1978), pp. 157–63.

40 Nasser interview with Kennett Love, Cairo, 17/2/66, Seeley G. Mudd Library, Kennett Love Papers, Box 5, p. 30.

41 Fawzi, M., *Suez 1956: An Egyptian Perspective* (London, 1986), pp. 68–76.

42 Lamb, R., *The Failure of the Eden Government* (London, 1987), p. 221; Kyle, *Suez*, pp. 283–4.

43 Lucas, *Divided We Stand*, p. 225.

44 Dooley, 'Great Britain's "Last Battle" in the Middle East: Notes on Cabinet Planning during the Suez Crisis', p. 508; Lucas, *Divided We Stand*, p. 226.

45 Horne, *Macmillan, 1894–1956*, pp. 429–30.

46 For the most recent treatment of this question see Raad, Z., 'A Nightmare Avoided: Jordan and Suez 1956', *Israel Affairs*, 1/2, Winter 1994, pp. 288–308.

47 Dooley, 'Great Britain's "Last Battle" in the Middle East: Notes on Cabinet Planning during the Suez Crisis', p. 509.

48 Ibid.

49 Lucas, *Divided We Stand*, p. 228.

50 Kyle, *Suez*, pp. 298–9.

51 Ibid., p. 314.

52 Cabinet Conclusions, 23/10/56, PRO CAB128/30.

53 Cabinet Conclusions, 25/10/56, ibid.

54 Kyle, *Suez*, pp. 308–9.

55 Rhodes James, R., *Anthony Eden* (London, 1986), p. 533.

56 Horne, *Macmillan 1896–1956*, p. 433.

57 Eisenhower interview, 28/7/64, John Foster Dulles papers, Oral History, Seeley G. Mudd Library, Princeton.

58 Minutes of the 302nd NSC meeting, 1/11/56, Eisenhower Papers: Box 8, Ann Whitman File, NSC Series.

59 Kunz, D., 'The importance of having money: the economic diplomacy of the Suez Crisis', in Louis and Owen, *Suez, 1956*, p. 218.

60 Dooley, 'Great Britain's "Last Battle" in the Middle East: Notes on Cabinet Planning during the Suez Crisis', p. 516.
61 Horne, *Macmillan, 1896–1956*, p. 444.
62 Rhodes James, *Anthony Eden*, p. 573.
63 Kyle, *Suez*, p. 465.
64 Conversation between Eisenhower, Hoover and Adams, morning of 7/11/56, *FRUS*, 1955–57, XVI, Suez Crisis, pp. 1043–4.
65 Lucas, *Divided We Stand*, p. 300. Eisenhower had authorized high level reconnaissance flights over Syria in a bid to determine whether the Soviets were building up air forces there (conversation with Allen Dulles and Hoover, 8.37am, 6/11/56, *FRUS*, 1955–57, XVI, p. 1014).
66 Ibid., p. 319.
67 Horne, *Macmillan, 1896–1956*, p. 445.
68 Adamthwaite, A., 'Suez Revisited', *International Affairs* 64/3, Summer 1988, pp. 449–64, p. 463.
69 Barnes, J., 'From Eden to Macmillan', in eds Hennessy, P. and Seldon, A., *Ruling Performance* (Oxford, 1987), p. 98. Barnes argues that while Suez altered public perceptions of Britain's great power status, it had surprisingly little impact on Britain's ability to act, even in the Middle East.
70 Dooley, 'Great Britain's "Last Battle" in the Middle East: Notes on Cabinet Planning during the Suez Crisis', p. 517.
71 Lucas, *Divided We Stand*, p. 324.
72 Ibid.
73 This concept as a tool for analysing Anglo-American relations was first developed in Reynolds, D., *The Creation of the Anglo-American Alliance, 1937–41: A Study in Competitive Cooperation* (London, 1981).
74 Quoted in Lucas, *Divided We Stand*, p. 307.
75 Darwin, J., *Britain and Decolonisation* (London, 1988), p. 231.

Notes to Chapter Six

1 Caccia–Lloyd, 23/11/56, PRO FO371/121274.
2 Caccia–FO, 28/11/56, PRO FO115/4550.
3 Lloyd–Salisbury, 27/11/56, ibid.
4 Brief for Ministerial Meetings in Paris, 'US accession to the Baghdad Pact', 11/12/56, PRO FO371/121274.
5 For the internal debate in the State Department see Jones–Burdett, US State Department, 780.5/11–1556; Mathews–Burdett, US State Department, 780.5/11–1456; Nunley–Burdett, US State Department, 780.5/11–1556.
6 For the Joint Chiefs' views see Murphy–Hoover, US State Department 780.5/11–1656, and Radford–Wilson, 30/11/56, Eisenhower Papers: Box 1, White House Office, Office of the Staff Secretary, Defense Series. Defense Department views are expressed in a covering letter to Radford's memorandum, Wilson–Eisenhower, 4/12/56.
7 For ambassadorial views see Gallman–Dulles, US State Department, 780.5/11–1556; Warren–Dulles, US State Department 780.5/11–2056.

8   Rountree–Gallman, US State Department, 780.5/11–2056.
9   Memorandum of a phone call, Eban–Rountree, US State Department 780.5/11–3056.
10 It may well be that the difficulties with Congress over the pact which were repeatedly cited by Administration officials are another case of what Neville Chamberlain called the 'Mr Jorkins' factor in American politics. Mr Jorkins was the unseen junior partner in the law firm of Spenlow and Jorkins in Dickens's *David Copperfield*, always cited by Mr Spenlow as a ruthless and obdurate taskmaster who prevented him from showing generosity to his clients and staff. (Cited by Reynolds, D., in 'Roosevelt, Churchill, and the wartime Anglo-American alliance, 1939–45' from Louis, W. R. and Bull, H., *The Special Relationship*, Oxford, 1986, p. 19.)
11 Memorandum of a conversation, Dulles, Rountree, and the Ambassadors of Turkey, Iran, Iraq and Pakistan, US State Department, 780.5/12–456.
12 'US position on Middle East problems', Rountree–Dulles, US State Department 780.00/12–756.
13 Conference with the President, 21/11/56, Eisenhower Papers: Box 4, John Foster Dulles, White House Memoranda Series.
14 Kyle, (*Suez* p. 506) calls this the 'key to American Middle East policy at this point'.
15 Eisenhower–Dulles, 12/12/56, Eisenhower Papers: Box 6, Ann Whitman File, Dulles–Herter Series.
16 Memorandum of a conversation with Senator Knowland, 8/12/56, Eisenhower Papers: Box 1, John Foster Dulles, General Correspondence.
17 Record of a conversation between Lloyd and Dulles, 10/12/56, PRO FO371/129327.
18 Memorandum of a conference, 20/12/56, Eisenhower Papers: Box 20, Ann Whitman File, DDE Diary Series.
19 Ambrose, *Eisenhower the President*, p. 376.
20 Crabb, C. V., *The Doctrines of American Foreign Policy* (London, 1982), p. 164.
21 Presidential-Bipartisan Congressional leadership meeting, 1/1/57, Eisenhower Papers: Box 2, Ann Whitman File, Legislative Meetings Series.
22 Meeting between Dulles, Caccia and Alphand; US State Department 780.5/12–2956.
23 Caccia–FO, 24/12/56, PRO FO371/121274, and memorandum of a conversation, Dulles–Caccia, 24/12/56, Eisenhower Papers: Box 1, John Foster Dulles, General Correspondence.
24 Macmillan, H., *Riding the Storm* (London, 1971), p. 213; Macmillan–Eden, 17/2/57, Avon Papers 23/48/2.
25 Hoopes, T., *The Devil and John Foster Dulles* (London, 1974), p. 406.
26 Crabb, *The Doctrines of American Foreign Policy*, p. 168.
27 Ibid., pp. 171–2.
28 Hoopes, *The Devil and John Foster Dulles*, p. 407.

29 Conference with the President, 13/5/58, Eisenhower Papers: Box 6, John Foster Dulles, White House Memoranda Series.
30 Caccia–Hadow, 19/1/57 PRO FO371/127740; and Morris–Hadow, 27/2/57, PRO FO371/127741.
31 'Anglo-American cooperation in the Middle East', 13/3/57, PRO CAB134/2339.
32 'Middle East expenditure', 11/3/57, ibid.
33 'Military support for the Baghdad Pact', 22/1/57, PRO CAB131/18.
34 Eisenhower, D. D., *Waging Peace* (London, 1965), p. 116.
35 Ambrose, *Eisenhower the President*, p. 385.
36 Meeting between Dulles and Lloyd, 10/12/56, PRO FO371/129327.
37 Bligh, A., *From Prince to King: Royal Succession in the House of Saud in the Twentieth Century* (London, 1984), pp. 59–64.
38 Ibid., p. 61. Bligh shows that discontent among the princes had already come out into the open in the shape of a report in the Lebanese newspaper, *al-Hayat*, in July 1956 stating that seven of the King's brothers had submitted a memorandum criticizing his domestic and foreign policies.

Notes to Chapter Seven

1 Rhodes James, *Anthony Eden*, p. 587; Kyle, *Suez*, pp. 532–3.
2 Horne, A., *Macmillan, 1894–1956* (London, 1988), pp. 450–1.
3 Fry, M. and Hochstein, M., 'The Forgotten Middle Eastern Crisis of 1957: Gaza and Sharm-el-Sheikh', *International History Review*, Vol. XV/1, February 1993, pp. 54–5.
4 Ibid., p. 60.
5 Cited in Fry and Hochstein, 'The Forgotten Middle Eastern Crisis of 1957: Gaza and Sharm-el-Sheikh', p. 46.
6 Ibid., p. 78.
7 Horne, *Macmillan, 1957–86*, p. 22.
8 Summary Briefing Paper, 'Traditional Concept of the Anglo-American alliance', undated [March 1957], Eisenhower Papers: Box 3, Ann Whitman File, International Series.
9 Horne, *Macmillan, 1957–86*, p. 21. The British approach had been, according to a telegram from Sandys, to be 'conciliatory in public and blunt in private'. [Sandys–Macmillan, 28/1/57, PRO FO371/126683] Sandys himself appears to have relished the opportunity to give Dulles 'the works', as he called it, at their meeting in Washington towards the end of January.
10 Eisenhower, *Waging Peace*, p. 122. Also, Eisenhower's diary entry, 21/3/57, *FRUS*, 1955–57, XVII, pp. 461–2.
11 'Long-Range Policy toward Egypt', undated, Bermuda briefing paper, Eisenhower Papers: Box 9, White House Central File, Confidential Series, Subject Sub-series.
12 Draft outline for the Prime Minister's speech at Bermuda on the Middle East, 16/3/57 PRO FO371/127755. Keith Kyle (*Suez*, p. 534) argues

that 'if there had been one person more set on destroying Nasser than Eden it had been Macmillan'.

13 Eisenhower, *Waging Peace*, p. 122.

14 Minutes of the second session of the Bermuda conference, 21/3/57, Eisenhower Papers: Box 2, White House Office, Office of the Staff Secretary, International Trips and Meetings Series.

15 Plenary meeting of the Bermuda conference, 21/3/57, PRO FO371/127755.

16 Ibid.

17 'Detail Unsolved at Bermuda Talk', *New York Times*, press cutting, 25/3/57, Box 113, John Foster Dulles Papers, Seeley G. Mudd Library, Princeton.

18 Lloyd–Caccia, 25/1/57, PRO FO371/127813.

19 Abidi, A. H. H., *Jordan: a Political Study 1948–57* (New York, 1965), pp. 146–7.

20 Ibid., p. 153.

21 State–Amman, US State Department 785.00/4–557.

22 Amman-State, US State Department 785.00/4–957, and State–Amman, US State Department 785.00/4–957.

23 Telephone Call, Dulles–Eisenhower, 25/4/57, Eisenhower Papers: Box 23, Ann Whitman File, DDE Diary Series. Satloff, R. B., *From Abdullah to Hussein: Jordan in Transition* (Oxford, 1994), pp. 160–75, provides the most recent and detailed account of the events leading up to the Zerqa affair.

24 Cabinet Conclusions, 30/4/57, PRO CAB128/31 Part 1.

25 Barbour–Dulles, US State Department, 780.5411/4–2757.

26 Bonn–State, US State Department 780.5411/5–357.

27 Valletta–State, US State Department 780.5411/5–957.

28 Baylis, *Anglo-American Defence Relations 1939–1984*, 2nd edn (London, 1984), p. 92.

Notes to Chapter Eight

1 Report to the Cabinet Official Committee on the Middle East on the Bermuda discussions, 29/3/57, PRO FO371/127756.

2 The description appears in the joint 'Review of Middle East problems bearing upon the supply of oil to the Free World' [10/5/57, PRO FO371/127757], and is excluded from the agreed position paper accepted by Dulles after the July talks, which refers instead to the US and UK cooperating 'to preserve beneficial UK relationships with the Persian Gulf and Arabian principalities' [11/7/57, PRO FO371/127756].

3 See 'Middle East discussions with the Americans: Persian Gulf States', 8/4/57, PRO FO371/127756; Middle East Committee brief for Anglo-American discussions on 15 April, 12/4/57, PRO CAB134/2339; draft despatch to H. M. Ambassadors in the Middle East on the talks between Trevelyan and Henderson, 11/7/56, PRO FO371/127756.

4   Long, D. E., *The United States and Saudi Arabia: Ambivalent Allies* (Boulder, Colorado, 1985) p. 110. Long notes that the dispute was eventually settled in 1974 with scarcely any comment outside the Arabian Peninsula.

5   Macmillan claimed that there could be no doubt that the Saudis were involved in fermenting the trouble alongside Nasser. (Macmillan–Eisenhower, 19/7/57, *FRUS*, 1955–57, Vol. XIII, pp. 226–7). However, American intelligence reports indicated that 'there is no evidence of official support of the present uprising, and arms smuggling into Oman may have been done by Talib and his group rather than by the Saudis directly'. (Ibid., pp. 234–5. Memorandum for the Special Assistant for Intelligence to the Acting Secretary of State, 1/8/57.)

6   Conversation between Dulles and Eisenhower, 3/8/57, Eisenhower Papers: Box 5, John Foster Dulles, White House Memoranda Series.

7   'Review of Middle East problems bearing upon the supply of oil to the Free World': Egypt, 10/5/57, PRO FO371/127757.

8   Middle East Committee brief for the Anglo-American discussions on 15 April, 'Egypt', 12/4/57, PRO CAB134/2339. US views on the strength of Nasser's position are made clear in the document 'Long-range policy toward Egypt', prepared for the Bermuda conference, Eisenhower Papers: Box 82, White House Central File, Confidential Series, Subject Sub-series.

9   Seale, P., *The Struggle for Syria*, 2nd edn (London, 1986), p. 291. Lesch, D., *Syria and the United States: Eisenhower's Cold War in the Middle East* (Oxford, 1992), pp. 118–19, is particularly critical of the US reaction to the Syrian–Soviet Economic Agreement.

10 Seale, *The Struggle for Syria*, pp. 292–5.

11 Dulles–Eisenhower, 20/8/57, Eisenhower Papers: Box 7, Ann Whitman File, Dulles-Herter Series. Lesch, *Syria and the United States: Eisenhower's Cold War in the Middle East*, p. 142.

12 FO–Baghdad, 20/8/57, PRO FO371/128224.

13 Lesch, *Syria and the United States: Eisenhower's Cold War in the Middle East*, pp. 147–52, provides a good treatment of the limitations of the Henderson mission.

14 Dulles–Lloyd, 21/8/57, Eisenhower Papers: Box 7, Ann Whitman File, Dulles–Herter Series.

15 Seale, *The Struggle for Syria*, p. 296.

16 Henderson–Dulles, 28/8/57, Eisenhower Papers: Box 7, Ann Whitman File, Dulles–Herter Series.

17 Memorandum of a conversation, Dulles–Knowland, 30/8/57, Eisenhower Papers: Box 1, John Foster Dulles, General Correspondence.

18 Baxter (Tel Aviv)–Dulles, 22/8/57, and Baxter–Dulles, 28/8/57, Eisenhower Papers: Box 7, Ann Whitman File, Dulles–Herter Series.

19 Cabinet Conclusions, 27/8/57, 'Syria', PRO CAB128/31 Part 2.

20 Horne, *Macmillan 1957–86*, p. 42.

21 Seale, *The Struggle for Syria*, p. 297.

22 Record of a conversation between Lloyd and Casey, the Australian Minister for External Affairs, 11/9/57, PRO FO371/128227. In reply to

a direct question about collaboration with Britain over Syria, Dulles had told a news conference on 10 September that 'the United Kingdom is kept informed through normal diplomatic channels of our thinking on the subject . . .'. News Conference, 10/9/57, Box 119, John Foster Dulles Papers, Seeley G. Mudd Library, Princeton.

23   Macmillan–Eisenhower, 10/10/57, PRO PREM11/2461.
24   Lloyd–Macmillan, 17/9/57, PRO FO371/128228.
25   Horne, *Macmillan 1957–86*, p. 44.
26   Lesch, *Syria and the United States: Eisenhower's Cold War in the Middle East*, pp. 132–4.
27   Seale, *The Struggle for Syria*, p. 304.
28   Ibid., p. 305. Lesch, *Syria and the United States: Eisenhower's Cold War in the Middle East*, pp. 181–5.
29   Memorandum of a conversation, Dulles, Mansfield and Macomber, 11/9/57, Eisenhower Papers: Box 1, John Foster Dulles, General Correspondence.
30   'British and American Policy toward Egypt', discussion between Dulles, Lloyd and other officials, US State Department, 611.74/10–1557.
31   Meeting with the President, 28/10/57, Eisenhower Papers: Box 5, John Foster Dulles, White House Memoranda Series.
32   Memorandum, Rountree–Dulles, 'Our relations with Egypt in the light of the Syrian situation', US State Department, 611.74/11–457.
33   Eisenhower–Dulles, 13/11/57, Eisenhower Papers: Box 7, Ann Whitman File, Dulles–Herter Series; Ambrose, *Eisenhower the President*, p. 463.
34   Memorandum of a Cabinet meeting, 15/11/57, Eisenhower Papers: Box 5, John Foster Dulles, White House Memoranda Series.
35   *FRUS*, 1955–57, Vol. XIII, Near East, Jordan–Yemen, Egypt–State, 11/12/57; State–Egypt, 12/12/57, pp. 744–47.
36   Ambrose, *Eisenhower the President*, p. 424; Baylis, *Anglo-American Defence Relations*, p. 92.
37   Macmillan–Eisenhower, 10/10/57, PRO PREM11/2461.
38   Lloyd–Macmillan, 15/10/57, ibid.
39   Macmillan–Eisenhower, 16/10/57, ibid.
40   Cabinet Conclusions, 21/10/57, PRO CAB128/31 Part 2.
41   Briefing Paper for the Macmillan Conference, undated [October 1957], Eisenhower Papers: Box 7, Ann Whitman File, Dulles–Herter Series.
42   Briefing Paper for the Washington Conference, undated [October 1957], Eisenhower Papers: Box 74, White House Central File, Confidential Series, Subject Sub-series.
43   Meeting with the President, 22/10/57, Eisenhower Papers: Box 2, White House Office, Office of the Staff Secretary, Subject Series, State Department Sub-series.
44   Meeting between Dulles, Quarles, Strauss and Twining, 22/10/57, ibid.
45   Brook–Heads of Foreign Office Departments, 25/3/59, PRO FO371/143671.
46   Elbrick–Dulles, 'Establishment of Working Groups to Implement the Eisenhower–Macmillan Talks', US State Department, 611.41/10–2957.

47   Chiefs of Staff Committee, Confidential Annex, 29/10/57, PRO DEFE4/101.
48   Cabinet Conclusions, 28/10/57, PRO CAB128/31 Part 2. 'Declaration of Common Purpose', 25/10/57, Box 119, John Foster Dulles Papers, Seeley G. Mudd Library, Princeton.
49   Horne, *Macmillan, 1957–86*, p. 56.
50   Baylis, *Anglo-American Defence Relations*, p. 91.

Notes to Chapter Nine

1   Seale, *The Struggle for Syria*, p. 307.
2   Ibid., p. 309.
3   Kerr, M., *The Arab Cold War*, 2nd edn (London, 1967), p. 8.
4   Ibid., p. 9.
5   Ibid., p. 11.
6   Seale, *The Struggle for Syria*, p. 316; Kerr, *The Arab Cold War*, p. 14.
7   Seale, *The Struggle for Syria*, p. 317.
8   Roberts, D., *The Baath and the Creation of Modern Syria* (London, 1987), p. 43.
9   Ibid.: Roberts argues that because of his close links with the Baath, 'we need not take too seriously Nasser's pose as the reluctant debutant.' However, this runs against the grain of the persuasive arguments of Seale and Kerr cited above.
10 Olson, R. W., *The Baath and Syria, 1947 to 1982. The Evolution of Ideology, Party and State* (Princeton, 1982), p. 31.
11 Editorial Note, *FRUS*, 1958–60, Vol. XII, pp. 32–3.
12 Lloyd–Macmillan, 28/1/58, PRO FO371/134386.
13 Record of a conversation between Lloyd, Dulles and Nuri at the Iraqi Embassy, Ankara, 29/1/58, PRO FO371/134388.
14 Dulles–Eisenhower, 29/1/58, Eisenhower Papers: Box 7, Ann Whitman File, Dulles–Herter Series.
15 Rockwell–Rountree, 'Egyptian–Syrian Union', US State Department 780.5/1–2158.
16 Briefing by General Cabell, NSC 353rd meeting, 30/1/58, Eisenhower Papers: Box 9, Ann Whitman File, NSC Series. Roberts, *The Baath and the Creation of Modern Syria*, p. 45, notes that Moscow Radio actually broadcast the accusation that the Baath were 'collaborating with imperialism'.
17 Caccia–Lloyd, 4/2/58, PRO FO371/134386.
18 Briefing by Dulles on his trip to the Near East, NSC 354th meeting, 6/2/58, Eisenhower Papers: Box 9, Ann Whitman File, NSC Series.
19 Ambrose, *Eisenhower the President*, p. 463.
20 Abidi, *Jordan: a Political Study, 1948–1957*, p. 153.
21 Wright–Lloyd, 25/2/58, PRO FO371/134025.
22 Caccia–Lloyd, 8/3/58, PRO PREM11/2403.
23 Dulles–State, 11/3/58, *FRUS*, 1958–60, Vol. XII, pp. 294–5. (There appears to be a mistake in the heading of the telegram in the *FRUS* volume which refers to Secretary of State *Herter*.)

24 Caccia–Lloyd, 20/3/58, ibid.
25 Report of a press conference given by Dulles, 10/4/58, PRO FO371/
    133799; Press Conference, 8/4/58, John Foster Dulles Papers, Box
    363, Seeley G. Mudd Library, Princeton.
26 Hayter–Caccia, 28/3/58, ibid.
27 A memorandum on 'Long Range Policy toward the Arab Union', dated
    26 March 1958 and written by the Director of Near Eastern Affairs,
    Rockwell, had emphasized the problems for the US in becoming too
    closely associated with the unpopular Arab Union. Rockwell did argue,
    though, that the US should offer assistance in the economic and milit-
    ary fields. (*FRUS*, 1958–60, Vol. XI, pp. 282–6.)
28 Bligh, *From Prince to King*, p. 64.

Notes to Chapter Ten

1   Cobban, *The Making of Modern Lebanon*, p. 87.
2   Alin, E. G., *The United States and the 1958 Lebanon Crisis: American Inter-
    vention in the Middle East* (London, 1994), p. 38.
3   Joint Planning Staff, Memoranda, DEFE6/43, 16/10/57; US Joint
    Chiefs of Staff History, p. 423. A briefer account of the ensuing Anglo-
    American planning process can be found in Ovendale, R., 'Great Brit-
    ain and the Anglo-American Invasion of Jordan and Lebanon in 1958',
    International History Review, Vol. XVI/2, May 1994, pp. 285–9. See also,
    Ashton, N. J., '"A Great New Venture"? Anglo-American Cooperation
    in the Middle East and the Response to the Iraqi Revolution, July
    1958', *Diplomacy and Statecraft*, Vol. 4, No. 1, March 1993, pp. 62–7.
4   Memorandum of a conversation between Lloyd and the Australian
    Minister of External Affairs, Casey, 11/9/57, PRO FO371/128227.
5   US Joint Chiefs of Staff History, p. 426. A conversation between Lloyd
    and Whitney, the US Ambassador in London showed that the British
    shared American concerns about attacks on King Hussein delivered
    over Radio Cairo. (*FRUS*, 1955–57, Vol. XIII, p. 159.)
6   Lloyd–Middleton, 14/11/57, PRO PREM11/2386.
7   No copy of this report has been released in either US or UK archives.
    All comment on it is by way of inference from subsequent discussions
    of its conclusions. (See, for example, Memorandum by Rose, 9/5/58,
    PRO FO371/134156.)
8   Chiefs of Staff Committee, Minutes, 3/12/57, PRO DEFE4/102. See
    especially the remarks of Group Captain Spotswood who had recently
    visited the Washington Working Party.
9   US Joint Chiefs of Staff History, p. 432.
10 Joint Planning Staff, Memoranda, 21/2/58, PRO DEFE6/49.
11 US Joint Chiefs of Staff, Central Decimal File, 7/4/58, CCS381 EMMEA.
12 US Joint Chiefs of Staff History, p. 435.
13 Ibid.
14 Joint Planning Staff, Memoranda, 21/5/58, PRO DEFE6/54.
15 Chiefs of Staff Committee, Minutes, 16/5/58, PRO DEFE4/107; Edi-
    torial Note, *FRUS*, 1958–60, Vol. XI, p. 60.

16   Lloyd–Caccia, 13/5/58, PRO PREM11/2386.

17   Conference with the President, 13/5/58, Eisenhower Papers: Box 6, John Foster Dulles, White House Memoranda Series.

18   The Administration had for some time been concerned about what it saw as increasing Communist influence in all walks of Lebanese life. Indeed, as far back as January 1955, the US Embassy in Beirut had gone so far as to argue that a positive response by the Administration to the Lebanese Basketball Federation's request for an American coach 'would provide an opportunity to combat Communist infiltration of Lebanese sports teams'. (Cited in Alin, *The United States and the 1958 Lebanon Crisis: American Intervention in the Middle East*, p. 46.)

19   See for example, McClintock–Dulles, US State Department 783A.00/5-1358. Eveland argues that Dulles became increasingly exasperated with McClintock during the crisis, especially because of his tendency to dispatch NIACT (Night action) telegrams marked for his personal attention. [Eveland, W. C., *Ropes of Sand* (London, 1980), p. 284.]

Charles Thayer, on the other hand, presents a picture of an ambassador who, although not an expert in Middle Eastern affairs, was thorough and systematic, and 'won the respect of his staff'. [Thayer, C., *Diplomat* (London, 1960), p. 77] He also claims incidentally that the ambassador was reluctant to send NIACT messages (p. 61).

Although Eveland's reliability as a witness is tarnished somewhat by his own evident personal dislike for McClintock, the sending of Robert Murphy to oversee the diplomatic side of the American operation in Lebanon after the landing of the marines does tend to suggest a certain lack of confidence in the ambassador. Still, Copeland has argued that the dispatch of 'Great White Fathers' to deal with a particular problem over the head of the ambassador on the spot was typical of Dulles's methods. [Copeland, M., *The Game of Nations* (London, 1969), p. 136.]

20   Dulles–McClintock, US State Department 783A.00/5-1358.

21   Ibid.

22   Kyle, *Suez*, p. 111.

23   Middleton–FO, 14/5/58, PRO PREM11/2386.

24   Lloyd–Caccia, 16/5/58, ibid.

25   Lloyd–Wright, 16/5/58, ibid.

26   Lloyd–Jebb, 24/6/58, PRO PREM11/2387.

27   Agwani, M. S., *The Lebanese Crisis, 1958* (London, 1965), pp. 120–21.

28   *FRUS*, 1958–60, Vol. XI, pp. 63–6.

29   Lodge–Dulles, 21/5/58, Eisenhower Papers: John Foster Dulles, Telephone Calls Series.

30   Conversation between Dulles and Caccia, US State Department 783A.00/5-2158.

31   Lloyd–Caccia, 20/5/58, PRO PREM11/2386.

32   Barbour–Dulles, US State Department 783A.00/6-658.

33   State–Cairo, US State Department 783A.00/5-2858.

34   Eisenhower, *Waging Peace*, p. 268; State–Beirut, US State Department 783A.00/6-1158.

35 Cabinet minutes, 17/6/58, PRO CAB128/32 part 2.
36 'Policy toward the United Arab Republic', undated (June 1958), Eisenhower Papers: Box 76, White House Central File, Confidential Series, Subject Sub-series.
37 'Situation in Lebanon', undated (June 1958), ibid.
38 Urquart, B., *Hammarskjöld* (New York, 1972), p. 265.
39 Eisenhower, *Waging Peace*, p. 268.
40 Conference with the President, 15/6/58, Eisenhower Papers: Box 33, Ann Whitman File, DDE Diary Series.
41 Dulles–Lodge, 20/6/58, Eisenhower Papers: Box 8, John Foster Dulles, Telephone Calls Series.
42 Allen Dulles–Foster Dulles, 20/6/58, ibid.
43 Lloyd–Caccia, 19/6/58, PRO PREM11/2387.
44 Lloyd–Caccia, 23/6/58, ibid.
45 Mason–Lloyd, 21/6/58, ibid.
46 Urquart, *Hammarskjöld*, p. 268.
47 Lloyd–Beirut, for Hammarskjöld, 24/6/58, PRO PREM11/2387.
48 Conversation between the Dulles brothers, Quarles, Rountree; US State Department 783A.00/6–2258.
49 Eisenhower, *Waging Peace*, p. 266. Robert Divine confirms that the issue at stake in Lebanon was one of credibility. However, in common with Stephen Ambrose, he argues that it was Nasser to whom Eisenhower wanted to make his point. [Divine, R. A., *Eisenhower and the Cold War* (Oxford, 1981), p. 103.]
50 Conversation between Caccia and Dulles, US State Department 783A.00/6–2458.
51 Butler–Laskey, reporting Macmillan's views for communication to Lloyd, 27/6/58, PRO PREM11/2387.
52 Urquart, *Hammarskjöld*, p. 272.
53 Mason–FO, 23/6/58, PRO PREM11/2387. Macmillan minuted on Mason's report, 'this seems queer considering how wet H. is in general'. However, Keith Kyle points out that Hammarskjöld's personal opinion of Nasser was low. Following a visit to the Middle East in February 1956 when he had met the Egyptian leader, he had compared him to an intelligent junior Nazi officer, pathologically suspicious of everybody. This may have inclined him to take a tougher line with Nasser. (Kyle, *Suez*, p. 106.)
54 Lodge–Dulles, US State Department 783A.00/6–2658.
55 Agwani, *The Lebanese Crisis*, p. 214.
56 Dixon–FO, UN observers' report, 3/7/58, PRO PREM11/2387.
57 Chiefs of Staff Committee, minutes, comments by Rose, 24/6/58, PRO DEFE4/108.
58 Conversation between Dulles and Hammarskjöld, 7/7/58, Eisenhower Papers: Box 1, John Foster Dulles, General Correspondence.

Notes to Chapter Eleven

1 A memorandum by Harold Glidden of the Research and Analysis Division of the State Department, entitled 'Intelligence Indications of

Coup in Iraq', offers explanations as to why the US intelligence community did not predict the coup (*FRUS*, 1958–60, Vol. XII, pp. 322–3).

2   Penrose, E. and E. F., *Iraq: International Relations and National Development* (London, 1978), p. 202.

3   Khadduri, M., *Republican Iraq* (London, 1969), p. 20.

4   Dann, U., *Iraq under Qassem* (London, 1969), p. 23; Khadduri, *Republican Iraq*, p. 32.

5   Some substance seemed to be lent to this belief by the pictures of Nasser which appeared immediately on Baghdad's streets. However, this was probably merely a piece of opportunism on the part of the Baath and the UAR Embassy, seeking to capitalize on the fall of the old regime to advance Nasser's influence. (Daniel, N., 'Contemporary Perceptions of the Revolution in Iraq on 14 July 1958', in Fernea, R. A. and Louis, W. R., *The Iraqi Revolution of 1958: The Old Social Classes Revisited* (London, 1991), p. 13.)

6   Scott–FO, 14/7/58, PRO PREM11/2387; McClintock–State, US State Department 783A.00/7–1456.

7   Scott–FO, 14/7/58, PRO PREM11/2387; McClintock–State, US State Department 783A.00/7–1458. Both telegrams follow within four hours of the two cited above.

8   Meeting between Dulles, Twining, Allen Dulles and officials, 14/7/58, Eisenhower Papers: Box 16, John Foster Dulles, Chronological Series.

9   Meeting between Eisenhower and Twining, 15/7/58, Eisenhower Papers: Box 35, Ann Whitman File, DDE Diary Series.

10 Khadduri, *Republican Iraq*, p. 36.

11 Macmillan–Lloyd, 18/7/58, PRO PREM11/2408.

12 Ambrose, *Eisenhower the President*, p. 470. A dramatized, but surprisingly accurate account of the meetings of 14 July is given in a *Look* magazine article, 'Day of Decision', 16/9/58, Box 78, Allen Dulles Papers, Seeley G. Mudd Library, Princeton.

13 Memorandum of a conference with the President, 10.50am, 14/7/58, *FRUS*, 1958–60, pp. 211–15.

14 Eisenhower, *Waging Peace*, p. 270.

15 'Blue Bat', Joint Planning Staff Annex, 16/5/58, PRO DEFE5/84.

16 Conference between Eisenhower, Dulles, Allen Dulles, etc., 14/7/58, Eisenhower Papers: Box 35, Ann Whitman File, DDE Diary Series.

17 Eisenhower, *Waging Peace*, p. 279; Macmillan, *Riding the Storm*, pp. 533–4; Baylis, *Anglo-American Defence Relations, 1939–1984*, p. 95; Stivers, W., 'Eisenhower and the Middle East', in (eds) Melanson, R. A. and Mayers, D., *Reevaluating Eisenhower: American Foreign Policy in the 1950s* (Chicago, 1987), p. 202; Horne, *Macmillan, 1957–1986*, pp. 93–4; Dann, *King Hussein and the Challenge of Arab Radicalism*, p. 84.

    Of these accounts, the two most recent, written with access both to certain US and British government documents on the crisis, both make omissions. Dann argues on the basis of the apparently defective memory of the then US Assistant Secretary of State, Rountree, that: 'the "division of labour" that eventually materialized... was apparently envisaged from the first.' He makes no reference to 'Blue Bat', which

effectively invalidates his case. Horne admits to 'gaps in one's understanding of the process by which, despite the dialogue of the previous
August/September, the two allies ended up acting independently,
though in close association, in the Middle East in 1958.' However, he
is more inclined to regard this as evidence of 'how much trust had
been restored between the two countries since Suez'.

Only Watt comes close to the realities of the situation, although he
perhaps overstates the case slightly, arguing that: 'the American decision to intervene in the Lebanon in July 1958 was taken without any
consultation with Britain, despite earlier agreement that such an operation, if undertaken, would be preceded by mutual consultation.' Watt,
D., 'Demythologising the Eisenhower Era', in Louis and Bull, *The Special Relationship*, p. 75.

18 Meeting between Dulles and Eisenhower, 15/5/58, Eisenhower Papers:
Box 32, Ann Whitman File, DDE Diary Series.

19 Lodge–Dulles, 23/6/58, *FRUS*, 1958–60, Vol. XI, pp. 168–9.

20 Meeting with Congressional leaders, 14/7/58, Eisenhower Papers: Box
35, Ann Whitman File, DDE Diary Series.

21 Cabinet Minutes, 7pm, 14/7/58, PRO CAB128/32 Part 2.

22 There are three versions of this phone conversation in British and
American archives. Significant differences exist between the two British accounts, one in the Prime Minister's files (PREM) and the other
in the Foreign Office files (FO). Of these two versions the PREM
account seems the more reliable, not least because in the FO account
certain obvious mistakes are made, for instance over the British troop
numbers assigned to 'Blue Bat'. The American account in Eisenhower's
papers, is slightly different in tenor to that contained in British records.
Although the whole conversation in all of the accounts is somewhat
cryptic, due to the constraints of speaking on an open line, it is still
of great importance in setting the tone for the exchanges of the
coming days between the two countries. It was also the point at which
Macmillan acquiesced in Eisenhower's desire to intervene unilaterally
in Lebanon. (Eisenhower–Macmillan, phone conversation, 10.30pm
GMT, 14/7/58, PRO PREM11/2387; FO371/134159; Eisenhower
Papers: Box 34, Ann Whitman File, DDE Diary Series; also, *FRUS*,
1958–60, Vol. XI, Lebanon and Jordan, pp. 231–4.)

23 Eisenhower–Macmillan, phone conversation, 14/7/58, PRO PREM11/
2387.

24 Eisenhower–Macmillan, phone conversation, 14/7/58, Eisenhower
Papers: Box 34, Ann Whitman File, DDE Diary Series.

25 Cabinet Minutes, 11pm, 14/7/58, PRO CAB128/32 Part 2.

26 Macmillan–Eisenhower and Dulles, 2.32am, 15/7/58, PRO PREM11/
2387.

27 Meeting between Macmillan, Sandys and the Chiefs of Staff, 15/7/58,
PRO PREM11/2380.

28 Hood–Lloyd, 15/7/58, PRO PREM11/2380.

29 Dulles–Eisenhower, phone conversation, 8.40am EDT, 15/7/58,
Eisenhower Papers: Box 34, Ann Whitman File, DDE Diary Series.

30 Cabinet Minutes, 11.15am, 15/7/58, PRO CAB128/32 Part 2.

31 Lloyd–Hood, 15/7/58, PRO PREM11/2380.

32 Hood–Lloyd, 15/7/58, ibid.

33 Meeting re Jordan, Dulles and officials, 15/7/58, Eisenhower Papers: Box 16, John Foster Dulles, Chronological Series.

34 Meeting between Eisenhower and Twining, 15/7/58, Eisenhower Papers: Box 35, Ann Whitman File, DDE Diary Series.

35 Dann, *King Hussein and the Challenge of Arab Radicalism*, p. 86. Dann concedes that 'much of the affair is still in doubt' in his footnotes to the information presented on the Rusan plot and admits that one of his main sources is 'not totally trustworthy'.

36 Conference with the President, 16/7/58, Eisenhower Papers: Box 35, Ann Whitman File, DDE Diary Series.

37 Lawson–Dulles, US State Department 785.00/7–1658.

38 Jordan–State, 16/7/58, *FRUS*, 1958–60, Vol. XI, pp. 312–13.

39 *Hansard*, Vol. 591, 17/7/58, p. 1506.

40 Cabinet Minutes, 10.30pm, 16/7/58, PRO CAB128/32 Part 2.

41 Dulles–Eisenhower, phone conversation, 16/7/58, Eisenhower Papers: Box 16, John Foster Dulles, Chronological Series.

42 Rundall–FO, 19/7/58, PRO PREM11/2377. An interesting analysis of both Ben Gurion's motives and the implications of the crisis for Anglo-Israeli relations can be found in Almog, O., 'An End of an Era – The Crisis of 1958 and the Anglo-Israeli Relationship', *Contemporary Record*, Vol. 8, No. 1, Summer 1994, pp. 49–75.

43 Macmillan–Eisenhower, 17/7/58, PRO PREM11/2380.

44 Lloyd–Macmillan, 2.08am, 18/7/58, PRO PREM11/2380.

45 Lloyd–Macmillan, 4.57am, 18/7/58, ibid.

46 Hood–FO, 23/7/58, ibid.

47 Conference between the President, Foster Dulles, Allen Dulles, etc., 23/7/58, Eisenhower Papers: Box 35, Ann Whitman File, DDE Diary Series.

48 Vorys–Dulles, 23/7/58, Eisenhower Papers: Box 8, John Foster Dulles, Telephone Calls Series.

49 Macmillan–Lloyd, 18/7/58, PRO PREM11/2408.

50 Sluglett, M. and P., *Iraq since 1958* (London, 1987), p. 57.

51 Khadduri, *Republican Iraq*, p. 92.

52 GEN 658, 1st meeting, 22/7/58, PRO CAB130/153.

53 Memorandum of a conversation, 9/6/58, *FRUS*, 1958–60, Vol. XII, pp. 301–2. The stridency of Macmillan's tone over Iraqi pressure on Kuwait is fascinating. Macmillan accuses Nuri of 'attempting a Nasser-type operation against Kuwait'. This illustrates both the importance attached to the Kuwaiti issue by Macmillan, and an element of disenchantment with Nuri in the weeks immediately preceding the Iraqi Revolution, mirrored on the US side.

54 Dulles–Eisenhower, phone call, 8.40am, 15/7/58, Eisenhower Papers: Box 35, Ann Whitman File, DDE Diary Series.

55 Conference with the President, 20/7/58, Eisenhower Papers: Box 35, Ann Whitman File, DDE Diary Series.

56   Dulles–London, summary of Lloyd–Dulles meetings, US State Department 780.00/7–2158.
57   Dulles–London, US State Department 780.00/7–1758.
58   Synopsis – Intelligence and State Department Items reported to the President – on Mid East crisis, 23/7/58, Eisenhower Papers: Box 35, Ann Whitman File, DDE Diary Series. Divine, *Eisenhower and the Cold War*, p. 101.
59   Ovendale, 'Great Britain and the Anglo-American Invasion of Jordan and Lebanon in 1958', pp. 302–3, puts a very different gloss on this. His analysis is based almost exclusively on a reading of British sources.

Notes to Chapter Twelve

1   Thayer, *Diplomat*, p. 81.
2   Nixon–Dulles, 6.49pm, 15/7/58, Eisenhower Papers: John Foster Dulles, Telephone Calls Series.
3   Urquart, *Hammarskjöld*, p. 279.
4   Ibid., p. 281.
5   Eisenhower, *Waging Peace*, p. 286.
6   Urquart, *Hammarskjöld*, p. 284.
7   Macmillan–Lloyd, 19/7/58, PRO PREM11/2388.
8   Lloyd–Washington, 1/8/58, ibid.
9   Hood–FO, 4/8/58, PRO PREM11/2381.
10   Gen 660, 1st meeting, 6/8/58, PRO CAB130/153.
11   'Settlement for Jordan', 6/8/58, PRO PREM11/2381.
12   Gen 660, 1st meeting, 6/8/58, PRO CAB130/153.
13   Johnston–FO, 7/8/58, PRO PREM11/2381.
14   Johnston–FO, 12/8/58, ibid.
15   Johnston, C., *The Brink of Jordan* (London, 1972), p. 123.
16   Johnston–FO, 24/8/58, PRO PREM11/2381.
17   Johnston–FO, 18/8/58, ibid.
18   Johnston–FO, 25/8/58, ibid; State–Amman, US State Department 785.00/8–2758; Amman–State, US State Department 785.00/8–2858.
19   Herter–London, US State Department 785.00/7–2558.
20   Hood–Lloyd, 2/9/58, PRO PREM11/2381.
21   Lloyd–FO, 26/9/58, ibid.
22   Urquart, *Hammarskjöld*, p. 290.
23   Divine, *Eisenhower and the Cold War*, p. 100.
24   Watt, *Succeeding John Bull*, p. 134.

Notes to Chapter Thirteen

1   Dann, *Iraq under Qassem*, p. 77.
2   Ibid., p. 78.
3   Sluglett, *Iraq since 1958*, p. 55.
4   Dann, *Iraq under Qassem*, p. 99.
5   Memorandum by Greene, Special Assistant to the Secretary, US State Department 780.5/7–2458.

6   Minutes of a Cabinet Meeting, 18/7/58, Eisenhower Papers: Box 35, Ann Whitman File, DDE Diary Series.
7   NSC, 373rd meeting, 24/7/58, Eisenhower Papers: Box 10, Ann Whitman File, NSC Series.
8   *New York Herald Tribune*, press cutting, 29/7/58, Box 125, John Foster Dulles Papers, Seeley G. Mudd Library, Princeton.
9   Department of State Press Release, Bilateral Agreements with Three Countries, 5/3/59, Box 140, ibid.
10   'The Baghdad Pact: review of existing plans and studies', Joint Planning Staff, 22/8/58, PRO DEFE6/51.
11   Khadduri, *Republican Iraq*, p. 77.
12   NSC, 374th meeting, 31/7/58, Eisenhower Papers: Box 10, Ann Whitman File, NSC Series.
13   'Factors affecting US policy toward the Near East', 21/8/58, Eisenhower Papers: Box 23, White House Office, Office of the Special Assistant for National Security Affairs, Policy Papers Series.
14   NSC, 377th meeting, 21/8/58, Eisenhower Papers: Box 10, Ann Whitman File, NSC Series.
15   NSC, 379th meeting, 18/9/58, ibid.
16   NSC, 380th meeting, 25/9/58, ibid.
17   NSC, 383rd meeting, 16/10/58, ibid.
18   'US Policy toward the Near East', NSC5820/1, 4/11/58, Eisenhower Papers: Box 26, White House Office, Office of the Special Assistant for National Security Affairs, Policy Papers Series.
19   Trevelyan, H., *The Middle East in Revolution* (London, 1970), p. 139. Trevelyan, who did not arrive in Baghdad to take up his post as ambassador until several weeks after his predecessor, Wright, had issued the warning to Qassem, pours cold water on the notion that the British were involved in tipping Qassem off about the Rashid Ali coup.
20   NSC, 393rd Meeting, 15/1/59, *FRUS*, 1958–60, Vol. XII, p. 376.
21   Stevens–Lloyd, 29/11/58, PRO FO371/133074.
22   Lloyd–Hood, 30/11/58, ibid.
23   Hood–Lloyd, 1/12/58, ibid.
24   Dann, *Iraq under Qassem*, pp. 110–11.
25   Conversation between Stevens and Rountree at Heathrow Airport, 20/12/58, PRO PREM11/2396.
26   Conference with the President, 23/12/58, Eisenhower Papers: Box 3, White House Office, Office of the Staff Secretary, State Department Series.
27   NSC 395th meeting, 29/1/59, *FRUS*, 1958–60, Vol. XII, p. 378.
28   Ambrose, *Eisenhower the President*, p. 466.
29   NSC 393rd meeting, 15/1/59, *FRUS*, 1958–60, Vol. XII, p. 377.
30   Meeting of Ministers, 21/12/58, PRO PREM11/2735.
31   Dulles–State, 28/7/58, *FRUS*, 1958–60, Vol. XI, pp. 405–6.
32   Dulles–Macmillan, US State Department 780.00/8–258.
33   Whitney–Dulles, US State Department 780.00/8–858.
34   JCS–Holloway, 23/8/58, JCS Central Decimal File, 'US/UK planning', CCS381 EMMEA.

35   Cabinet Defence Committee, 'Iraq', 23/1/59, PRO CAB131/21.
36   Meeting between Lloyd, Herter, Rockwell and officials, 4/4/59, PRO PREM11/2735.
37   De Zulueta–Macmillan, 1/4/59, PRO PREM11/2735.
38   Memorandum of a conversation, 22/3/59, *FRUS*, 1958–60, Vol. XII, pp. 217–18.
39   Paper by Gray, 1/4/59, *FRUS*, 1958–60, Vol. XII, p. 401. The 'other sources' available to the Administration may well have been rather limited. Secretary Dulles had earlier noted that: 'after the fall of the government of Nuri Said, the US had relatively few remaining [intelligence] assets in Iraq.' (NSC, 393rd meeting, 15/1/59, *FRUS*, 1958–60, Vol. XII, p. 376.)
40   Paper by Gray, 1/4/59, *FRUS*, 1958–60, Vol. XII, p. 402.
41   NSC, 401st meeting, 2/4/59, *FRUS*, 1958–60 Vol. XII, pp. 402–6.
42   Gray–Herter, 3/4/59, *FRUS*, 1958–60, Vol. XII, p. 410.
43   Assistant Secretary Rountree was in fact appointed to head the group later in the month. (Editorial Note, 23/4/59, *FRUS*, 1958–60, Vol. XII, p. 441.)
44   'Situation in Iraq', 15/4/59, *FRUS*, 1958–60, Vol. XII, pp. 414–22.
45   NSC, 402nd meeting, 17/4/59, Eisenhower Papers: Box 11, Ann Whitman File, NSC Series.
46   Meeting between Lloyd, Herter, Rockwell, and officials, 4/4/59, PRO PREM11/2735.
47   NSC, 402nd meeting, 17/4/59, *FRUS*, 1958–60, Vol. XII, p. 436.
48   NSC, 404th meeting, 30/4/59, *FRUS*, 1958–60, Vol. XII, p. 444.
49   Rountree–Dillon, 20/5/59, *FRUS*, 1958–60, Vol. XII, p. 457.
50   NSC, 432nd meeting, 14/1/60, *FRUS*, 1958–60, Vol. XII, p. 501.
51   Editorial Note, 23/4/59, *FRUS*, 1958–60, Vol. XII, p. 441.
52   Lloyd–Macmillan, 25/5/59, PRO PREM11/3266.
53   De Zulueta–Macmillan, 25/5/59, ibid.
54   Record of a conversation between Sir Roger Stevens and Mr Lewis Jones in the State Department, 31/8/59, PRO FO371/141841.
55   Macmillan–Eisenhower, 14/5/59, PRO PREM11/3427.
56   'Anglo-American Planning in the Middle East', 25/7/59, PRO CAB131/21.
57   Mountbatten reported considerable resistance among the US military to progressing the planning process during his visit to Washington. (Mountbatten–MOD, 31/8/59, PRO PREM11/2753.)
58   Cabinet Defence Committee, 10th meeting, 18/9/59, 'Anglo-American Planning in the Middle East', PRO CAB131/21.
59   Trevelyan–FO, 13/6/59, PRO FO371/140917.
60   Trevelyan–Stevens, 23/6/59, PRO FO371/140918.
61   Trevelyan–Lloyd, 9/7/59, PRO FO371/140919.
62   Trevelyan–Lloyd, 1/1/60, PRO FO371/149839.
63   Records of conversations between the Prime Minister and President Nasser in New York, 28/9/60 and 3/10/60, PRO FO371/152109. President Eisenhower also met Nasser at the UN and enjoyed a similarly cordial exchange of views. (*FRUS*, 1958–60, Vol. XIII, pp. 600–7.)

64   Points for a Middle East Policy, Part II, O.M.E.(58)46, 19/11/58, PRO
      CAB134/2342.

Notes to Chapter Fourteen

1   See the definition of US 'bedrock' objectives in 'Factors affecting US
      policy toward the Near East', 21/8/58, Eisenhower Papers: Box 23,
      White House Office, Office of the Special Assistant for National Secur-
      ity Affairs, Policy Papers Series.
2   'The Future of Anglo-American Relations', Working Group on US/
      UK Cooperation, 9/10/59, PRO FO371/143672.
3   'The Future of Anglo-American Relations', 12/6/59, ibid. A draft
      version of 10 July refers to 'our break with Nasser as compared with
      the continuity of US relations with him'.
4   Watt, D. C., 'The Anglo-American Relationship', from Louis and Bull,
      The Special Relationship, p. 3.
5   Beeley, H., 'The Middle East', ibid., p. 290.
6   Morris–FO, 8/9/59, PRO FO371/140717.

Notes to Postscript

1   Watkinson–Home, 17/1/61; and Home–Watkinson, 8/2/61, PRO
      PREM11/3427.
2   'Planning for intervention in the Gulf', minute by Beaumont, 3/5/61,
      PRO FO371/156694.
3   'Anglo-US Planning for Intervention in the Persian Gulf', minute by
      F. Hoyer Millar, 25/5/61, PRO FO371/156694.
4   Richmond–Home, 14/8/60, PRO FO371/148911.
5   Ibid.
6   Richmond–Middleton, 6/4/61, PRO FO371/156873.
7   Ibid.
8   Middleton–Stevens, 21/1/61; and 7/3/61, PRO FO371/156873.
9   'Exchange of notes regarding relations between the United Kingdom
      of Great Britain and Northern Ireland and the State of Kuwait', 19/
      6/61, PRO PREM11/3427.
10   Trevelyan–FO, D.11.26pm, 26/6/61, PRO PREM11/3427.
11   Trevelyan–FO, D.11.25am, 27/6/61, ibid.
12   Trevelyan–FO, D.11.26pm, 26/6/61, ibid. In his memoirs Trevelyan
      details the evidence gathered by the embassy about Qassem's inten-
      tions. However, much of it appears to have been no more than cir-
      cumstantial. (Trevelyan, H., *The Middle East in Revolution*, London,
      1970, pp. 187–9.)
13   Trevelyan–FO, 28/6/61, D.4.47pm, ibid.
14   Caccia–FO, D.12.31am, 27/6/61, PRO FO371/156845.
15   Home–Rusk, D.5.40pm, 28/6/61, PRO PREM11/3427.
16   Memorandum for the President by Under Secretary Chester Bowles,
      US State Department 611.86B/5–661.

17   Memorandum for Bundy, 10/7/61, Box 62, Folder: Bundy, McGeorge, John F. Kennedy Papers.
18   FO–Kuwait D.6.40pm, 29/6/61, PRO PREM11/3427.
19   Home–Rusk, D.6.25pm, 29/6/61, PRO PREM11/3427.
20   FO–Kuwait, D.2.35am, 30/6/61, PRO PREM11/3427.
21   Richmond–FO, D.9.26am, 30/6/61, ibid.
22   De Zulueta–Macmillan, 29/6/61, PRO PREM11/3427; and Cabinet Defence Committee minutes, 7pm 29/6/61, PRO CAB131/26.
23   Cabinet Defence Committee, minutes of (first) meeting, 3pm, 30/6/61, CAB131/26.
24   Cabinet Defence Committee, minutes of (first) meeting, 3pm, 30/6/61, PRO CAB131/26.
25   London–State, D.1pm, US State Department 686D.87/7–161.
26   'Effects of the Kuwait Crisis on British Policy', London–State, US State Department 641.86D/9–1161.
27   Cabinet Defence Committee, minutes of (second) meeting, 9.15pm, 30/6/61, PRO CAB131/26.
28   Cabinet Defence Committee, 10.30am 1/7/61, ibid.
29   NSC, 486th meeting, 29/6/61, Box 313, John F. Kennedy Papers.
30   Caccia–FO, D.6.53pm, 1/7/61, PRO PREM11/3428.
31   Caccia–FO, 5/7/61, PRO FO371/156878.
32   Baghdad–State, US State Department 686D.87/7–461.
33   Talbot–Rusk, 'Consultation with the UK on the Kuwait Situation, US State Department 786D.00/7–761.
34   The precise terms in which Rusk framed his question are not clear from the record. (Record of a Conversation between the Secretary of State and Mr Rusk at Bougival, 6/8/61, PRO PREM11/3429).
35   *Financial Times*, 5/7/61; *Observer*, 9/7/61; *Guardian*, 19/7/61.
36   Richmond–FO, 4/7/61, PRO PREM11/3428.
37   See FO–Rabat, 18/8/61, PRO PREM11/3429; Record of a meeting held at the Foreign Office, 18/8/61, FO371/156888; and Record of a conversation between the Secretary of State and Sir William Luce, 19/8/61, ibid.
38   Arabian Department–Home, 2/9/61, PRO FO371/156889.
39   Brook–Macmillan, 13/9/61, PRO PREM11/3430.
40   Home–Macmillan, 3/10/61, PRO PREM11/3430.
41   Dann, *King Hussein and the Challenge of Arab Radicalism*, p. 118.
42   Amman–FO, 29/9/61, PRO FO371/158788; FO–Amman, 4/10/61, PRO FO371/158790.
43   Memorandum for McGeorge Bundy, 'Tentative Analysis of the Situation in Syria as of September 30, 1961', US State Department 783.00/3061.
44   Trevelyan–Lloyd, 13/6/60, PRO FO371/149843.
45   Trevelyan–Home, 26/10/61, PRO FO371/157670.
46   Trevelyan–Lloyd, 13/6/60, PRO FO371/149843.

Select Bibliography

PRINTED WORKS

Books

Abadi, J., *Britain's Withdrawal from the Middle East, 1947–71: The Economic and Strategic Imperatives* (Princeton, 1983).

Abidi, A. H., *Jordan: a Political Study, 1948–57* (New York, 1965).

Adams, S., *Firsthand Report: The Story of the Eisenhower Administration* (New York, 1961).

Agwani, A. S., *The Lebanese Crisis, 1958: A Documentary Study* (London, 1965).

Alexander, C. C., *Holding the Line: The Eisenhower Era 1952–1961* (Bloomington, 1975).

Alin, E. G., *The United States and the 1958 Lebanon Crisis: American Intervention in the Middle East* (London, 1994).

Alteras, I., *Eisenhower and Israel: US–Israeli Relations, 1953–60* (Gainesville, 1993).

Ambrose, S. E., *Eisenhower the President* (London, 1984).

Ambrose, S. E. and Immerman, R. H., *Ike's Spies* (New York, 1981).

Aronson, G., *From Sideshow to Centre Stage: US Policy Towards Egypt, 1946–56* (Boulder, 1986).

Bailey, S. D., *Four Arab–Israeli Wars and the Peace Process* (London, 1990).

Barakat, H., *Toward a Viable Lebanon* (London, 1988).

Bar-Joseph, U., *The Best of Enemies: Israel and Transjordan in the War of 1948* (London, 1987).

Bar-On, M., *The Gates of Gaza: Israel's Road to Suez and Back, 1955–1957* (London, 1994).

Bar-Zohar, M., *The Armed Prophet: A Biography of Ben Gurion* (London, 1967).

Batatu, H., *The Old Social Classes and the Revolutionary Movements of Iraq* (Princeton, 1978).

Baylis, J., *Anglo-American Defence Relations, 1939–1984*, 2nd edn (London, 1984).

Behbehani, H. S. H., *The Soviet Union and Arab Nationalism, 1917–1966* (London, 1986).

Bell, C., *The Debatable Alliance* (London, 1964).

Binder, L., *Politics in Lebanon* (New York, 1966).

Black, I. and Morris, B., *Israel's Secret Wars* (London, 1991).

Bligh, A., *From Prince to King: Royal Succession in the House of Saud in the Twentieth Century* (London, 1984).

Brands, H. W., *Cold Warriors: Eisenhower's Generation and American Foreign Policy* (New York, 1988).

Brecher, M., *Decisions in Israeli Foreign Policy* (Oxford, 1974).

Brown, S., *The Faces of Power: Constancy and Change in United States Foreign Policy from Truman to Reagan* (New York, 1983).

Burns, E. L. M., *Between Arab and Israeli* (London, 1962).

Capitanchik, D. B., *The Eisenhower Presidency and American Foreign Policy* (London, 1969).

Carlton, D., *Anthony Eden* (London, 1981).

Carlton, D., *Britain and the Suez Crisis* (Oxford, 1988).

Caroz, Y., *The Arab Secret Services* (London, 1978).

Cobban, H., *The Making of Modern Lebanon* (London, 1985).

Cohen, M. J., *Palestine: Retreat from the Mandate* (London, 1978).

Cook, B., *The Declassified Eisenhower* (Garden City, 1981).

Cooper, C. L., *The Lion's Last Roar: Suez, 1956* (New York, 1978).

Copeland, M., *The Game of Nations* (London, 1969).

Crabb, C. V., *The Doctrines of American Foreign Policy* (London, 1982).

Crabb, C. V., and Mulcahy, K. V., *Presidents and Foreign Policy Making: From FDR to Reagan* (London, 1986).

Darwin, J., *Britain and Decolonisation* (London, 1988).

Dann, U., *Iraq under Qassem* (London, 1969).

Dann, U., *King Hussein and the Challenge of Arab Radicalism: Jordan 1955–1967* (Oxford, 1989).

Darby, P., *British Defence Policy East of Suez, 1947–1968* (Oxford, 1973).

Dayan, M., *Diary of the Sinai Campaign* (London, 1967).

Dayan, M., *The Story of My Life* (London, 1976).

Deighton, A., (ed.) *Britain and the First Cold War* (London, 1990).

Devereux, D. R., *The Formulation of British Defence Policy Towards the Middle East* (London, 1990).

Divine R. A., *Eisenhower and the Cold War* (Oxford, 1981).

Dixon, P., *Double Diploma: The Life of Sir Pierson Dixon* (London, 1968).

Eban A., *An Autobiography*, (London, 1977).

Eden, A., *Full Circle* (London, 1960).

Edmonds, R., *Setting the Mould: the United States and Britain, 1945–50* (Oxford, 1986).

Eisenhower, D. D., *The White House Years: Mandate For Change, 1953–6* (London, 1963).

Eisenhower, D. D., *The White House Years: Waging Peace, 1956–61* (London, 1965).

Eveland, W. C., *Ropes of Sand* (London, 1980).

Fawzi, M., *Suez, 1956: An Egyptian Perspective* (London, 1987).

Fernea, R. A. and Louis, W. R., *The Iraqi Revolution of 1958: The Old Social Classes Revisited* (London, 1991).

Finer, H., *Dulles Over Suez* (Chicago, 1964).

Flapan, S., *The Birth of Israel. Myths and Realities* (London, 1987).

Freiberger, S. Z., *Dawn Over Suez: The Rise of American Power in the Middle East, 1953–1957* (Chicago, 1992).

Fullick, R. and Powell, G., *Suez: The Double War* (London, 1979).

Gallman, W. J., *Iraq Under General Nuri: My Recollections of Nuri al-Said, 1954–1958* (Baltimore, 1964).

Gerson, L. L., *John Foster Dulles* (New York, 1967).

Gilbert, M., *Winston S. Churchill, Volume VIII: Never Despair, 1945–65* (London, 1988).

Ginat, R., *The Soviet Union and Egypt, 1945–1955* (London, 1993).

Gordon, J., *Nasser's Blessed Movement: Egypt's Free Officers and the July Revolution* (Oxford, 1992).

Goria, W. R., *Sovereignty and Leadership in Lebanon, 1943–1976* (London, 1985).

Gorst, A., Johnman, L. and Lucas, W. S. (eds) *Post-War Britain, 1945–64: Themes and Perspectives* (London, 1989).

Green, S., *Taking Sides: America's Relations with a Militant Israel 1948–67* (London, 1984).

Greenstein, F. E., *The Hidden-Hand Presidency: Eisenhower as Leader* (New York, 1982).

Guhin, M. A., *John Foster Dulles: A Statesman and His Times* (New York, 1972).

Hahn, P. L., *The United States, Great Britain, and Egypt, 1945–56: Strategy and Diplomacy in the Early Cold War* (London, 1991).

Hawley, D., *The Trucial States* (London, 1970).

Heikal, M., *Nasser: the Cairo Documents* (London, 1972).

Heikal, M., *Cutting the Lion's Tail* (London, 1986).

Hennessy, P. and Seldon, A. (eds) *Ruling Performance* (Oxford, 1987).

Heuser, B. (ed.), *NATO and the Cold War* (London, 1991).

Higgins, R., *United Nations Peacekeeping, 1946–67. Documents and Commentary I The Middle East* (Oxford, 1969).

Hoopes, T., *The Devil and John Foster Dulles* (London, 1974).

Hogan, M. J., *The Marshall Plan: America, Britain and the Reconstruction of Western Europe, 1947–52* (Cambridge, 1987).

Hopwood, D., *Egypt: Politics and Society, 1945–1981* (London, 1982).

Horne, A., *Macmillan, 1894–1956* (London, 1988).

Horne, A., *Macmillan, 1957–86* (London, 1989).

Hughes, J. E., *The Ordeal of Power: A Political Memoir of the Eisenhower Years* (New York, 1963).

Hussein, King, *Uneasy Lies the Head: The Autobiography of His Majesty King Hussein I of the Hashemite Kingdom of Jordan* (New York, 1962).

Ionides, M., *Divide and Lose: The Arab Revolt of 1955–1958* (London, 1960).

Johnston, C., *The Brink of Jordan* (London, 1972).

Kerr, M., *The Arab Cold War*, 2nd edn (London, 1967).

Khadduri, M., *Republican Iraq* (London, 1969).

Korbani, A. G., *US Intervention in Lebanon, 1958 and 1982: Presidential Decisionmaking* (London, 1991).

Kuniholm, B., *The Cold War in the Near East* (Princeton, 1980).

Kunz, D., *The Economic Diplomacy of the Suez Crisis* (London, 1990).

Kyle, K., *Suez* (London, 1991).

Lamb, R., *The Failure of the Eden Government* (London, 1987).

Lenczowski, G., *The Middle East in World Affairs*, 4th edn (London, 1980).

Lenczowski, G., *American Presidents and the Middle East* (London, 1990).

Lesch, D. W., *Syria and the United States: Eisenhower's Cold War in the Middle East* (Oxford, 1992).

Lloyd, S., *Suez 1956: A Personal Account* (London, 1978).

Long, D. E., *The United States and Saudi Arabia: Ambivalent Allies* (Boulder, Colorado, 1985).

Louis, W. R., *The British Empire in the Middle East* (Oxford, 1984).

Louis, W. R. and Bull, H. (eds), *The Special Relationship* (Oxford, 1986).

Louis, W. R. and Owen, R. (eds), *Suez, 1956: The Crisis and its Consequences* (Oxford, 1989).

Love, K., *Suez: The Twice Fought War* (Toronto, 1969).

Luard, E., *A History of the United Nations, Vol. II. The Age of Decolonisation, 1955–1965* (London, 1989).

Lucas, N., *The Modern History of Israel* (London, 1974).

Lucas, W. S., *Divided We Stand: Britain, the US and the Suez Crisis* (London, 1991).

Lubell, S., *Revolt of the Moderates* (New York, 1956).

MacDonald, I., *The History of the Times: Volume V, Struggles in War and Peace, 1939–66* (London, 1984).

Macmillan, H., *Tides of Fortune, 1945–55* (London, 1969).

Macmillan, H., *Riding the Storm, 1956–9* (London, 1971).

Marr, P., *The Modern History of Iraq* (London, 1985).

Melanson, R. A. and Mayers, D. (eds), *Reevaluating Eisenhower: American Foreign Policy in the 1950s* (Chicago, 1987).

Melman, Y. and Raviv, D., *Imperfect Spies: The History of Israeli Intelligence* (London, 1989).

Meyer, G. E., *Egypt and the United States: the Formative Years* (London, 1980).

Monroe, E., *Britain's Moment in the Middle East* (London, 1963).

Morris, B., *1948 and After: Israel and the Palestinians* (Oxford, 1990).

Morris, B., *The Birth of the Palestinian Refugee Problem, 1947–49* (Cambridge, 1988).

Morris, B., *Israel's Border Wars, 1949–56* (Oxford, 1993).

Murphy, R., *Diplomat amongst Warriors* (New York, 1964).

Neff, D., *Warriors at Suez: Eisenhower Takes America into the Middle East* (New York, 1981).

Neustadt, R. E., *Alliance Politics* (London, 1970).

Northedge, F. S., *Descent from Power* (London, 1974).

Nutting, A., *No End of a Lesson: The Inside Story of the Suez Crisis* (London, 1967).

Nutting, A., *Nasser* (London, 1972).

Olson, R. W., *The Baath and Syria, 1947 to 1982. The Evolution of Ideology, Party and State* (Princeton, 1982).

Oren, M. B., *Origins of the Second Arab–Israel War* (London, 1992).

Ovendale, R., *The English Speaking Alliance: Britain, the United States the Dominions and the Cold War, 1945–51* (London, 1985).

Partner, P., *Arab Voices: The BBC Arabic Service, 1938–88* (London, 1988).

Paterson, T. G., *Meeting the Communist Threat: From Truman to Reagan* (Oxford, 1988).

Penrose, E. and E. F., *Iraq: International Relations and National Development* (London, 1978).

Pineau, C., *Suez 1956* (Paris, 1978).

Pridham, B. R. (ed.), *The Arab Gulf and the West* (London, 1985).

Rabinovich, I., *The Road Not Taken: Early Arab–Israeli Negotiations* (New York, 1991).

Ramet, P., *The Soviet–Syrian Relationship since 1955: A Troubled Alliance* (Boulder, 1990).

Ranelagh, J., *The Rise and Fall of the CIA* (New York, 1987).

Reynolds, D., *The Creation of the Anglo-American Alliance, 1937–41: a Study in Competitive Cooperation* (London, 1981).
Reynolds, D. and Dimbleby, D., *An Ocean Apart* (London, 1988).
Rhodes James, R., *Anthony Eden* (London, 1986).
Roberts, D., *The Ba'th and the Creation of Modern Syria* (London, 1987).
Safran, N., *Israel: the Embattled Ally* (London, 1978).
Satloff, R. B., *From Abdullah to Hussein: Jordan in Transition* (Oxford, 1994).
Seale, P., *The Struggle for Syria*, 2nd edn (London, 1986).
Shlaim, A., *Collusion Across the Jordan* (Oxford, 1987).
Shlaim, A., *The Politics of Partition* (Oxford, 1990).
Shuckburgh, E., *Descent to Suez: Diaries, 1951–56* (London, 1986).
Shwadran, B., *The Middle East, Oil, and the Great Powers* (New York, 1973).
Sluglett, M. and P., *Iraq since 1958* (London, 1987).
Stivers, W., *America's Confrontation with Revolutionary Change in the Middle East, 1948–83* (London, 1986).
Stoff, M. B., *Oil, War, and American Security* (London, 1980).
Thomas, H., *The Suez Affair* (London, 1966).
Thorpe, D. R., *Selwyn Lloyd* (London, 1989).
Torrey, G. H., *Syrian Politics and the Military 1945–58* (Colombus, 1964).
Touval, S., *The Peace Brokers: Mediators in the Arab–Israeli Conflict, 1948–79* (Princeton, 1982).
Trevelyan, H., *The Middle East in Revolution* (London, 1970).
Urquart, B., *Hammarskjöld* (New York, 1972).
Vatikiotis, P. J., *Politics and the Military in Jordan* (London, 1967).
Vatikiotis, P. J., *Egypt since the Revolution* (London, 1968).
Vatikiotis, P. J., *Nasser and his Generation* (London, 1978).
Vatikiotis, P. J., *The History of Egypt: From Muhammad Ali to Mubarak* (Baltimore, 1985).
Watt, D. C., *Succeeding John Bull: America in Britain's Place* (Cambridge, 1984).
Wilson, M. C., *King Abdullah, Britain and the Making of Jordan* (Cambridge, 1987)
Yapp, M. E., *The Near East Since the First World War* (London, 1991).
Young, J. W. (ed.), *The Foreign Policy of Churchill's Peacetime Administration* (Leicester, 1988).

Articles

Adamthwaite, A., 'Suez Revisited', *International Affairs* 64/3, Summer 1988.
Aldrich, W., 'The Suez Crisis: A Footnote to History', *Foreign Affairs*, April 1967.
Almog, O., 'An End of an Era – The Crisis of 1958 and the Anglo-Israeli Relationship', *Contemporary Record*, 8/1, Summer 1994.
Ashton, N. J., 'The Hijacking of a Pact: The Formation of the Baghdad Pact and Anglo-American Tensions in the Middle East, 1955–58', *Review of International Studies*, 19/2, April 1993.
Ashton, N. J., '"A Great New Venture"? – Anglo-American Cooperation in the Middle East and the Response to the Iraqi Revolution, July 1958', *Diplomacy and Statecraft*, 4/1, March 1993.
Brands, H. J., 'The Age of Vulnerability: Eisenhower and the National Insecurity State', *The American Historical Review*, 94/4, 1989.

Brands, H. W., 'The Cairo–Teheran Connection in Anglo-American Rivalry in the Middle East', *International History Review*, xi/3, August 1989.

Cohen, R., 'Israeli Military Intelligence before the 1956 Sinai Campaign', *Intelligence and National Security*, January 1988.

Dixon, P., 'Eden After Suez', *Contemporary Record*, 6/1, Summer 1992.

Dooley, H. J., 'Great Britain's "Last Battle" in the Middle East: Notes on Cabinet Planning during the Suez Crisis of 1956', *International History Review*, xi/3, August 1989.

Dutton, D., 'Living With Collusion: Anthony Eden and the Later History of the Suez Affair', *Contemporary Record*, 5/2, Autumn 1991.

Fry, M., and Hochstein, M., 'The Forgotten Middle Eastern Crisis of 1957: Gaza and Sharm-el-Sheikh', *International History Review*, xv/1, February 1993.

Gorst, A. and Lucas, W. S., 'Suez 1956: Strategy and the Diplomatic Process', *Journal of Strategic Studies*, December 1988.

Gorst, A. and Lucas, W. S., 'The Other Collusion: Operation Straggle and Anglo-American Intervention in Syria, 1955–6', *Intelligence and National Security*, 4/3, July 1989.

Hahn, P. L., 'Containment and Egyptian Nationalism: The Unsuccessful Effort to Establish the Middle East Command, 1950–53', *Diplomatic History*, Winter 1987.

Immerman, R. H., 'Eisenhower and Dulles: Who Made the Decisions?', *Political Psychology*, I, 1979.

Jalal, A., 'Towards the Baghdad Pact: South Asia and Middle East Defence in the Cold War, 1947–55', *International History Review*, xi/3, August 1989.

Little, D., 'Cold War and Covert Action: The United States and Syria, 1945–1958', *Middle East Journal*, 44/1, 1990.

Lucas, W. S., 'Redefining the Suez "Collusion": A Regional Approach', *Middle Eastern Studies*, January 1990.

Oren, M. B., 'Secret Egyptian–Israeli Peace Initiatives Prior to the Suez Campaign', *Middle East Journal*, July 1990.

Ovendale, R., 'Great Britain and the Anglo-American Invasion of Jordan and Lebanon in 1958', *International History Review*, xvi/2, May 1994.

Petersen, T. T., 'Anglo-American Rivalry in the Middle East: The Struggle for the Buraimi Oasis, 1952–1957', *International History Review*, xiv/1, February 1992.

Raad, Z., 'A Nightmare Avoided: Jordan and Suez 1956', *Israel Affairs*, 1/2, Winter 1994.

Reynolds, D., 'A "Special Relationship"? America, Britain and the International Order since the Second World War', *International Affairs*, Vol. 62, Winter 1985/6.

Reynolds, D., 'Eden the Diplomatist, 1931–56: Suezide of a Statesman', *History*, February 1989.

Salem, E. A., 'Lebanon's Political Maze: The Search for Peace in a Turbulent Land', *The Middle East Journal*, Autumn 1979.

Shaw, T., 'Government Manipulation of the Press during the 1956 Suez Crisis', *Contemporary Record*, 8/2, Autumn 1994.

Shlaim, A., 'Conflicting Approaches to Israel's Relations with the Arabs: Ben Gurion and Sharett, 1953–6', *Middle East Journal*, Spring 1983.

Warner, G., 'The United States and the Suez Crisis', *International Affairs*, 67, 2, 1991.

Printed Documents

Foreign Relations of the United States [FRUS]
1955–57, xiii Near East: Jordan–Yemen, (Washington, 1988).
1955–57, xiv Arab–Israeli Dispute, 1955 (Washington, 1990).
1955–57, xv Arab–Israeli Dispute, January 1 – July 26 1956 (Washington, 1990).
1955–57, xvi Suez Crisis (Washington, 1990).
1955–57, xvii Arab–Israeli Dispute (Washington, 1990).
1958–60, xi Lebanon and Jordan (Washington, 1992).
1958–60, xii Near East Region: Iraq; Iran; Arabian Peninsula (Washington, 1993).
1958–60, xiii Arab–Israeli Dispute; United Arab Republic; North Africa (Washington, 1992).

Hansard, House of Commons Debates.

DOCUMENTS

Public Record Office, Kew, London

AIR8 Chief of Air Staff Papers.
CAB128 Cabinet Meetings.
CAB129 Cabinet Memoranda.
CAB130 Cabinet Committee (Ad Hoc) Files.
CAB131 Defence Committee.
CAB134 Cabinet Committee (Standing) Files.
DEFE4 Chiefs of Staff Committee Meetings.
DEFE5 Chiefs of Staff Memoranda.
DEFE6 Joint Planning Staff.
FO371 Foreign Office, General Political Correspondence.
PREM11 Prime Minister's Correspondence.

Crown copyright documents in the Public Record Office are quoted by permission of the Controller of H.M Stationery Office.

US National Archives, Washington, DC, USA

RG59 State Department Central Decimal Files.
RG84 Embassy and Consular Files.
RG218 Records of the Joint Chiefs of Staff.

All documents referred to as 'US State Dept.', unless otherwise stated, are from the Central Decimal File. Since the reference contains the date of the document I have decided not to repeat this in my notes. The date is the sequence of numbers following the '/' in any reference. It is arranged in the order of month followed by day, then year. So for example, 785.5/6–1356 would be a document dated 13 June 1956.

Dwight D. Eisenhower Presidential Library, Abilene, Kansas, USA

Referred to as 'Eisenhower Papers'.

Ann Whitman File:
DDE Diary Series.
Dulles–Herter Series.
International Series.
International Meetings Series.
Legislative Meetings Series.
National Security Council Series.

John Foster Dulles Papers:
Chronological Series.
Telephone Calls Series.

White House Office Files:
Office of the Staff Secretary.
Subject Series.

John Fitzgerald Kennedy Presidential Library, Boston, Massachucetts, USA

Pre-Presidential Papers.
President's Office Files.
National Security Files.
White House Central Files.

Seeley G. Mudd Manuscript Library, Princeton University, Princeton, New Jersey, USA

John Foster Dulles Papers.
Allen Dulles Papers.
Kennett Love Papers.
Hamilton Fish Armstrong Papers.
Oral History Collection.

Library of Congress, Manuscript Division, Washington DC, USA

Loy W. Henderson Papers.

Index

Nigel John Ashton is currently lecturing in the Department of History at the University of Liverpool, where he has held a permanent post since 1993. During the academic year preceding this appointment, he held a temporary lectureship in the Department of Politics and Contemporary History at the University of Salford. *Eisenhower, Macmillan and the Problem of Nasser* is his first book.